M. + J. Walzer
August 1986
Princeton

# The Sociology of Hope

# The Sociology of Hope

**Henri Desroche**

Translated from the French by
Carol Martin-Sperry

Routledge & Kegan Paul
London, Boston and Henley

This translation first published in 1979
by Routledge & Kegan Paul Ltd
39 Store Street, London WC1E 7DD,
Broadway House, Newtown Road,
Henley-on-Thames, Oxon RG9 1EN and
9 Park Street, Boston, Mass. 02108, USA
Photoset in 11/12pt Baskerville by
Rowland Phototypesetting Ltd
Bury St. Edmunds, Suffolk
and printed in Great Britain by
Redwood Burn Ltd
Trowbridge and Esher
Translated from Sociologie de l'espérance
French edition © 1973 Calmann-Lévy
This translation © Routledge & Kegan Paul 1979

British Library Cataloguing in Publication Data

Desroche, Henri
The sociology of hope.
1. Hope
I. Title
301.5'8        BV4638        79-40085

ISBN 0 7100 0311 0

# Contents

# Introduction

# The miracle of the rope

Die Hoffnung ist ein Seil.
(Hope is a rope.)

Angelus Silesius

The title of this book was a subtitle used by Mircea Eliade[1] to evoke a typical miracle of fakirism, paralleled in many religious traditions.

In this rite, the officiant – fakir, shaman . . . or juggler – throws a rope like a lasso in the air. This rope rises higher and higher 'in the air'. It should fall down. But the officiant assures us that it has mysteriously anchored itself somewhere, and to prove it, he or his disciple climbs up the rope. The rope does not give way. *It holds*. And it carries the weight of the man as he climbs.

This 'miracle' has many variations. In particular that in which the climber is dismembered. Once he is out of sight, his limbs fall to the ground one by one until the officiant, by a second miracle, proceeds to put them together again. It must suffice just to mention this collateral theme.

Mircea Eliade finds the fundamental theme, the ascension, in classical India, in Islam, in ancient Mexico, in the Dutch Indies, in Irish folklore. He even finds this myth of the holy rope in both Homer and Plato. The rite remains unexplained: 'Whatever the explanation proposed – collective suggestion or the work of a conjurer – the problem of the rope trick has not yet been solved'. But whatever the explanation of the rite, one question remains: that of the lessons of the myth that this rite claims to inculcate. For 'if the metaphors of the thread and the rope return continually to the imagination and speculation of man', this means that 'these metaphors correspond to very deep experiences and in the end they

I

reveal a human situation which cannot be expressed in other symbols or concepts'.[2]

The cases quoted by Eliade all include the experience of an alliance of man with an act of grace in his fight with – and his victory over – gravity. However, they vary according to two types. Sometimes the act of grace is reduced to its most simple expression: the rope attaches itself to a 'cloud' in the sky, and even in certain cases the officiant can make it come out of his own body and make it go back in by swallowing it. Sometimes, on the contrary, the rope 'falls from on high', 'descends from the sky': in Plato's *Laws* it is even the 'golden sacred rope of reason' with which the gods animate the human puppet. In Homer it is the challenge made by Zeus: 'Hang a golden cable from the sky and climb up it, all you gods and goddesses, you will not bring Zeus, the supreme creator, down to earth from the sky however hard you try. But if I wanted to pull, I would pull the earth and the sea along with you. . . .'

The two types are not necessarily antithetical, and if there is an antithesis, it is transcended by the parable of the Pseudo-Dionysus. Here again we find the rope in the form of an 'infinitely luminous chain that hangs from the sky and comes down to us'. But one also finds the effort of the climber as he seizes the chain and 'pulls it towards him first with one hand, then with the other'. He goes at it as though 'we were on a ship and for our rescue we had been thrown ropes attached to a rock . . . . In fact we would not be pulling the rock towards us, we would be hauling ourselves and the ship towards the rock. . . .'

When, as I prepared this work, I reread Mircea Eliade's stimulating phenomenological meditation, I happened to read alongside it Angelus Silesius. I rediscovered his meditation on hope, the mystical: 'Hope is a rope'.[3] Paradoxically it was the combination of these two meditations that provided, both for the title and for the hypothesis of the work, the idea of the present approach, albeit sociological.

In this approach, I would at least like to contribute to the sociology of imaginary representations. I had the opportunity to become familiar with such representations in three areas: in the cults of possession, through the Durkheim of the *Elementary forms*, and especially through Roger Bastide, whom

I shall often cite; in messianisms – millenarianisms, a particularly rich source of material;[4] in written and lived
utopias,[5] extending into millenarianising and secularised
social ideologies.[6]

I confess: perhaps, impressed by the very abundance of
these phenomena, one becomes sceptical about the validity of
the axiom, according to which these *representations* – onciric,
liturgical, cultural, utopian, ideological, in short, *imaginary* in
one way or the other – are explicable 'in the last analysis' *by*
and, all things considered, reducible *to*, *situations* of social,
economic, technological or demographic *reality*. Certainly, as
we can see, these situations weave a system of restraints
which determines these representations, but this social
determinism is just that gravity which the grace of the
imaginary 'undetermines', as it were, giving freedom and
setting free. Forces of *pressure* pose and define a question. But
it is the forces of *aspiration* which formulate and offer an
answer. It is as though human beings – personalities and/or
collectivities – who are burdened by the weight of necessities,
found something *like the rope* to be a message, an announcement, a 'revelation', a gospel. Whether they believe this rope
to have come from elsewhere, or whether they think it came
from within themselves is of no consequence. In both cases it
is a rope that they throw *in the air*, in other words, into space,
into the clouds, into the sky. To the observer, it seems that
there is nothing to keep it up, except for the impalpable and
inconsistent worlds of fantasy, wanderings and absurdity.
And yet this rope is anchored. *It holds.* And when humans
grab hold of it and pull themselves up, it *takes the strain*, it
maintains its rigidity, even if, believing that they are bringing
heaven down to the earth, they are only moving their ancient
lands up towards new heavens, as in the image of the Pseudo-
Dionysus. If an imagination is thus *constituted*, it is no less a
*constitutive* imagination, the constructor of a social reality.[7] It
is not without hazards and pitfalls. For if hope is identified
with this constitutive imagination, it cannot be so without
sharing in both the characteristic *fullness* and *emptiness* of the
imaginary.[8]

After all, this miracle of the rope may be an invitation –
especially in the sociology of religions – to a match between a

3

so-called 'materialist' sociology and another sociology of which it was said by Durkheim that if it could not be idealistic, it could at least, and should, restore to social ideals their specific social creativity. If hope 'is a rope', is not its miracle precisely that of such a creativity, or, to adopt the perspective opened by E. Morin, that of an 'event'?[9] The privilege of hope would then be to promote an event into an advent. In any case the Weberian axiom recalled by Morin is also suited to our purpose:

Man, who lives in areas that are steeped in culture, and who is caught in the network of their techniques, questions the world that surrounds him as little as the child, who is used to taking the tram every day, asks himself how one makes it start. *Only he who is capable of being amazed by the sequence of events can question himself on the meaning of the universe.*[10]

# Chapter 1

# Religious hope: its peaks and troughs. An anthological approach

> In der Hoffnung leben ist etwas Grosses, aber es ist auch etwas tief Unwirkliches.
> (There is something great but also profoundly unreal in living in hope.)
>
> Gershom Sholem

We have learnt that hope is a 'theologal' virtue, Péguy even believed it to be the most wonderful. For this reason it is considered to belong to a theology and this theology seems even now to be in full reactivation. However, it will be examined here as being neither theologal nor theological, even if the phenomena used to elucidate it are primarily religious phenomena.

These phenomena are those of the collective imagination in its utopian, millenarianist or utopian-millenarianist expressions. Their occurrence is virtually universal. This at least is what seems to be the outcome of a double investigation, the first part of which has already resulted in a first version of a *Dictionary* of messiahs, messianisms and millenarianisms of the Christian era, and the second part of which is at this moment generating the preliminary index cards of a parallel dictionary of written and lived utopias. A population – in the statistical sense of the word – is emerging from it, which is in turn slim and tumultuous, fascinating and formidable, plaintive and pathetic, recurrent and unpredictable, arrogant and absurd, obstinate and flexible, nagging and marginal. Should one say marginal? 'Marginalised' would be more accurate. In fact this hope strolls along the corridors of waking social dreams: most of the time they are childhood memories for manifold societies who have succeeded, if not in repressing them, at least in channelling them into nugatory acculturations. For such an imagination is like a noetic energy: it is equally charged with both the dangers aggravated by its progressive disintegration and the blessings promised by its use for peaceful ends; the theological treatments of this theologal potential have, on the whole, merely had as a goal the extraction of this needful beneficence from this possible maleficence, or even, as Bastide remarks in the case of parallel phenomena, the extraction of 'possession' from 'obsession':[1]

> In short, the African, like the Christian, has an ambivalent attitude towards the mystical phenomenon: he considers it to be an election and an honour, but at the same time he is afraid, and when an individual shows his aptitude for going into a trance he cannot stop himself reshaping the trance, socialising it, protecting it against all the possible mistaken ideas with the barriers of collective norms or the parapets of the history of the gods.

As A. Dumas remarked elsewhere, the imagination is a snare: its sheer absence is enough to produce inanity by 'perceptive myopia or abstract sclerosis'; but its sheer presence is not enough for self-regulation.[2] This is why the theologian has always been wary of this theologal leap: a wariness which is the heir of that of officiants appointed to control trances in cults of possession.

This dialectical relation between an *experience* – usually exuberant – of hope and its theological *expression* is to be found with variables – either strengthening or weakening – in most phenomena of this kind. But there is another problem: that of the plurality of such expressions which corresponds to the plurality of such experiences. For there are a thousand and one theologies *expressing* the thousand and one experiences of such a hope, more or less open to notice and more or less amenable to observation or even measurement in an inductive field.

To take an extreme case, let us look, for example, at the paradoxes of the hope that was lived and then reflected upon in a communal micro-movement, at the juncture of neo-Christianities and pre-socialisms at the turn of the nineteenth century: that of the Shakers.[3] To use Bastide's terminology yet again, one finds the distinction between what could be called a 'wild' hope and a 'baptised' hope. The wild hope is that of the founder Ann Lee, that young girl caught up in the anguish of the world's first proletariat in the outskirts of Manchester. 'Churches and clergy helped her not,' the historians record. It was at the time when the Luddite followers were breaking machines, when the dominating society took on the face of hell as much in its rhythms of production as in its rhythms of reproduction: 'Many births, many deaths'. Ann Lee had had this experience as much in the family of which she was the daughter as in the family of which she became the mother. The Luddites broke the cycle of production. Ann Lee's revelation was one of holy Luddism: one that would break the cycle of reproduction. Such was her hope in this hopeless world: to reach the end of the world, in the double sense of a world finally completed, finally perfect, by the generalisation of a mixed monasticism. She received her revelation in prison when she was locked up for having disturbed a church service. She was too illiterate to support this revelation with a theology. But she was charismatic enough to recruit several generations of disciples, clerics and historians, who worked towards this theology by demonstrating that the revelation was a recurrence of all the theologies of hope spawned by a *dualist* tradition: from Buddha to Gandhi via the whole range of Manicheans and Messalians to the Bogomils or the Cathars. It was *one* hope, *one* theology, and even if they appeared to some to be a fanciful system of ideas, they nevertheless harboured a system of *forces* which upheld – heavens on earth – a network of North American communities which were admired by Engels before receiving homage from Tolstoy. . . .

But very different are this Shaker theology and, for example, the Mormon or adventist theologies, each of which justifies *its* hope in the same cultural area and at the same period of time. They are all different from the Levellers' theology one century earlier, or Léon Bloy's theology one century later. One could add to the list: the hope of Luther – and its accompanying theology – is not that of Thomas Münzer, any more than Eusebius of Caesarea's is that of Irenaeus, Papias or Tertullian.

Irenaeus's is not even Montanus's, although Christianity in Lyons and Asia Minor had a common mould; that of the early St Augustine is not the same as that of the late St Augustine, or if one prefers the macrosociological register, the hope of Zoroaster is not that of Mani, the hope of Islam is not that of Buddhism, whereas within Islam, that of Sunnite Islam is not or was not the same as that of Shiite Islam, and within Buddhism, that of Mahayana is not that of Hinayana.

This panorama, which could go on for ever, is one of hopes *together with* theologies that orchestrate them, underwrite them or clothe them with narrative. One should add to them two types of hopes *without* theologies. The first is that of religious experiences that did not have the luck, good or bad, of being invested with such an expression: the movements of the cargo cults in the South Sea Islands, of the Ghost Dance in North America, of Anthony the Adviser in the Sertao desert; many other explosive social millenarianisms had great hopes, whose myths remain 'myth-dreams' without having the chance of emerging into that mode of conscious logic which is a theology. The second type is the hope (espérance) that has despaired of the gods and has removed from them a hope (espoir) of man in man, and this without other resort to alliances with the afterworlds of man. One may wonder whether the word hope (espoir) does not include the very *experience* of a non-religious *hope* (espérance). One can certainly take such an experience to be the *object* of a theology. It is not subject to it, and confronted with those that are, it could well take as its axiom Sophocles's saying: 'I have nothing but scorn for the mortal who comforts himself with hollow hopes. . . .'

This last phrase could lead one to temptation: that of asking either the multitude of theologies or the plurality of sociologies for a tabulation of hopes to be arranged axiologically either as hollow hopes or as fulfilled hopes. This comparative axiology cannot be the theme of the following analyses: it depends on the personal or collective wager of a given human nature, and its equipment is neither precise enough nor powerful enough to link up with a population of hopes as numerous and as little capable of standardisation as those of thousands of collectivities and billions of personalities in the world of the living or of the dead. Comte assured us that humanity counted more dead people than living. It is just as true of gods and theologies. It is also true of hopes. That is why, rather than count and label the hollow hopes over against the fulfilled hopes, one prefers to this comparative axiology, to explore a praxeology induced from phenomena that are catalogued and outlined in the following chapters. Not fulfilled *or* hollow hopes, but the peaks *and* troughs of all hope!

## I The peaks of hope

The old theologies advocated hope as the psycho-sociological strategy of an alliance: that of man and his god. This presentation is topical enough to be considered. But it immediately follows that not all religions are *perceived* of as religions of hope, and this in at least two cases: that of blocked hope and of vanished hope.

The first is that of *blocked* hope in a religion that is so bound up with the here below that it is identified with its own confinement. Religion is identified with society, 'Church and State'. The gods are the keystone of the city; the city offers its pillars to this keystone. For a long time, religions, known as religions of the city, witnessed this mutual binding. In his great book on 'The ancient city', Fustel de Coulanges makes a pertinent analysis of it. The religion of the city – at the apex of its pyramid of families and 'gentes' – had erected its gods and its clergies, in this case those of *its* patrician class. The plebeians were considered not to have any religious family – 'gentem non habent' – and therefore 'in a word, without cult' – and without hope until later with the arrival of the mystery cults – including Christianity – they won the right to a cult and to prayer: 'The plebeians, who were once a crowd with no cult . . . could pray; this was a good deal in a society where religion gave man his dignity.'

The same vicissitudes are found throughout the religious revolution that reached Egypt towards the beginning of the second millenarian century. The Pharaoh alone monopolised the hope which was his by his right to immortality and forbidden to anyone but him – a hope opened to the plebeians themselves after this revolution in funeral rites. In the historian's judgment, 'The fact that all the Egyptian deceased, dating from the Middle Empire, are identified with the King and the gods, reveals a social transformation, the greatest that the history of Egypt has to show' (A. Moret). A blocked religion unblocked itself. From being a closed religion it became an open one.

There is the same closing and ultimate opening in the Vedic religion which became the Aryan branch of the Indo-European religions. It was a religion of three classes or Aryan castes of the conquering population: the priesthood of the Brahmans, the nobility of the Kshatriya, the third estate of the Vaisha. A sacred text sanctioned this hierarchy by extolling the speech of Purusha: his mouth became the caste of the Brahmans, his two arms the caste of the warriors, his thighs the Vaicya. As for his feet, they became the caste of those without caste – those who – 'gentem non habent' – were the inferior caste of the conquered population, the Shudra. They were forbidden not only to read but to listen to the sacred text. There was no hope for them until the great movements of the sixth century heralded the formulation of a casteless monasticism within this caste religion and in opposition to a priesthood, the first caste of this religion.

But there is another case, that of *vanished* hope, in a religion that confirms the hereafter in such a way that it militates against any protest here below. One may perhaps suggest as a counterbalance to these three examples taken from ancient religions an example taken from a modern religion. In the nineteenth century a great social hope (espoir) accompanied the advent of industrial societies and the formation of the first proletariats. Hope of a redistribution of the social classes and of new regimes of ownership accompanied a renewed mastery of man over nature. This social hope was fringed with religious hopes (espérances) in the messages of short-lived socialistic utopias. It then became the very hope that despairs of the gods by investing itself in science and in the praxis of a so-called 'scientific' socialism. It is then that a religious hope crystallises, which expects nothing from this human hope. Among many others, texts of Pope Leo XIII bear witness to this. According to him these human hopes are vestiges which are attributable to 'this deadly plague which creeps through . . . human society and leads it to its ruin'. Religious hope is the antidote to it, which consigns the rich sinner 'to eternal punishment' and the poor saint to 'the rewards of eternal happiness'. Against the 'socialist schismatics' who make their followers 'impatient with the human condition', it animates the societies of workers and craftsmen, who, established under the patronage of religion, 'know how to make all their members happy with their lot and work'.[4]

> Finally the question of the relations of the rich and the poor, with which the economists are so concerned, would be completely resolved in that it would be well-established that poverty is not without dignity, that the rich man should be merciful and generous and the poor man should be content with his lot and his work, since neither one nor the other is born for these perishable goods, and the one must get to heaven through patience and the other through generosity.[5]

'Permanence of the social conceptions of the Old Regime,' would have glossed Haubtmann, one of the rare scholars who was 'familiar with the 99 volumes of "the integral, and universal collection of the sacred orators"' He found there this conception without hope – other than meta-social – of the social order. 'This order which is founded on the inequality of conditions and fortunes' is considered to be 'necessary', 'natural', 'divine' – at least after Adam's fall. The states of richness and poverty are therefore equally God's will, but the 'state of poverty is *spiritually* surer and more noble than the state of richness'.[6] Vanished hope is like the hope of methodism that vanished in England when, according to English historians, vicars were teaching patience while the unions were instilling impatience.[7] Hopes were walled in before a breach could be made in the cement.

In a different cultural area, is there not an analogous opening which makes a breach in the Buddhist theology and practice whereby the annihilation of desire is the necessary and even sufficient path to Nirvana? . . . Not only do the Bodhisattvas renounce this celestial annihilation for as long as this beatitude is not shared by the whole world, but –

especially in a whole current of Chinese Buddhism – a terrestrial Buddha – Maitreya – whose parousia is periodically seen as imminent – opposes the extra-cosmic Buddha. This perception becomes a leaven for the transformation of terrestrial institutions, both civil and religious, '. . . usually stirred up by some visionary monk putting himself forward as an incarnation or as the precursor of the messiah Maitreya . . . . There were no less than nine peasant revolts of Buddhist inspiration . . . between 402 and 517 . . . directed not only against the authority of the state, but also against the authority of the established Church' (P. Demiéville).

A religion of hope which is neither a blocked hope nor a vanished hope would therefore be a religion simultaneously of a different here-below in a different hereafter, or vice versa. It is part of utopia in that, in its own way, it is an imaginary project of a society that would be culturally (new heavens) and socially (new earth) *an alternative society*. This is the form of religious experience that can be observed in phenomena as numerous and as varied as: cults of possession, matrices of religions of salvation, socio-religious utopias, millenarianisms with or without messianism, contestant 'pentecostalisms', social dramatisations of a political and/or aesthetic kind . . . . These are the ones that will be given priority.

## 1 Hope as a waking dream

Looking through an old edition of Bossuet, and in another volume at some fragments of his *Discourse on universal history*, I came across this definition of hope by Aristotle, as reported by Diogenes Laertius and transcribed with admiration by Bossuet: 'What is hope? *The dream of an awakened man*'.[8] It has a triply solid guarantor – philosopher, historian and theologian combined.

But the dream is a mental category that is so suspected of being vacuous that it would surely be useless to add a triply plebeian guarantee, since sociologists, as we all know, are the plebeians of the 'logies'.

In his excellent contribution 'Prestiges et problèmes du Rêve',[9] Roger Caillois brilliantly demonstrates the narrowness of the frontier between the dream and reality. And what if reality, or what is called reality, had two registers, the *experienced*, certainly, but also the *dreamed*! And what if our matter-of-fact conception of reality was nothing but an occidental episode of this complex reality! Once developed, did not the theologies lean towards 'generally confirming the idea that the dream gives access to the divine world, or in any case a world that is *more significant if not more true than the world of wakefulness*'? This is also the conviction of the 'so-called primitive peoples':

> 'It has often been maintained that (they) do not distinguish between dreaming and wakefulness. I think one should vary this opinion: *they know perfectly well* what is dreaming and what is wakefulness, but they do not attribute any less reality to the dreamed than to the experienced . . . In other words, they make the distinction, but it does not follow that dreaming appears to be illusory and wakefulness incontestable. It could be that dreaming is reckoned to have the edge on wakeful-ness in terms of *density of existence*.'

There are dreams that precede, announce, command and finally constitute a reality that, without them, would only have been a latent possibility. Dreams and hope are in proximity to each other: 'The wonders of dreams are also connected . . . to the phenomena of haunting, of *possession*, of substitution of personality to which they remain close, to the expectation of a sign from the hereafter, to the hope of an irrefutable revelation. . . .'[10]

If this is the case for 'sleeping' dreams – including those in which 'one dreams that one awakens from a dream, whereas in reality it is the same dream unfolding' (R. Caillois) – what will it be for waking dreams, those in which one thinks that one is beginning to dream, whereas in reality thoughts insist on weaving their way in? And what will it be when these waking dreams are, in addition, social dreams in which, as every novel reveals, groups lie to themselves in order to speak their own truth? It is to these dreams that the Canadian sociologist Fernand Dumont calls the attention of his col-leagues, as though to an operational 'superstructure' as fundamental as the productive 'infrastructure':[11]

Without giving a long lesson of sociology or philosophy, one may recall that, in the tradition of the scientific analysis of society, two tendencies have gradually emerged.

According to one view, social life is to be explained from below: men have interests derived from the relations of production in their society; they belong to classes, they are part of organisations. In a word, they work. And, when they dream, their reveries, their ideologies rise up from a harder ground, formed by their labours and their conflicts. Who would disagree with this, even if he had never read Marx? The only condition would be that he must have worked.

But there is another view of things that starts from the reveries in which men, be they plumbers or doctors, impose ideals on their most empirical existence. *In order to adopt this analysis it is not necessary to believe in a mysterious collective spirit that broods over societies*. It is enough to admit that men dream when they work and vice versa; to recognise also that if work has its solidity, its techniques and its organisation, *dreams also cluster together and bring to bear on the gatherings of men a logic which, as it is not as clear as the other, must be deciphered*.

Finally, Roger Bastide sums it up in two short but dense essays on the sociology of the dream.[12] He agrees with Dumont in his diagnosis of the partiality of a certain sociology:

'Sociology is only interested in the awakened man, as though the sleeping man were dead. . . . Following the injunctions of our culture which, through all the curtains, be they of iron or of bamboo, is a culture of productivism, . . . it considers that work exorcises the fantasies born of a long night, in case they should disturb the Promethean act. . . . *Is this radical cleavage between . . . dreaming and working justified?* And should one not . . . see how the twilight states, how the obscure and dark matter of man prolongs the social aspect just as the social aspect feeds off our dreams? Briefly, should one not attempt a sociology of the dream?'

One can immediately see the two chapters. On the one hand, the chapter of 'the social structures of oneiric thought', in other words how the dream is *constituted* from its social structures; on the other hand, the chapter of the 'function of the dream in society', in other words how the dream *constitutes* a society, failing which 'productivism and mental illness are perhaps twins that one can absolutely not separate'. 'Freud impersonalised the dream, one must now resocialise it.'

This social function of dreams, Bastide continues, is without doubt repressed in 'our contemporary civilisation' where its substitute – resorting to the 'keys to dreams' – is considered merely to be 'refuse having to do not with a respectable sociology, but with a kind of social street cleansing service . . .'. On the other hand, in the so-called primitive societies – and here we come back to Caillois – this social function goes 'from medical diagnosis to the reception of a message from the hereafter, in the most varied circumstances, as much in daily life as in passing moments, in initiation rites, and finally in the dynamism of cultural changes, from the creation of a new song, or a new dance step, to the genesis of certain messianic movements'.

The second article insists not only on this social function of the dream, but on the necessary culture of this function: 'Physiologists have shown that dreaming is absolutely essential to the health of the individual, and see in a decrease in dreaming the sign of serious illness. One is more and more convinced that what is true biologically speaking, is just as true psychologically speaking'. And if we refer to F. A. Weiss,[13] we see that he refuses to see in the dream a simple phenomenon of reactivation of a traumatic past or a troubled present, but he makes of it an 'active', 'creative' process, to the extent that he asks the therapist not to be a 'killer of dreams' but an instructor of the nocturnal life of his patients. In dreaming, the patient 'forges his future'. The *awakened* dream comes from the same dynamics as the nocturnal dream: 'So we see that at present a whole movement is taking shape to give back to the dream, *one could add to the awakened dream*, . . . its vital role, and to reintroduce it into the dynamics of a *personality* . . . .' Bastide adds: and into the dynamics of *collectivities*. The relationship of the *dream* and the myth and their interpenetration in the myth-dream, a key concept proposed by Burridge[14] for the interpretation of a secularised millenium, bears witness to this. For 'myths and dreams are not played in two different registers of the imaginary . . . .' Indeed, why could one not find a myth-dream 'in our western societies as well as among the Melanesians'?

If hope is an awakened dream, as Aristotle or Plato suggested, this awakened dream would paradoxically be one of its 'peaks'. It is up to sociology to shed light on this dream 'in the same way and for the same reasons that the dream sheds light on the social factor'.

## 2 Hope as a 'collective ideation'

This sociological category plays a latent role in the work of Durkheim. It is, however, only in a note to one of his discourses that it is stated formally.[15] It is shown there to be a fundamental sociological category, not without some nostalgia: 'There is a whole part of sociology involving the search for the laws of collective ideation, still altogether unexplored.'

Durkheim's work taken together nevertheless situates the place and the function of this collective ideation in the anatomy of the religious phenomenon as well as in the anatomy of any shared conviction. In his commentary on his major work (*Forms*) Durkheim considered the nature of 'religious ideals', and reiterated a vital distinction:[16]

> Religion is not only a *system of ideas*, it is above all a *system of forces* . . . . Religious life implies the existence of *very specific forces* . . . recalling a well-known phrase, I will restrict myself to saying that they are *the forces that can move mountains*. By that I mean that when man lives a religious life, he believes he is participating in a force that dominates him, *but which at the same time supports him and raises him above himself* . . . . In a word, the characteristic of religion is the dynamogenic influence that it exercises on consciousness.

From this fundamental remark on the physiology of the religious phenomenon one can infer its anatomy as it is implicitly expressed elsewhere.[17]

This phenomenon can be stratified according to three superimposed levels:

*Level 1:*
An unstable, ephemeral layer which is specifically that of the system of ideas: a speculative layer, in other words, *explanatory* of man and the world. It is 'that of a man who *represents* the world to himself in such and such a way'. Diagnosis: 'Religion is the science of a society without science'. This being so, 'scientific thought is merely a more perfect form of religious thought. It seems only natural that the second should progressively fade behind the first, as the latter becomes more able to carry out its task'. One is in the '-logy' in its purest state. The scientific '-logies' (anthropo-, socio-, psycho-, logies, etc.) take the place of the religious '-logies' (theologies).

*Level 3:*
In contrast a stable and perennial layer. It is more that of an '-urgy', or in strictly Durkheimian terms, that of *cult* . . . . 'There is something eternal in religion . . . it is the cult' (*Forms*, pp. 609, 615). Not that the '-urgies' do not die. But if they die in one society, they are resuscitated in the starts of another society, from the spring which is 'the particular life that emanates from men when they are assembled together', when 'under the effect of the collective force they are sometimes seized by a real delirium which incites them to acts in which they do not recognise themselves'. The *elementary forms* of religion must be found in this endemic or epidemic sociurgy: for 'the true function of religion is not to make us think, to enrich our knowledge or to add to the representations that we owe to science the representations of a different origin and character, but *to make us act, to help us to live*' (ibid., p. 595). And if this function is not assumed by a religious liturgy, it will be assumed by a social dramaturgy. It is in this celebrating and celebrated action that the 'dynamogenic influence' that is exercised on consciousness activates or reactivates itself.

*Finally, level 2:*
The intermediary level. The first level is, at the extreme, that of a system of *ideas* without *force*. The third, that of a system of *forces* without *ideas*. Between them is an ambiguous level of *ideas-forces*: that of collective ideations. The composition of this layer takes its elements partly from 'borrowings from the established sciences'; but that is not sufficient, because 'science is fragmentary and incomplete, it advances slowly and is never concluded; life, however, cannot wait' (ibid., p. 615). Hence it is nourished equally by a 'faith'[18] which is above all 'a desire to act, and science, however far one pushes it, always keeps at a distance from action . . . . Theories that are *destined to make one live, to make one act, are therefore obliged to anticipate science and complete it prematurely*' (ibid., p. 615).

At this level, one is in a '-logy' mixed with an '-urgy' and vice versa. To Durkheim this ambiguous combination is not only the fact of the knowledgeable religions like the theologies, but of other ideologies, like for example, the 'socialisms', analysed in the same terms in his (Bordeaux) lectures and his controversy with Lagardelle. This diagnosis is not, however, disqualifying. If he is demystifying anything, it would be just as much the value of faith illicitly attributed to a science, as the value of science arbitrarily postulated by a faith.

For according to this same analysis, a real society can no more do without these collective ideations than an organism can do without reflexes and, in that sense, prejudices, or in other words prematurely born judgments. 'A society with no prejudices would be like an organism with no reflexes, it would be a monster incapable of living' (*La Science sociale et l'action*, p. 197). And that is why 'religions, even the most rational and the most secularised, are not able and will never be able to do without a very particular kind of speculation which, while having the same objects as science itself, cannot however be truly scientific . . .' (*Forms*, pp. 615–16).

This circumspect analysis of warm societies by a cold sociology is at the same time an analysis of the contesting societies by a sociologist whose temperament is more con-servative. At the level where he detaches structure and function from the collective ideation, he anticipates and joins the social sleep-walking assigned to the myth-dream by his contemporary commentators. For the religion that he is talking about is a 'faith-hope', one that can move mountains, in which man is supported by what dominates him: these ideas or ideals *up in the air*, these 'creations up in the air' (Freud), whose dynamogenic value does not come from the rational validity of their systems of explanation, but from the mobilising and animating power of their oneirism. If hopes and the myths that carry them are collective ideations, they are at the same time much more and much less than sciences. 'Much less' is a trough, 'much more' is a peak.

## 3 Hope as exuberant expectation

The way is opened by a third French sociologist, Marcel Mauss. It is he who, in a discourse to the Society of Psychology,[19] marked off this field of expectation as a sociological field, or even an inter-disciplinary field. . . .

> one of the phenomena . . . which implies this considera-
> tion of the whole of man: his body, his instincts, his
> emotions, his desires, his perceptions, his intellect . . .
> one of the phenomena of sociology that is the closest to
> both the psychological and the physiological, and . . .
> also one of the most frequent.
>     A whole part of law is expectation. Emmanuel Lévy
> demonstrated it: the right of civil responsibility is an
> expectation; but the violation of laws, crime, is merely an
> offence against expectation, for people never expect laws
> and circumstances to change. And the idea of order is
> but a symbol of their expectations. A whole part of art is
> no more than a system of raised and fulfilled expectations,
> of alternate games of disappointed and satisfied expecta-
> tions. Bergson developed this idea as far as comedy was
> concerned. It is to be found in Aristotle; he proposed the
> theory, so simple and so right, of purification, at bottom
> the purging of expectation, which justified many rites and
> the use – which was once ritual – of the comic and the
> tragic. A whole part of the effects of art, the novel, music,
> games, the entire practice of fictitious passions, replace in
> us the dark dramas of real passion, barbaric, ancient or
> wild. Even economic facts have a whole side that is

connected with phenomena of expectation: lottery, speculation, credit, discounts, money, all correspond to expectations. From the point of view of general sociology, one could cite the common states of tension; what is called diplomatic tension; the 'attention' of the soldier in the ranks or on sentry duty. In technology one only has to look at the anxiety that goes with most technical projects.

Particularly fruitful is the study of expectation and moral illusion, the deceptions inflicted on the expectation of individuals and collectivities, the study of their reactions . . . .

A good psychological and especially physiological description would enable us better to describe the 'vague anxieties' – smacking of madness – the precise images that replace them, and the violent movements and absolute inhibitions that expectation causes within us. Such things are rare in the happy, secular and civil life that was ours. But war made us feel and live experiences of this kind. They must have been and still are infinitely more frequent in the lives of the men who surround us and of those who preceded us.

Finally, expectation is one of those things in which emotion, perception and more exactly the movement and the state of the body directly condition the social state and are conditioned by it. As with all the facts that I have cited, the triple consideration of the body, the mind and the social environment must be taken into account.

This call to psychology was not without echoes. Jean Lacroix makes a brilliant and rapid evaluation in a work well worth considering.[20] This evaluation shows that there are two levels in expectation: on the one hand a level of *aspiration* or expectation of a *desirable ideal*, desired as this desire invests it in *will*; on the other hand, a *level of anticipation* of a *possible realisation*, as it is circumscribed by *capacities*. One also finds this dialectic of hope between what one *should* do to reply to the *subjective* demand of desires, and what one *can* do to respond to the *objective* framework of powers. There is a *trough*, revealed by classical Marxist analysis. But there is also a *peak*, especially when the expectation is joyfully exuberant. It is then similar to that faith of which it is said 'it moves mountains'. The will gives rise to capacities. The desirable exorcises the impossible. Aspiration expands expectancy. The *representations* of hope transform *hopeless situations*. At the extreme, to take up a well-known axiom, if social existence determines consciousness, consciousness determines this social existence just as much if not more. Imagination takes charge.

But another distinction is proposed here, especially where hope is identified with this exuberance. It is the distinction between *inhibitory* expectation and *exalting* expectation. Here the peaks and troughs are also difficult to dissociate. For there are cases – innumerable cases – in which the expectation is exalting, mobilising, motivating, creating 'coalescences', gathering together, decompartmentalising, producing energies, sudden movements, resistances, exoduses and hegiras, revolts and crusades, commotions and stirrings in peoples, social groups, nations or churches, corporations or sects, which it hoists up above themselves in an unprecedented cultural creativity. But there are also cases – and they are not rare – in which expectation is inhibitory, demobilising, reinforcing with its debilitating virus the weaknesses of a society that is anaemic, disintegrating, full of abdications and defeats, idealising the senescences or the laxities of a social web, postulating euthanasia and making it sacred. When Hernando Cortes came to Mexico City, the Aztec expectation nourished an inhibition of this kind which gave the conquistadors an unexpected weapon: that of a brain-washing operated by an 'intoxicant' in which the anaemia of the expectation had anaesthetised the resilience of the aspiration . . . . In that kind of expectation, the conquistadors are seen as ancient gods returning to take possession of the Empire. Montezuma was already conquered when he greeted Cortes:[21]

> Lord, you have at last reached your city: Mexico. You have come to take your place on the throne . . . I have already seen you, I have already cast my eyes on your face! . . . Such was the legacy and the message of our kings . . . . According to them you would take your place

on your chair, on your majestic throne . . . . And now it
is done . . . . Come into your land: take possession of
your royal dwelling place . . . . Come into your land,
Lords!

It was the same with the Inca Empire, where the Indians saw
the arrival of the Spanish 'as a return of the gods', as
'virachochas'. This does not prevent this inhibitory expectation from becoming, or becoming again, an exalting expectation and even a revolutionary expectation, also in the name of
ancient gods, but seen this time as the gods of the revenge of
the occupied against the occupying. The themes of Expectation are reversed: the Spanish 'are not the sons of Virachocha,
but of the devil' . . . 'the Spanish had conquered the Indians;
*but now the world was coming full circle*, God and the Spanish
would be beaten this time and all the Spanish killed, their
towns swallowed up, and the sea would swell and drown them
and banish their memory'.[22]

## 4 Hope as a generalised utopia

The sociologist that we would refer to here for our anthology
could well be the Italian sociologist, Antonio Gramsci. He is
one of those who did not accept the validity of the distinction
– adequate for the catechist but otherwise to be treated with
caution – between what was called 'utopian' socialism and
'scientific' socialism, at least at the level where such a
distinction has become vulgar through being popularised.
Today the analyses that can distinguish the utopian elements
of this 'science' as well as the scientific elements of this
'utopia', are increasing. To take only two cases, the second
centenary of Robert Owen in 1971 and of Charles Fourier in
1972 provided an opportunity to make a multiple return to
sources which had been treated far too long as simple samples
of a 'primitive mentality' . . . . 'Scientific' arrogance must
increasingly admit that its relativising absolutism is itself a
dated and context-bound Europeocentric product, that is
itself relativisable. In the opposite sense, the dream, the
trance, indeed even madness, and in any case myths as well as
utopia, acquire the density of proceedings which, although
they are not rationalised and are even irrational, are none the

less human proceedings which in the end come from another type of rationality or 'science'.

We are not dealing in this work with real utopias as such, any more than with those social waking dreams which were the religions in utopia.[23] It is obvious however, that the utopian cycle, in particular the one which culminates in the so-called 'utopian socialisms' – that socio-cultural matrix of contemporary socialism – is one of the cycles that unfolded from the manifestations of the Hope phenomenon in its millenarian stage. We shall come across it again.[24] What should above all be noted here, is the assurance with which a label that has depreciated as much as the label of 'utopia' is emerging today from the pejorative atmosphere to which it found itself relegated. It is not the only one to be in that position: one could say the same about labels such as 'sect', 'primitive', 'pagans', 'heresies', 'dreams' and many others, which are considered to be labelling *marginal* phenomena, and of which we have already said that they have above all been marginalised phenomena. Certainly most of the cases we have noted refer to one form or another of social oneirism. But does not the very fact that this oneirism has been or is being treated as a negligible quantity or an aberrant qualification corre-spond to a mental attitude that is itself neglectful and in the long run erroneous? Bastide says:[25]

> The question I ask myself is that of knowing whether the sociologist has the right to ignore the other half of our life, to want to envisage man only standing or sitting, not lying and dreaming . . . . Is this radical break between the psychological and the social, which is like the reflection at the scientific level of these two halves of man, the dreaming and the working, really justified?

Are not utopia and hope, in particular, twin sisters? In utopia there is the hope of a different society. In hope there is the utopia of a different world. In both of them there is the strategy of alterity. Between both of them, the dividing line is very fine: the utopian society has its religious trances; the world of hope has its terrestrial implications ('on earth as it is in heaven') . . . . And in the long run, if one wants to ride the 'utopias' of the pejorative charges that a very determined

23

society has burdened them with, is there not an elective affinity between this utopia and religion itself? Gramsci answers this question in the affirmative.[26]

> It does not mean that utopia cannot have a philosophical value, for it has a political value, and all politics are implicitly philosophies, albeit in a state of fragments and rough outline. In this sense, *religion is the greatest utopia, in other words the greatest 'metaphysic', that has appeared in history*, because it is the most grandiose attempt to reconcile in a mythological form the real contradictions of historical life: indeed it states that men have the same 'nature', that man in general exists, as he was created by God, the son of God, and consequently the brother of other men, equal to other men, free among other men and like other men, and that he can conceive of himself as such by seeing himself in God, 'the autoconsciousness' of humanity; but it also states that all this is not of this world, but will happen in another (– utopian) world. So there fermented among men the ideas of equality, fraternity and liberty, among the layers of men who do not see themselves as either the equals or the brothers of other men, or free in relation to them. So it was that these demands were made, in one way or another, in well-defined forms and ideologies in all radical agitations of crowds.

So two movements intersect each other: the movement of Gramsci which postulates religion as a generalising and generalised utopia; and the movement of utopism itself: does it not postulate in the last analysis '*the utopianisation of the world*', according to Cabet's vow in his *Voyage en Icarie*?

The objection to this eventual reciprocity of perspective is immediate and obvious. It is the one according to which hope is a successful utopia and utopia a failed hope. But as we shall see, the handling of categories such as failure or success hardly lends itself to such summary oppositions, which have already been pertinently denounced by the philosopher.[27] Rather than wanting to cross definitions, it would perhaps be better to consider utopia more as a secularising religion and religion more as a sacralising utopia. But in each case, it is the imaginary which is at work, that of a creative imagination, and if it is not creative 'of creators' as Bergson maintained, it is at least *creative of creativity*.

Having proposed these four sociological concepts to theologian audiences, I am aware that they may seem tentative, hesitant, indeed even feeble, and in some way more likely to denounce the troughs rather than announce the peaks of hope treated in this way. For he who *lives* by *a* hope, his hope does not *appear* as a waking dream, or a collective ideation, or an expectation oscillating between inhibition and exaltation, or a utopia, be it generalised or generalising. And during the correspondence undertaken on the occasion of the Dictionary of Millenarianisms, several religious bodies did indeed challenge the index cards that concerned them with a rather similar argument: only we *ourselves* can interpret *our own* hope. They are right in their system of *forces*. The sociologist who analyses Bahaism or Kimbanguism does not *live* himself by that force which the hope of the CJCSK, the Church of Jesus Christ on earth through Simon Kimbangu, or the Bahai World Faith gives its believer . . . . But the first does not share the hope of the second and vice versa. And in the thousand and one hopes that can and should be thus confronted, a thousand and one systems of forces are expressed in a thousand and one languages. Looking at the hypothesis of a common *sociological* stock, it is inevitable for the comparativist to propose 'roots' which *appear* to maintain distant relations with each of these languages. And yet this hypothesis is itself inevitable: even if, in order to be fruitful, it has to 'wait' for the consequences of an altogether contingent ecumenism; even if such a sociological project feeds, more or less surreptitiously, a dream, an ideation, an expectation and a utopia. For even if a society is constituted 'above all *by the idea that it has of itself*', even if a 'religious experience' founded on this exists, 'it does not in any way follow that the reality that founds it conforms objectively to the idea that the believers have of it'.[28]

## II The troughs of hope

Why 'troughs'? Because of Sophocles, whom we have already quoted: 'I have nothing but scorn for the mortal who comforts himself with hollow hopes.' But here, as before, the peak and the trough are difficult to separate. And after all, if the peaks may have seemed debilitating, it is not impossible for the troughs, on the contrary, to appear to be comforting. In any case, this preliminary chapter which is intentionally conceptual, will be illuminated in the following chapters which are deliberately more empirical. To the four 'peaks' classified by sociological induction, let us now add four 'troughs' where sociologies will still be on the receiving end.

### 1 The trough of its conditions or failed hope

Simone Weil, who likes to quote Sophocles comments: 'Throughout history men have suffered and died in order to emancipate the oppressed. Their efforts, when they have not been in vain have only ended in replacing one regime of oppression by another.' She is echoed by Jeanne Deroin, another militant worker a century earlier, after the failure in 1848: 'Revolutions cannot produce the well-being aspired to by the suffering classes: they almost always serve as a stepping stone for a few ambitious people to gain power . . . .'

This disenchantment could appear suspect to some if its underlying argument did not coincide with the distinction already adopted from the psychologists: that which distinguishes in hope between the desirable defined by a level of aspiration, and the possible defined by a level of expectation. This psychological distinction also corresponds to a sociological distinction. The latter can be commented on by a case study.

There is a Marxist text according to which 'humanity only poses itself problems it can solve'. Taken out of context, this text has even become a slogan propitious to the disproportion of certain autosatisfactions. This extrapolation which lends itself to unqualified extrapolation by some pundits – luckily for some and unluckily for others – is negated by other texts which state exactly the opposite: humanity does pose itself problems which are insoluble. The most topical of these texts is probably the one in which Engels presents his own treatment of a hope-phenomenon as spectacular as the one implied in the theology of Thomas Münzer and in the practice of the revolting German peasants in the sixteenth century.[29]

The phenomenon, in addition to its historical effervescence, is also distinguished by its cultural commemoration in the collective memory. It is on this phenomenon that first Engels, then K. Kautsky focused one of their best analyses of historical sociology. It is this phenomenon that A. Weill rehabilitated in a Fourierist publication, not without bombast and plagiarism, for a clientele of French pioneers of 'social science'. It is around this phenomenon that Ernst Bloch brings out, in an early work,[30] what was to become his twofold expertise in utopian phenomena and the hope-phenomenon. And finally, if one is not mistaken, it is still this same phenomenon that is borne, like a splinter in the flesh, by at least a section of the theological descendants of the Reformation.

A summary of the case was proposed by Engels in a less well-known publication.[31]

> Luther had always defined his objective as the return to
> primitive Christianity in theory; and in practice the
> peasantry took on exactly the same definition, demanding
> in consequence not only the ecclesiastical but also the
> *social* practice of primitive Christianity . . . . Thus did
> they revolt and begin a war against the lords which could
> only be a war of extermination . . . .

So there are two hopes face to face, in opposition even, both of equally Christian reference. Each one has *its* theology. The first one has Luther's theology: 'He believed as strongly in the divine right of princes and lords to march on the people as he believed in the Bible.' The second one has Münzer's theology: on the one hand a theology of 'the kingdom of God', already identified with something like a classless society ('his political programme bordered on communism'); on the other hand a theology of the Holy Ghost 'enthusiasm of reason', not without 'an extraordinary resemblance to the modern speculative concepts, sometimes bordering even on atheism'. Quite obviously a Münzerised Engels brings to mind an acceptably

Marxised Münzer. But the outcome of the analysis is even more remarkable. It is concerned with the defeat and the rout that made this Münzerian hope a failed hope. And one comes again across the proposed distinction between the two categories, that of the *objectively possible* and of the *subjectively necessary*.

Here is the situation:

> The worst that can happen to a leader of an extreme movement is to be obliged to take hold of the power at a time when the movement is not yet mature enough to dominate the class that he represents or to apply the measures that the domination of this class demands.

And here is the impasse:

On the one hand, the *objectively possible*:

> What he can do does not depend on his will, but on the stage that the antagonism of the different classes has reached, on the degree of development of the conditions of material existence, and on the state of production and the transports that determine at every given moment the degree of development of the antagonisms of classes.

This objectively possible is therefore – negatively – at the limit of what is *materially* circumscribed by a system of constraints.

But what is *subjectively necessary* is beyond these limits, for there is also a certain *psychological* determinism fed by the density and ebullience of the aspirations that are fostered and sustained.

> *What he must do*, what his own party demands of him, does not depend on him once again, *nor does it depend on the degree of development of the struggle of the classes and its conditions*. It is linked to *the doctrines he has taught and the claims he has made up to then*, doctrines and claims that do not come from the momentary relations of social classes that are face to face, but from the more or less deep understanding of the general tendencies of the social and political development.

To sum up

He is thus necessarily placed before an insoluble
dilemma. *What he can do* contradicts all his past action,
his principles and the immediate interests of his party,
and *what he should do* is impracticable.

*Conclusion:* it is therefore *possible* for a humanity to pose itself
*necessarily* insoluble problems. There are failed hopes because
they are *hic et nunc cornered* hopes. It is true, as Sartre
postulates, that 'the past is continually being adjourned'. And
the old phalansterian satirist did not fail to attribute to his
Thomas Münzer the demand of such an adjournment.[32] But
this is already another dimension, which we shall be
approaching later on.

## 2 The trough of its springboards or empty hope

In this case it is a page of Durkheim that yet again provides a
guide-line analysis. We know the thesis set out in *Elementary
forms.* Having selected *one* type of religious life as a field of
analysis, Durkheim asks himself about the matrix phenomenon which underlies the system of beliefs and rites, and he
detects this phenomenon in an effervescent cult related to a
cult of possession. Finally he generalises: 'It is in the effervescent social milieus and from this effervescence itself that
the religious idea seems to be born' (*Forms*, p. 313). Mistakes
have been made about the meaning of the hypothesis and it
has been supposed that primitive religions of the analysed
type were elementary forms of all subsequent religions. It
would appear that the hypothesis is different: elementary
forms and later forms exist in *all* religions, as is indicated by
another commentary: 'Indeed it was during moments of
effervescence of this kind that the great ideals upon which
civilisations rest, have *at all times* been constituted.' We have
already evoked this Durkheimian *anatomy* of the religious
phenomenon in what has preceded.

The analysis that follows has the advantage of outlining its
*physiology*, and in that physiology the logic or even the logistics
of hope. After mentioning some of the 'creative or innovating
periods' in which a 'collective enthusiasm' dragged history
towards its 'not-yet', the analysis continues:[33]

At those moments it is true, this higher life is lived with such intensity and in such an exclusive way that it takes up almost all the room in consciousnesses, it more or less completely chases out the selfish and common pre-occupations. The ideal tends to become one with the real; that is why men have the impression that the time is near when it will become reality itself and when the kingdom of God will be achieved on this earth. But the illusion is never lasting because this exaltation itself cannot last: it is too exhausting. Once the critical moment has passed, the social thread slackens, intellectual and sentimental commerce abates, individuals fall back to their ordinary level. Then all that has been said, done, thought, felt during the period of fertile upheaval only survives in the shape of memory, prestigious no doubt, just like the reality that it recalls, but with which it has stopped being confused. It is only an idea, a collection of ideas. This time, the opposition is clear-cut. There is, on one side, what is given in sensations and perceptions, and on the other, what is thought in the shape of ideals. Certainly these ideals would quickly be etiolated if they were not periodically revived. That is the purpose of festivals, public, religious or secular ceremonies, preaching of all kinds, of the Church or of school, dramatic representations, artistic manifestations, in a word everything that can bring men closer together and make them communicate in the same intellectual and moral life. They are like partial and weakened revivals of the effervescence of the creative eras.

This page of anthology comes at the right moment to connote the 'effervescent' qualification added above to Marcel Mauss's notes on the sociology of expectation: 'The ideal tends then to become one with the real: that is why men believe that the time is near when it will become reality itself . . . .' These comments are just as valid for the celebration of a cargo cult as they are for the expectancy expressed by Lenin in his diaries during the period of war communism, when he counted month after month and sometimes day after day on the conflagration of the western proletariat. Finally this same analysis carves out the very trough of hope which is the trough of its springboards: 'The illusion is never lasting because this exaltation cannot last, *it is too exhausting* . . . . Once the critical moment has passed, *the social thread slackens* . . . .' Is this not confirmed in particular for what has been called in the same text 'the great Christian crisis' . . . including its reactivation by that enigmatic Montanism of Asia Minor and its expectation of a celestial Jerusalem in the valley of Pepuza? Was such a crisis not locatable until the fourth century, even in a whole patristic vein which will be mentioned later? And all this without mentioning the apocalyptic Judeo-Christian tradition, canonical or apocryphal, which is more or less mixed in with the outbursts of revolt, both cultural and social, against the imperial and imperialist Roman occupation . . . .

But also and especially if this analysis carves out the trough of this congenitally wounded hope, it designates the endogenous therapy invented by all societies to dress the wound. For if 'the exaltation cannot last', it can be perpetuated in two forms: in the collective *memory* by being guaranteed an *echo*; in the collective *consciousness* by being assured of a *viaticum*. Hope is only empty when it is without echo or viaticum. The collective memory offers it this echo in which 'it is perpetuated in the form of memory'; we should even mention the case in which the collective memory not only commemorates but also restores, reconstructs or even constructs an 'elementary form', events and/or people; for if the past is sometimes the matrix of a future which is its repercussion, in other cases the future is the matrix of a past which is its projection or rather its retrojection. Furthermore, the collective consciousness is such that it will not leave hope without a viaticum: 'Ideals would be quickly etiolated if they were not periodically revived. That is the purpose of *festivals* . . . etc.' 'Religious or secular' festivals, 'dramatic' or 'artistic' – and what festival does not have a little of all these elements – are situated not only in the system of ideas but in a system of forces that they activate or reactivate, instigate or restore; they do more than commemorate, they celebrate, and these celebrations are a food, a fullness that fills the trough of a hope that is emptying itself. The echo in the collective memory and the viaticum of the

31

collective consciousness join together in order to resist the deactivations and decelerations of hope, which is born – *in illo tempore* – in the high places of the collective imagination. As Harvey Cox said, they are the three daughters of time who hold hands and invite one to the libations.[34] This Cantata of three voices and its constituent roles will be the theme of a later chapter (cf. *infra* ch. 5). The social physiology of hope will better illustrate how a hope without an echo or a hope without a viaticum, slides towards an empty hope, according to whether its springboards are absent or even short-lived.

### 3 The trough of its levels or trapped hope

Whether it finds its polarisation in an 'elsewhere' or a 'not-yet', the strategy of hope is one of transition between the Same and the Other: the situations such as they are, are not destined to remain identical to themselves, they can and should become others, completely different others, including the situation that makes me what I am, and its metamorphosis which arranges to meet that which I am not. That is the certainty that also makes hope into a faith.

It is this certainty which is ambiguous, and this ambiguity is shown in the double root – *alter* and *alienus* – which produced the double noun: *alterity* on the one hand, and *alienation* on the other. It is as though hope were making a promise – to come out of itself – and at the same time was concealing a threat – not to be able to return to itself. There is a double trap: that of finding alienation when one was searching for alterity; and that of giving up all alterity to avoid alienation.

The masters of suspicion – Marx and Nietzsche in particular – devoted themselves to uncovering the snares of alienation. Would hope – like religion – be the recourse of the man who either has not yet found himself, or has already lost himself again? or, to take Marx's words, 'the illusory sun which moves around man, as long as man does not move around himself'? 'Soul of a world with no soul and spirit of a situation with no spirit'? 'Halo of a vale of tears'? or even 'opium of the people'?[35] All these grievances turn out to be even more forceful when they take as a target one or another of the situations that corresponds exactly to the forms of either a *faded* hope or a *blocked* hope . . . . We have already mentioned this and there is no point in returning to it . . . .

The pattern does indeed seem to be more complex than this brilliant polemic would suggest. It forces one to return to the subtle and ambiguous games of alterity and alienation.

Although hope coincides with a strategy of alterity, it does not arbitrarily remain in monistic compartments. One could write a social history of hope, therefore of religion, as the history of a universal resignation that is doped or drugged by the illusory spell of a fallacious hereafter. But one could just as well write another history of the same hope – therefore of the same religion – as the history of continual outbursts of societies disenchanted with their temporal institutions as well as with their spiritual ones; a history which questions itself about this disenchantment in order to throw up other ways of life on a new earth under new heavens. After all, the fragments of the history of religions that can be collected from Marx-Engels are not any less close to the second version than they are to the first. And the hope-phenomenon, as it has been defined, is situated in the turning points of such outbursts . . . .

One can even see their double strategy through their typology. On the one hand a *minimalist* strategy: the one that ends in something like a general strike of established societies and religions, in order to create global micro-societies founded on a non-co-operation with the dominant society of whom one asks the *minimum* to be able to live *outside* it. On the other hand, a *maximalist* strategy: the one that on the contrary would win from this dominating society the *maximum* to be able to live *within* it and to replace it. There is a certain continuum present in the combination and eventual conjugation of these two strategies. It is in this continuum that one can place face to face the *troughs* of a triple alienation, which are correlative to the *peaks* of a triple alterity. Chances against risks; risks against chances. Recto and verso. Traps and promises; promises and traps. In any case it is impossible to take refuge in ponderousness in order to escape from this reciprocal relativisation.

(1) The first form of *alterity* practised by a social strategy is the hope of *alternance*. A society that cannot last in its super-

society – 'this exaltation cannot last, it is too exhausting' –
divides, or allows itself to be divided within itself, into sectors
of alternance in which this super-society can fulfil its function
of counter-society.

Sectors in time: Sabbath of days, Sabbath of years, Sabbath
of Sabbaths. Society accepts being lived in the wrong way. It
even accepts being turned upside down: hierarchies are
reversed; taboos are violated; holidays supplant all work;
rational behaviour gives way to excitement, to the carnival, to
the feast of fools.

Sectors in place: sacred high places are exterritorialised.
Within their precinct the application of laws is suspended.
They are inviolable places of refuge where nevertheless the
rules are violated. Often these places of alternance are
combined with times of alternance.

Economic sectors: a 'quaternary' economy replaces the
classical sectors of the primary, secondary and tertiary
economies; economy of the potlatch, of the gift and the
counter-gift, of consummation, sacrificial economy, oblative
economy.

Social sectors: sometimes formed by a slice of alternating
life for a given group, sometimes coagulated round a
demarcated social group; groups that are both counterweights
and compensation; accepted and supported even, by the
global society, whose paradoxical function is to live contrary
to the norms of life advocated by this society . . . . A way for a
society to deny itself in affirming itself, to affirm itself in
denying itself . . . to alternate calculation with fantasy, the
moroseness of compunction with optimistic or black humour,
work with play, the living one earns with the living that comes
after the living one earns . . . . Through these alternate
dispensations, the hope of being other, will have been a
viaticum, and purgatories furtively nibble away at the edge of
paradise.

The trap of this alterity is alienation in evasion, or
escapism: 'Nothing is any good without measure' (Durkheim).
And there is indeed a measure beyond which hope experienced
in this way, is trapped in a 'trip' from which it does not
return. The artificial paradise of drugs is not only a symbol of
it, but a case. That the hope of alternance can become so

devastating that it acts like an opium, is one question. But it is another question to know how a society could live without alternances through which it is experienced and expressed *other* than it is in its daily life.

(2) The second form of this alterity is the hope of *altercation* . . . . It is joined to the preceding one by definite links. Jean Cocteau in his *Bacchus*, stages a festival of fools in which the reversal of social hierarchies is suddenly taken seriously by his hero, who attempts a 'revolution' by assuring the political continuity of this ludic reversal. A festival can be close to a revolution. And conversely, is there not a festival in all revolution? In a recent study, a young sociologist (D. Mothé) pointed out the aspects of festivity implied in the subversion of a strike.[36]

> The setting in motion of a strike causes in the militants and sometimes in the workers who are taking part in it, feelings of joy that are comparable to the ones caused by religious or sexual rites, or even by intellectual and artistic creation. The strike could be compared to kinds of spectacles in which the principal actors are the militants who, in order to make a success of the show, attempt to make the spectators take an active part, in other words the body of the workers . . . . The emotive charge immediately freed by *the act of downing tools* . . . is so powerful for most militants that it would be ridiculous to measure it by the results accomplished, which very often consist in a very modest increase in salary. In the factories, the militant workers (or the ones who are determined to start strikes), are also the ones who very often do not look at their pay slips and are the least well-informed about their rights, because they are the ones who are the most disinterested.

'The act of downing tools!' It is precisely *strikes* of this kind that function in the strategy of the hope of altercation. Its bridgehead could be an operation of alternance as it is in Cocteau's *Bacchus*. But its occupied area is that of a managing strike – not always self-managing – under the various guises manifested by the social history of such hopes. Strike of religious society, of course; strike of images (iconoclasms); strike of buildings (churches or temples); strike of certain rites (circumcision, christenings . . .); strike of sacred places or times, or of sacralised people. When prophetic, and in some cases millenarian, hope moves the believers of a cargo cult or the disciples of a black African prophet, the 'missions' are deserted, the catechisers go away, the Bible is re-interpreted . . . . A hope of *altercation* emerges in a radical contestation of imported messages and institutions, and creates its own operational area in a group, a cult, an audience, a clientele, a circle of disciples, a micro- or para-church . . . . The Greek 'orgeons' and 'thiases' did not operate differently towards the cults of the city so as to overtake them with what would become a religion of salvation . . . .

But in this procedure this religious strike interlocks with a social, economic or political strike. Strike of the courts by the institution of an internal jurisdiction; strike of the culture dispensed by the network of the dominating society; strike of census-taking; strikes of such and such a form of property or appropriation; of such and such a form of production (industrial in particular); of such and such a form of consumption (vegetarianism, the eating of raw food, refusal to use imported food or clothing); of such and such a form of marriage in favour of monasticism, mixed or not, of polygamy or plural marriage; of such and such a form of reproduction replaced either by a taboo of sexuality or by a 'stirpiculture'. In the extreme form, strike of life itself in sacrificial suicides by fire or hunger-strike.

These are managing strikes. In other words their altercation cuts into the dominating society and creates micro-societies of opposition: practised utopias, 'ecclesiolae', communities, communes, monasticisms, phalansteries, micro-societies in which the laws of the macro-society are not only suspended but replaced by a new regime of direct action and of propagation by action. The expectation is not only partial, it becomes global, even if this globality turns out to be marginal . . . .

The trap of this alterity is obviously that of alienation in an opposition that is sometimes symbolic, sometimes re-assimilable, but vain in each case. But social and religious history

do not allow one to disqualify *a priori* the values of contagious-
ness and dispersion implied in such a strategy. It often occurs
that this altercation – by becoming federalised and generalised – initiates in a society the opposition of a counter-society
with its triple power: occupation, compensation or nego-
tiation. And it is possible for this altercation to emerge into an
alternative.

(3) The third and final form of this alterity – after alternance
and altercation – is the *alternative*.[37] Opposition takes power.
For example what at first was just an alternance of cult or of
culture – at the extreme a social waking dream, an oneiric
revelation, a seasonal festivity, an episodic prophet, a fabled
high place – becomes a centre of gravity and coalescence for a
minority of altercation, which is prolonged by its activism,
widened by its propaganda, deepened by combining its
ebullience and its reflection, rooted by commemorating itself
. . . . The core combines with others by incorporating them,
insinuates itself between the counter-culture that it postulates
and the acculturations that it attempts to subdue, makes
compromises between its level of aspiration and its level of
expectation, federates and purges, combines the extension
that it strives to attain and the intensity that it risks losing,
divides within itself the required alternances, transcends or
co-opts the internal altercations which inevitably appear,
steers a course in order to reach the size of a counter-power
. . . . At this point the trial of strength ensues with its two
outcomes: defeat, followed by repression; victory followed by
accession to omnipotence. After all, the trajectories that have
been followed throughout the centuries by the three great
religious hopes – Buddhism, Christianity and Islam – are not
that different from that victorious profile. And as for the
profile of defeat, the profile of socio-religious dissents confined
or driven back into a marginalisation, witness is born to it by
thousands of populations – by 'thousands of Christs' – which
are easily discernible as we shall see. It all comes to pass as
though militant hope had no issue other than a suffering hope
on the one hand and a triumphant hope on the other.
    But even in this second case, hope remains trapped by its
very triumphalism. After being waylaid by alienation as

escape, then by alienation as opposition, it is now waylaid by alienation in the form of domination. It tends to become once again a blocked hope with no other way out than an evaporating-evaporated hope. It has so often conceived expected objectives to be absolute! How could it hold attained objectives to be relative? Its very *expectation* is contaminated by its *attainment*. *It has arrived:* happy hour. But it is also the unhappy hour for upstarts and *arrivistes*. The point of arrival for some can only be the point of departure for others, be it only those who, according to Newman, endemically feed the anxiety of not being anxious or of not being anxious any more. Sociological analysis finds a theological postulate here: 'If at the end of everything there had to be a goal that could be reached, it would probably be better if this goal were never reached, for once this goal were reached, life would have no goal' (J. Moltmann). Could it be that hope feeds its opposite: a *spes contra spem*? That would be the ultimate trough: the trough of its essence.

## 4 The trough of its essence or unhoped for hope
Proust comments on it throughout his work: the real paradises are the ones that one has not yet found or that one has already lost. Heraclitus offers a counterpoint: 'Without hope one would not find the unhoped for which is undiscoverable and inaccessible'. Gershom Sholem operates along the same lines: 'There is something great but also profoundly unreal about living in hope'. And Georges Bernanos warns us: 'Hope is an heroic and disinterested act of the soul; we think it easy to hope, but only those can hope who have the courage to despair of the illusions or lies in which they found a security that they falsely took to be hope . . . .'

In considering so many phenomena – religions, churches, sects, nations, ethnic groups, social movements, insurrections, exoduses, resistance, dissent, etc. – propelled by a hope, in analysing them carefully, one cannot fail to notice one fact: hope is a promise that cannot be kept. It is like Lala in *La Ville*: 'Truth with the face of an error . . .'. And its grace consists in just that. It lies in order to tell the truth. Its line is curved: it is not the shortest path from one point to another. It is a detour, a long trek. It always keeps something different from what it promised, beneath or outside what it promised. There is something of a mirage, an imaginary geography in it. That is why it is moving in the sense that it puts personalities or groups in motion. Hope takes them off on a pilgrimage to other places, to other times, to other societies, towards other gods. But when the pilgrim arrives on the shores, these shores are not the shores of the promised land. Or if he believes that they are, he has put out his eyes.

In 1921 a black prophet, Simon Kimbangu, announced a new gospel in the Congo. It was the announcement of a Kingdom. He had received its revelation in a lost gospel that had been found again. This Kingdom would be the Kingdom of the resurrection of the blacks, who would seize religious and social mastery of their destiny. His words spread a socio-logical strike: believers and catechists moved away from their Baptist or Catholic missionaries; Belgian traders were angry that their customers disappeared; the plantations and the railways were short of workers; even the hospitals were emptied of their sick who went to seek cures in the holy village of Nkamba, carried off by troops of people. A counter-church took shape, which was also, and perhaps above all, a counter-society. It was a hope and it was disruptive. But after six months of public life, the prophet was arrested and the opposing coalition obtained his death sentence, commuted to life imprisonment which lasted thirty years in Elisabethville, while his disciples who were sent into exile, propagated the message wherever they went . . . . Such was the promise as it was 'held out', and it was lived in a quite extraordinary collective exaltation.

As for the promise that was *held*, it is double. On the one hand a political Congolese independence did satisfy in its way the political strand of this prophetic hope; but other prophets arose to dispute the identification of this new state with the hoped for kingdom. On the other hand, the religious strand of the same hope saw a new Church appear thirty years later, the CJCSK, the Church of Jesus Christ on earth through Simon Kimbangu. It was a black Church but it no longer denied the religious powers of the white Churches. It even requested and was granted approval by the Christian Churches connected with the World Council at Geneva.

None of this would probably have been possible, neither Church, nor even perhaps State, without the explosive charge put down by the gospel of the Kingdom. But none of this is on a level with the promised and hoped for Kingdom. It is nothing but a repercussion. Nothing would have happened without hope. But everything that did happen is short of the hope. And most of the time, the sociological observation of analogous phenomena – religious, social or political – forces one to ratify in a paraphrase, the cruel words of Alfred Loisy: they looked for Kingdoms and they got Churches and/or States.

In generalising this observation, one could infer that hope is doubly unhoped for: *it does not get what it hopes for, and it does get what it did not hope for.*

Perhaps one could even generalise further and come to something like a meta-sociology which accords with a philosophical conclusion of Sartre: 'We must recognise that reality is an aborted effort to reach the dignity of cause-of-self. Everything occurs as though the world, man, and man-in-the-world *only succeeded in realising a failed god.*' What follows is more abstruse though no less topical: 'Not that the integration ever came about, but precisely on the contrary because it· is always prescribed and always unattainable. It is *perpetual failure* which explains both the indissolubility of the in-self and the for-self and their relative independence'.[38]

In more colourful and less one-sided terms, hope presents itself as a surge of creativity: the jet rises and rises, but its grace in flight has as a price the weight of the droplets that tend to fall down. And yet, conversely, this falling is ceaselessly countered by the ascending force of the jet. There is in this an image dear to Bergson:[39]

The steam thrown up in the air condenses almost entirely into droplets which fall down; this condensation and this fall represent quite simply the loss of something, an interruption, a deficit. But a small part of the jet of steam remains uncondensed for a few seconds: it attempts to lift the drops that fall; the most it can do is slow down their fall. Thus from the same reservoir of life jets should continually spurt up, and as they fall back each one is a world . . . of these two currents, the second opposes the first, but the first does all the same obtain something from the second: there results between them a *modus vivendi* which is precisely organisation . . . *A reality that makes itself through one that unmakes itself.*

If hope is a victory, this defeat is the congenital injury done to the depths of its essence. But conversely, Euripides replies to Sophocles: 'I have nothing but scorn for the mortal who comforts himself with hollow hopes,' said the latter. But the former replies: 'Who knows whether life does not consist in dying and whether death is not living.'

The whole of this conceptual framework will be applied in the three following chapters, to reappear, better equipped, in the final chapter.

# Chapter 2

# A panorama of millenarian phenomena

Expectation is one of the phenomena of sociology that is the closest to both psychology and physiology and it is also one of the most common. If only one of you gentlemen could enlighten us on facts of this nature.

Marcel Mauss

The hypothesis of this chapter, and in particular of the following chapter, could well be borrowed from RenéGrousset: 'Periodically humanity marches towards an ideal world with infinite tentative efforts. It succeeds in reaching it, in giving it effect in a brief and singular success, but instead of keeping to it, it suddenly breaks away, abandons it and sets off again in search of adventure with no direction or guide, until it thinks it sees on the horizon the plan of some other perfect society which it hastens to construct.'

We find in the writings of a contemporary historian the analogous hypotheses of some great precursors. Here is Montesquieu's:

Almost all the nations of the world move round in a circle: at first they are barbaric, they conquer and come under orderly government, this government makes them grow bigger and they become civilised nations; civilisation weakens them, they are conquered, they become barbaric again.

or take J.-B. Vico:

The intelligence of nations is like fields which are cultivated after laying fallow for a long time and produce fruit whose size, taste and flavour are wonderful; but if they are cultivated for too long the fruit is small, dry and lacking in substance.

Although these different statements colour their analyses with what is already their interpretations, they all have the same theme: social development is not necessarily *linear* as the optimism of a cumulative progress rising to infinity would postulate; nor is it inevitably *cyclical* as the pessimism and resignation that says 'nothing new under the sun' would suppose; it could be a *spiral* consisting of a loop – rising and falling – connected to another loop and still more, thus reproducing at different levels of the same spiral, analogous *cycles* also rising and falling, the whole according to a *line* which provides the axis to such a *spiral*. These are only images, but they have the advantage of being convenient if not actually operative.

Could not a hypothesis that is plausible for the birth and death of societies be equally plausible for the birth and death of gods? J. Chaix-Ruy,[1] in an exegesis of J.-B. Vico, supposes that it could: 'In Vico it is the mechanism by which the gods are re-made.' One must complete this statement: this mechanism by which the gods are re-made also functions as the mechanism by which societies are unmade. A god who re-makes himself in a society that is unmaking itself, or to be more precise, a god who hopes to re-make himself in a society that refuses to unmake itself (or vice versa), such is the more or less apparent scenario of what there is of religion in the written and/or experienced utopias.

It is this same scenario that imposes itself in another tradition related to the tradition of utopias: the tradition of messianisms-millenarianisms in which religious imagination creates a renewed god or even a new god who questions the established or dominating social and religious order, and proposes a new way of envisaging or even establishing the reign of a new god over a new man. As we are aware, such a plan is hardly absent from a certain utopian tradition.[2] But here it becomes animate, frees itself, joins the collectivities of which it takes possession, and eventually rebels, revolts or even spreads and extends into a revolution.[3] The difference between millenarianism and utopia is not however so much one of hot and cold, for there are cold millenarianisms and hot utopias. It depends on the place of gods in both phenomena, more marginally in the social utopia, more centrally in the

43

religious millenarianism. This is expressed by the differences which in both cases affect the messenger and the message, for in both cases there is usually a messenger and a message. In one case the utopian is a writer who creates a literary fiction; in the other the instigator of a millenarianism – and in that sense the messiah – is one who offers a religious revelation.

However, both seem to obey this law of the spiral. They begin in the eruption of a wild imagination and they end – one is tempted to write: they cannot not end – by the re-absorption of an imagination that is tamed from then on and whose frustrations once again rebound in a new leap . . . a new loop in the spiral.

Messianisms and millenarianisms – in the manner of utopias – thus eternally create kingdoms from which they find themselves no less eternally exiled, whether they succeed or fail.

If, as G. le Bras wrote, society 'to a certain extent *creates* its gods'; if, as Durkheim maintained, such a creation grafts itself selectively on to 'the exuberant social situations in which religious life seems to be *born*', if, as Bergson postulated, the universe could be 'a *machine for making* gods', if moreover we take seriously this triple invitation to proceed empirically and concretely to take hold of this 'creation', this 'birth', this 'mechanism' which play a role in the appearance of men's gods, if finally our desire to understand is as much directed towards their disappearance as it is towards their appearance, then the socio-religious phenomena grouped in this class of messianisms-millenarianisms, twin brother of the utopian family, have every chance of offering us a useful, albeit insufficient, springboard.


This problematic of messianism-millenarianism has been, or risks being, blocked when it is immobilised and manipulated within *a* theology. For this theology, whatever its loyalties, there is *one* messiah, the true one, its own one, on the one hand; and on the other hand, there are false messiahs, the messiahs of others. Its own one is proper to *its own* church, and those of others are sent to the sociatric clinic; or in other words into penitentiary seclusion, and in the best of cases to the museum of deviance, to the department of curiosities, or to the twilight of truths that have remained or become mad.

Fortunately or unfortunately, for the last thirty years or so, religious sciences other than the theologies have been brought to bear on this phenomenon: ethnology, anthropology, sociology, social psychology, cultural history, phenomenology, etc. Some theologians themselves do not disagree with their observations or conclusions; one cannot hide that out of this come open or latent problems for them and for others. But we do not propose to solve them here, nor even to pose them. That is why the following pages must be taken for what they are: that is to say deliberately extra-theological. To make it easier to keep our distance, we shall refrain from comparing the phenomenon of primitive Christianity, on which hangs the calendar of our era, to the archetypal messianic phenomenon. This approach, we are aware, is on the contrary the one that tempted our utopian friends, who took it up so promptly, as well as tempting Engels, who having grown old in harness, did not demur to take it up passionately himself. To differ from them does not mean that one recognises that one is dealing with a field that is reserved for the theological interpretations of one or the other of the confessional churches, or of the sects that appeal to Christianity: this would be enough to open a wide range of interpretations. This field is, on the contrary, open to all the non-theological sciences, and some of them have not hesitated to penetrate it. But as Ecclesiastes says, there is a time for everything, and our time here will be limited to the messsianisms-millenarianisms that came *after* the primitive Christian era, which were usually *localised* in movements that were held to be deviant by the dominating Christianities, and which almost all appeal against a poorly informed Christianity on behalf of a better informed Christianity, pretending to reproduce in their scenario what would, according to them, have been the scenario of the Judeo-Christian expectation of the first centuries of our era.

In a judicial inquiry, an often used procedure is that of reconstructing the scene. One returns to the scene of the crime or at least one reconstructs an analogous scene. One takes into account the time and the light so that the conditions are identical. The people involved are asked to wear the same clothes and take up the same positions. The accused is requested to carry out in the same order the movements that he is supposed to have made. And one checks to see whether what happens within those limits of time and space confirms or invalidates the suspicions or statements.

The comparison is fragile, dubious even. But it is a fact: hundreds of movements have tried to do again what occurred messianically in the emergence of Christianity, by identifying it and checking it with what occurred in their own foundation. Hundreds of collectivities have thrown themselves, body and soul, into the expectation of an imminent kingdom of god on earth, thus repeating, according to them, the authentic Christian expectation. And indeed most of the time these pathetic, paradoxical and sometimes delirious witnesses have been cut down. The least one can say is that perhaps their laboratory was such that they were burnt by its emanations: it was none the less a laboratory in which, *ex post facto*, it is impossible to study 'what happened'. As Roger Bastide wrote about his book on the sociology of mental illnesses: 'These illnesses which are almost all illnesses of the sacred'. Even if messianisms-millenarianisms are of the sacred in its natural state, or even – *dato non concesso* – of the sacred of a sociatric scope, they none the less put the question at length and in depth, of the sacred before it was domesticated, or if one prefers, the question of the sacred as a crisis of a society before the society is, as some would say, cured of it, or, according to others, deprived of it.

Messianisms! Millenarianisms! We shall not return here to definitions that have already been suggested and elaborated elsewhere.[4] Let us simply say that the *messiah* is the *person* of whom *millenarianism* is the *movement*, and that there is not necessarily person *and* movement. We shall not delay any longer on the countless references that mark such a comparative study, or on the genesis of what is sometimes called today a 'messialogy' or an 'elpidology'.

We shall merely propose a panorama of the messianic-millenarian phenomena within the limits drawn out above. In the following chapter we shall consider some suggestions as to inductions or non-theological interpretations.

Is this phenomenon specifically linked to Christianity and the Christian expression? Does millenarianism only exist through contagion imported in the messages of missionaries? Among these messages, do those of such and such a confession or denomination turn out to be more particularly contagious? These questions have often been discussed. Without going into detail, one can at least recognise that the phenomenon is particularly lively in the religions of Abrahamic roots. Judaism and Islam can indeed plead traditions that are analogous to those of Christian millenarianism.

## 1 Jewish millenarianism

This tradition of Judaism cannot but plunge its roots into the social experiences, the religious expression of which is recorded in the prophetic and so-called apocalyptic literature of the Old Testament. But it is far from being confined by it. Without discussing violent messianisms (from the Zealots to Bar Kochba), or the more pacifist messianism (the Essenes), which surround the primitive Christian messianism, and probably interfere with it, Jewish tradition offers throughout the centuries, examples that are sometimes spectacular.

In the fifth century, Moses of Crete presented himself to his disciples as a Moses *redivivus*. The troubles brought by invasions made a new order in the Holy Land a matter of urgency. Moses predicted that on a given day the sea would open and make way. When the day came, the faithful sold all their belongings and gathered on a promontory, where Moses gave them the order to throw themselves into the water. Many are said to have drowned.

In the eighth century, Serenus, called the Syrian, also presented himself as the Messiah or his immediate precursor. He also promised the Jews their triumphal return to Palestine and their liberation from Muslim domination. But the Islamic authorities had him arrested and put to death. Some believed that he was merely a charlatan.

At Isphahan in the same century, Abu Isa also claimed to have a messianic calling to lead an armed revolt of the Persian Jews against the Caliph. He maintained he had had personal meetings 'in the heavens' with Jesus and Mohammed. His troops were crushed and he was killed.

Later on, in the twelfth century, in Yemen, a Messiah challenged an Arab king to cut off his head, assuring him that he would come back to life. His head was cut off. He did not come back to life. But the faithful remained convinced that the resurrection had been invisible.

In Kurdistan, also in the twelfth century, David Alroy promised the Persian Jews once more that he would free them from the Moslems and bring them back to Jerusalem. He presented himself as a liberating Messiah. He was assassinated.

In the following century, in Sicily, Abraham Abulafia called himself a Messiah and announced that the millennium would occur in 1290. He tried to convince the Pope who put him in prison. This did not prevent a great exodus of German Jews as the fateful day approached.

At Safed, in Galilee, Isaac Luria preached that the inauguration of the messianic era would occur in the last quarter of the sixteenth century.

Towards the end of that century, David Reubeni, a reluctant Messiah, advocated a great alliance of the Jews and the Christians against the Turks. He sought from Charles V the power to arm the Marranes (Jews from Spain and Portugal), and join them with the Jewish tribes of Arabia. He was received by the Pope. European Jews held him to be the Messiah who would deliver them from the Inquisition and bring them back to Palestine. But the Inquisition had the last word. Reubeni died in one of its prisons.

One could continue this list, to include the ambiguous odyssey of Sabbatai Zevi and his followers. One could also, in a sense, take it as far as Theodor Herzl, the founder of Zionism, author of a utopia *Altneuland* – translated into Hebrew as *Tel Aviv* – who took up both the social utopism of the nineteenth century and the millenarianism of Jewish tradition. Let us not omit, above all, in the social utopism that was thus recovered, that of Moses Hess, bachelor of Marx-Engels communism, author of the *Holy history of humanity*, herald of a New Jerusalem on earth, and according to David Ben Gurion, 'the first to have conceived of the plan for a

Jewish State organised in the Holy Land according to the laws of the Pentateuch'. Is this State the success or the failure of traditional Jewish millenarian hope? As we are aware, there is on this subject a sharp debate which is at the same time a current, inner debate of this tradition.

## 2 Moslem millenarianisms

Islam, that other great religion attached to Abraham, the Father of Believers, has been interpreted on the whole as a branch of Judeo-Christian messianism because of its aim to establish a Kingdom (of God) without a Church. P. Lagrange wrote: 'The mission of Mohammed is a chapter in messianic hopes which was the most unexpected and deceptive for the Jews'.

Supposing that that were so, it does not prevent Islam from nurturing around itself and sometimes against itself, socio-religious uprisings that are analogous to the Jewish or Christian millenarianisms. One of the most well-known is probably Babism and its successor Baha'ism, a dissidence within a branch of Islam that is itself dissident, Shiite Islam. The Bab was indeed a Shiite, therefore influenced by Persian Islam which was rebelling against Arabic Islam. In his turn he rebelled against Persian Islam, whose authorities pursued and executed several of his disciples. He was the obscure initiator of the movement, prophesying his divine mission in 1844. In August 1852, after a failed assassination attempt on the Shah, twenty-seven of his disciples were found guilty and executed. The Bab was already held to be a secret imam, and the return of the secret imam is related to a messianic parousia. Among those close to him, several aspired to the halo, which finally came to rest on Baha: he was to give this hope the scope of a universalist church. Exiled in Baghdad, Constantinople, Acre, he addressed to the heads of state and even to the Pope, his messages of universal peace and brotherhood for transcending and fulfilling existing religions in a cult of spirit and of truth. This doctrine is honoured and practised in a current and particularly fervent movement. Abbas Effendi, the son of Baha, maintained he was a reincarnation

49

of Jesus Christ in propagating the doctrine in the United States.

But many other millenarianisms – or mahdisms – are to be accounted for by Islam.

In the year 129 of the Hegira, Abu Moslim, who was thought to be a precursor of the Mahdi, caused an uprising in Khorassan before being assassinated, yet was held to be a survivor.

Abu Adg Allah in the year 296 of the Hegira announced to the Berbers: 'Now is the time when the Mahdi will come, for it is said that when this war comes to an end, he will appear'.

In the year 405 of the Hegira (1023), Al Hakim, a Fatimid caliph, was considered in North Africa to be an imam, and even an incarnation of the divinity. At all events several of his disciples, Hamza, Al Akhrem, tried to credit him as such to the Egyptian population.

Also in North Africa, in the nineteenth century, Bou Meza presented himself as being sent by God, 'that master of time', as a precursor of the Last Judgment, and thus caused the resistance of the Kabyl tribes against the French colonial occupation.

The terms 'mahdi' and 'mahdism' are quite closely related to Christian millenarianism. Originally they meant 'guided by God along the right path', but they came to mean hope in a social and religious order which was different from the one towards which an equally religious fatalism would lead one. This hope therefore accompanies many politico-religious insurrections or revolts. Some have remarked that their frequency in Maghrebin Islam was well-known. It is almost impossible to draw up a complete list of Mahdisms. According to a phrase attributed to him, the prophet Mohammed declared: 'After me, there will be arrogant caliphs, emirs and kings. *That is when the Mahdi will come.* He will come from my family and he will fill the world with justice, just as injustice reigned before him.'

There was a Mahdi in Egypt who promised his troops he would make them invulnerable to Bonaparte's cannons. There was also a Mahdi or a pre-Mahdi in Sudan, Mohammed Ahmed, who roused the Sudanese tribes against the Anglo-Egyptian conquest led by General Gordon. There were quasi-

Mahdis in Java, in the eighteenth and nineteenth centuries involved in the resistance movements against Dutch colonisation. There were many in black Africa, etc.

In Islam, as in Judaism, it is not possible to overlook the ferment of impatience and especially of social revolts contained in the religious imagination of expectation. The same can be said of Christianity.

## 3 Christian cycles: The patristic cycle

Were the first Christian generations millenarian? In any case it is a fact that a considerable part of their representatives hoped for and even counted on the return of Christ. It is generally admitted that the decline of this millenarianism coincided with the rise of Augustinian theology. As the author of an article in a theological dictionary derisively writes: 'St Augustine delivered a death blow to millenarianism. After him, the system grew weaker and weaker . . . . It was extinguished in the extravagances of a few followers of the Reformation . . . .' Indeed! The fact that this decline of millenarianisms also coincides with the ascension of the Christian Church to a *dominant* position, and the fact also that its vitality or survival had grafted itself during three centuries on the tribulations of this same Church which was now *dominated*, could already lead to many questions, and in particular the following one: are millenarianisms not religious representations that are liable to *change sides* according to social situations and their changes? One should also ask oneself about the vitality of such a phenomenon in orthodox or heterodox Christian traditions *before* Constantinisation and *after* it.

It is certainly to be found in the movements that are classed as 'heresies', and because of this typically discredited and obscured. Cerinthus, for example, was considered to be one of the first millenarians. He was vilified as such by Eusebius of Caesarea, and Irenaeus, a millenarian himself, considered him to be an enemy of John the Apostle. In fact the millenarianism of Cerinthus was not dissimilar to the Fourierist Eden. According to Eusebius: 'He states that after the Resurrection Christ will reign on earth, and men will live again in Jerusalem in physical pleasure and joy without sin. This enemy of the divine Scriptures adds that a thousand years will be spent in nuptial feasts . . . .' Another 'heretic', Montan, was on the contrary an ascetic millenarian. He and his prophetesses also announced the arrival, one is tempted to say the landing, of celestial Jerusalem in the valley of Pepuza in Phrygia. Around this holy city, New Jerusalem – oh, the role of holy *cities* in such expectations! – vast crowds would gather after pooling their possessions and renouncing their marriage vows.

But millenarianism was not the monopoly of heterodoxy. It is also to be found on the frontiers of what, for better or for worse, is confirmed or reclaimed as orthodoxy. Papias, the 'bishop' of Phrygia (Phrygia yet again!), in the middle of the second century, a disciple of John, and author of messages that were lost but re-transmitted by his hearers, announced a millennium of abundance and universal peace. Eusebius of Caesarea, who later – at the time when Christianity was already Constantinised – historialised the ecclesiastical history of those first centuries, was embarrassed to echo him . . . .

> This author certifies that through the oral tradition, some strange parables of the Saviour have come to him, strange teachings and discourses, as well as other accounts that touch on the legend (*fabula*), among which he says that there will be a period of a thousand years, after the resurrection of the body, during which the reign of Christ will occur bodily on this earth.

The historialist strikes a balance between rejecting and exalting. 'I think that he must have assumed all this after having misunderstood the narratives of the Apostles, and that he has not grasped the things that they said figuratively and symbolically.'

But Irenaeus quotes Papias, and considers him to have been 'a disciple of John, a companion of Polycarp', and he does not think that the millennium is an allegory: 'For it is right that in this same creation in which they have suffered and been afflicted . . . , the righteous should receive the reward for their labours; that they should reign in the creation

in which they have endured servitude . . . .' This reign will be
a reign of abundance 'on earth' . . . . And even: 'then virgins
will rejoice in the company of young men. Old men will
rejoice. Such are the promises that God made for the kingdom
of the Just.' . . . There remains only one assumption for
Eusebius to make: the one according to which Irenaeus was
misdirected by Papias, who was a stupid witness; enough of a
witness to answer for the historicity of the primitive message;
too stupid not to add his own fabulation! But one can go on
asking oneself: if there is an amalgamation, where is it the
most flagrant: on the side of Papias or of Eusebius . . . ? In the
affray, Irenaeus at least gains, in the nineteenth century, a
distant defender in the person of a Fourierist converted to
Catholicism, Désiré Laverdant. In his work *La Déroute des
Césars*, he applies himself to defending his utopian socialism
by its continuity with 'the Judeo-Christian millenarianism or
utopia'. According to him, this utopia goes back to the origins
of Christianity: 'And let us not forget that this hope of a reign
of justice here below goes back to Papias, the immediate
disciple of St John . . . .' There is even an appropriate reason
for a similar utopia to reappear in France, and this reason
turns around Irenaeus: 'If this radiant hope is bursting out in
our country at the moment, it is because the divine seed was
placed in the heart of the Gauls by the faithful Irenaeus.'
Because of him and through him: 'Gaul made the terrestrial
utopia of the reign of God its own.'

But there is no need to look for such distant and unreliable
evidence. Laverdant himself points the way, referring to
Justin and Tertullian among others.

Justin, who died in 165, knew that not everyone agreed on
the matter, and that many, 'even of Christian doctrine,
righteous and pious, did not recognise' this millenarianism.
He does however have his own opinion: 'As for me and *the
Christians of integral orthodoxy* . . . , we know that a resurrection
of the flesh will take place *over a thousand years in a rebuilt and
greater Jerusalem*.' And he does not hesitate to affirm and
confirm this to his interlocutor Trypho the Jew, who cannot
believe it.

Tertullian: 'We must admit that we are promised a kingdom *on earth before heaven*, but in a different state: after the

53

resurrection *lasting a thousand years*, in celestial Jerusalem, the city made by God.' And Lactance calls to the rescue the sibylline oracles in order to validate his short term views.

In those times, religious expectation – at the edges or even in the centre of Christianity – is also the expectation of another society.

## 4 The medieval cycles

If one moves the facts around a little one can summarily distinguish three cycles.

*The Imperial cycle* From the legend and cult of Charlemagne, who was considered to be a fabulous person as predicted by the sibylline oracles, there emerges an emperor of the final days who would go to Jerusalem to crown the Cross with his own crown. This view nourished the many adventures of the crusades. Above all it nourished the aspirations of the different and opposed protagonists in the struggles between the Papacy and the Empire. For the Ghibelline tradition, this consecration glorified a German sovereign who would renew the glory of the Empire by dominating a pope and a clergy that were sometimes identified with the Antichrist . . . . For another tradition – the Guelf tradition – the Emperor *redivivus* would on the contrary be a liberator of the Church. According to Folz, this tradition 'kept until the end of the Middle Ages its anti-Germanic aspect, and repeatedly put forward a French emperor of Carolingian descent, faithful servant of the Church, preparing for the second coming of Christ' . . . . This double tradition reflects, exalts and gives a religious meaning to 'the rivalry for the Empire, in the full sense of the word, between France and Germany'.

*The cycle of the crusades* 'Throughout the west, the Crusades were set in motion by eschatological motivations, the idea of the coming arrival of the Antichrist, the conquest of the final days, and the belief in the saints dwelling in Jerusalem' (A. Dupront). These themes are particularly active in the so-called crusades of the poor. Peter the Hermit was thought to have received a heavenly letter from Christ himself telling him to organise the first crusade. The crusade of the Shepherds increased this millenarianism with its claim of an extra or even anticlerical religion. The children's Crusades were as fanatical as some Jewish messianisms: they were convinced that the Mediterranean would open before them, just as the followers of Moses of Crete were. Colourful messianic personalities started or revived such enthusiasms, one of which – the crusade of the Shepherds – is considered by N. Cohn to be 'the first chiliast attempt at social revolution in Europe'. Among the messianic or messianised personalities there were: prophets, itinerant ascetics, charismatic preachers, princes, orators, adventurers, popular mystics . . . . As for the Antichrist, his role was held either by Islam (Mohammed, the precursor, and Moslem followers of the Antichrist), or by the Jews, hence antisemitism and sometimes the pogroms that often accompanied the vicissitudes and journeys of these crusades.

*The popular cycles* They are also many and various. Already at the beginning of the eleventh century, Tanchelm, a popular prophet, was denounced for his messianic claims. The canons of Utrecht signed this denunciation: 'He says he is God, stating that if Christ was God because he had the Holy Spirit, he himself is no less God for he has received the fullness of this Spirit.' In any case his messianism was antifeudal and even anti-ecclesiastical: did he not incite the population to a tithe strike before Saint-Simon? And even to a strike of the sacraments? Flanders was the scene of his apotheosis, and he was at the centre of a quite extraordinary personality cult. He was assassinated by a priest in 1115.

At the same time Éon de l'Étoile was active in Brittany. The despair of a great famine (1144) preceded the hope that he heralded by identifying himself with the saviour of the final days, by announcing a millennium, and by proposing an esoteric church.

Subsequently, several millenarian movements were started by the writings published by or attributed to Joachim of Flore and his theory or sociosophy of the Third Age. After the Age of the Father, then the Age of the Son, would come the Age of the Holy Spirit, the age of a universal monasticism, with the conversion of the Jews, the unification of the Church and the revelations of the eternal Gospel. The literalistic and dissident

Franciscans were related to it. We can see a fulfilment of the Joachimite prophecies in the movement started by Segharelli in Parma, which became the movement of the Apostolics, the continuation of which was taken up by Fra Dolcino. Under his direction, the Apostolics, who at first were a renewed or even new order, thought themselves to be not only the seed of a new church, but also the nucleus of an unprecedented world which would abolish property and probably marriage. Despite his resistance in the heart of a Piedmontese peasant underground, Dolcino and his sister in arms, Margarita, were arrested, tortured, and burnt alive in Vercelli in 1307. K. Kautsky, who studied this movement, liked to see in it the first 'communist' uprisings in the west.

In the following centuries, the popular revolutions were accompanied by millenarianism. In the workers' uprising in 1381 in England, 'poor priests', and radical Franciscans yet again, gave the popular revolt a theme by attributing a millenarian significance to it, in other words by predicting the end of the world – the world of feudal and ecclesiastical appropriation – and the coming of another world, which would reinstate the pre-feudal regime of village communities, the pentecostal Christian community and even the free society of the lost paradise. 'When Adam delved and Eve span, who was then a gentleman?' cried John Ball, 'the mad priest of Kent', in a call for direct action. He was hanged for being one of the leaders of the march on London.

But the millenarian theme immediately found in Central Europe a social, religious and political situation that assured its transfer. Indeed it organised there several currents of revolts that derived from the revolt and execution of John Huss. Among these currents, the Taborites are the most well-known. Their preachers held the hope of a millennium. Some believed that the year 1420 would be the year of the return of Christ and of the establishment of the Kingdom after universal destruction. Only certain high places would escape this destruction: the Tabors, holy cities from which resistance against repression was organised and in which a secular and egalitarian theocracy was founded. They were crushed in Lipan in 1434.

In the following century, the great war of the German

peasants took place, nourished by Bohemian reminiscences and not without links and correspondence with Prague; its herald was Thomas Münzer, of whom Engels wrote that his 'theory of the Holy Spirit bordered on modern atheism'. He was a millenarian rather than a messianic personality. His prediction of the Kingdom of God fused with agrarian demands: 'For Münzer, the Kingdom of God is nothing more than a society in which there would no longer be any class differences, any private property, any power of coercion independent of the members of society' (Engels). A coalition of the Catholic and Protestant German nobility, supported by Luther's famous appeal, inflicted the disaster of Frankenhausen on the peasant army in 1525. It is said that Münzer promised in vain to catch the cannon balls in the sleeves of his coat . . . .

The final popular medieval development was the Republic of Saints, at Münster, ten years later, probably the most famous experience of religious and sexual communism in European history. Münster in fact became not the Abbey of Theleme, but a kind of large mixed monastery that reinstated the polygamous sexual regime of the Old Testament, despite a monogamous opposition of certain men and a polyandrous opposition of certain women. John of Leyden was the triumphalist Messiah, supposedly predicted by the ancient Jewish prophets. But this other new Jerusalem, in the grips of a famine, did not resist the assault of its besiegers. The tortured body of John of Leyden was locked in an iron cage and placed on the top of a tower to perpetuate the memory of his untimeliness.

## 5 The cycle of the English revolution

The millenarian theme flourished there, and one finds in particular the zealot and pacifist versions. The zealots of this puritanism are represented by the Fifth Monarchy Men, a label taken from a prophecy of Daniel's. According to them, restoration of the Mosaic agrarian laws would prepare the way for a kingdom of saints, with no priests, sacraments, or even kings and governments. This anarchist messianism was

57

conjured up by one of their doctrinaires, Henry Archer, who announced that 'the personal Kingdom of Jesus Christ on earth' would occur at the end of the century. In 1661 Thomas Venner was the leader of their insurrection, which was put down by Cromwell's army. 'Thus ended the last politically important attempt of social Christian reformers to establish by the sword the Kingdom of God on earth' (Underwood).

However it was another movement, that of the Levellers, who more spectacularly practised this identification of the coming of the Kingdom with social revolution. Their uprising against Cromwell, their old ally, was considered by Marx-Engels to be the religious theme of the first proletarian revolution. Under the leadership of John Lilburne, they called for a judgment of God on earth – 'Arise, O God, judge Thou the earth' – in order to destroy all relationships of the master-slave type, which according to them were invented entirely by the powers of the political and religious masters.

On the pacifist side, one distinguishes first of all the Diggers, militants of agrarian leagues who occupied empty properties, dug the land (hence their name), and shared the harvests. That at least was their plan, echoed later in the plans of the agrarian leagues of north-eastern Brazil. The Francisco Juliao of the Diggers was G. Winstanley, who drew up a utopia, *The new law of justice*, which he intended to present to Cromwell. According to this utopia, the true religion is nothing more than the restitution of property to the community. 'The Kingdom of heaven is nothing more than the earth itself, become the common treasury again of all men.' The intervention of armed forces prevented the Diggers from going as far as the harvests.

A pacifist utopia, that was also presented to Cromwell, and that is linked to the American cycle, is the utopia of Peter Plockoy. His republic, like Winstanley's, is a republic without class, privilege, or established churches, except in the form of a meta-ecclesiastical cooperative ecumenism. This small republic was probably launched in the United States, where it was carried away in the turbulent clash of war. The patriarch of cooperation and ecumenism died a blind old man in Pennsylvania.

We are dealing here with the cycle of the English *political*

Revolution. A later cycle was that of the English *industrial* Revolution. That was when Luddism took on its millenarian expression in the extraordinary adventure of a little factory girl, Ann Lee, who became the female Messiah revered by the communal sect of the Shakers, whose American foundations were later to be taken as references and guarantees by several European socialists.

## 6 A missiological Catholic cycle

This is the one that anticipates in the (Latin-American) New World either the end of a perversion of Christianity involved and conveyed in European colonialism, or even, in a reverse movement, the re-Christianisation of the Old World judged to be too de-Christianised.

Vasco de Quiroga, a bishop, intended even to refer explicitly to Thomas More's utopia as a model for his regrouping of villages.

Jerome de Mendieta, a Franciscan, took up the Joachimite tradition in situating a future millenarian Kingdom in Mexico under the aegis of the Viceroy. Mendieta was already postulating, if not segregation, at least a cordon sanitaire, when he suggested that the Indians have separate communities from the whites. His hope was that the Indians, surrounded by the mendicant Brothers, and inspired by the Gospel, would, by the strength of their natural virtues, achieve the life of children of God.

This same dream reached a famous peak in the Christian communist Republic of the Guarani Indians, those 'Retreats' where two messianisms undoubtedly met: the latent messianism of Jesuit missiology and the Indian hope in the coming of civilising heroes. We know that after an almost legendary notoriety, these Retreats, which were abandoned on the superior order of the founding Fathers, were *manu militari*, completely routed.

In the Portuguese-speaking area, messianic import was complicated by reminiscences of a Portuguese messianism: sebastianism, which joined the local millenarianism of implicitly or explicitly political uprisings. We shall also find them in the cycle of the third world.

Finally the back drop is provided by that combination of evangelisation and colonisation that confronted a messianism of the conquerors – that of the conquistadors – and the *two* messianisms of the conquered: that of their sacred inhibition towards these newcomers, whom they took to be ancient gods returning to their lands; that of their revolts against those occupiers, whom they denounced as bringers of evil spells and mystifications; and this just as much in the Aztec empire of Mexico as in the Inca empire of Peru. Two works, one by Miguel Leon Portilla and the other by Nathan Wachtel, have rediscovered and rehabilitated this double 'vision of the conquered' (cf. Bibliography).

## 7 The North American cycle from the seventeenth to the nineteenth centuries

This cycle plays in the Protestant region of North America a role which is analogous to the one played by the preceding cycle in the Catholic regions of South America. However this analogy is full of differences which reflect the contrast between the two types of colonisation.

Indeed in North America, there are hardly any combined or hybrid messianisms,[5] but there are Indian messianisms on the one hand, and Anglo-Saxon messianisms on the other.

The former are endogenous and unite with the resistance of the Indian tribes against the effects of colonisation on the Great Prairie . . . . We shall come across them again in the cycles of the third world.

The latter are essentially the doing of the European immigrants, who, throughout the years, spread out their micro-communities like so many bridgeheads of the Kingdom of God. Communities! These groups usually practised the sharing of possessions, but their family regimes varied: monogamous families (Zoarites, Hutterites), polygamy (Mormons), mixed monasticism (Shakers, Rappites), plural marriage or free love (Oneida, Brotherhood of New Life) . . . .

Furthermore, these operations sometimes had an attractive aspect. Eric Janson, the founder of a Swedish community, Bishop Hill, gave himself an important role in the second coming of Christ. A Quaker, Hawland, founded a community of shared possessions on the apostolic basis: *Adonai Shomo* (the Lord is here). Peter Armstrong founded an even more explicitly millenarian community – *Celesta* – and gathered together in a Pennsylvanian valley the 144,000 chosen for the coming of the Lord. An observer who quotes these facts, states that there were many similar ones in the first half of the nineteenth century. In 1844, W. Miller, the father of Adventism, said that he held the names and addresses of 2,000 preachers who were proclaiming the imminence of the end of the world. Among them, an important contingent was announcing the end of *one* world and the inauguration of another, of the Millennium, under the apocalyptic sign of 'the Woman in the Wilderness'. It would be too captivating or too tedious to go into greater detail. It is probably one of the busiest workshops of social millenarianism. It is against this background in the first half of the nineteenth century, that stand out, on the one hand, the Adventist odyssey whose eschatology is difficult to separate from a certain millennium, and on the other hand the Mormon epic, which under the leadership of first Joseph Smith, then Brigham Young, was to lead the Latter Day Saints to their republic in Salt Lake City. Finally it is this workshop of the American communal micro-millenarianisms which was to become the fourth source of modern European socialism. Owen visited it and was inspired by it. The Fourierists found themselves there with the Unitarians. Cabet dreamed of it. Engels used it as an argument in his youth conferences in order to make communism plausible. W. Weitling found in it an entrenchment and a retreat . . . . Finally it is this same workshop, and its shared conviction to invent a new god, which became involved in the widest and most diffused literary or philosophical religious currents, and which shaped the American consciousness into the collective consciousness of a 'redeeming society', dedicated to a millenarian role in the destinies of the world.

## 8 The Slavonic or Russo-Polish cycle

We find here the symptoms of an ethnic or even national messianism which is analogous to the one diagnosed by

Tuveson in his analysis of America and its image as a Redeemer Nation.

The Polish cycle of the nineteenth century is distinguished by the well-known trio: Wronski, Towianski and Mickiewicz. Wronski, who was a mathematician philosopher, announced a fifth era, the Era of the Absolute, that of a superior religion that was hyper religious as well as hyper rational. In this regime to come, which was said to be the 'Absolute Union', the Slav nations played an important role, which Wronski's disciples contemplated in Paris in their messianic association: the Antinomian Union . . . Towianski also went to Paris where he was exposed to the Saint-Simonian influence. He announced a re-establishment of primitive harmony, the reign of equality and fraternity, in a renewed humanity under the aegis of a Catholic Church, reformed in both its leadership and its membership. In the near future, three races were to come to the fore: the Jews, the French and the Slavs . . . Mickiewicz was influenced by Towianski; he exposed his concepts in his work *Messianism and the official Church*. But in his own thought, the primary messianic role was given to the Polish nation, whose liberation became for him the stage of a millennium: among the Slav nations, Poland was the crucified nation; revived, it would join with France to establish a fraternity of nations.

This same national and ethnic messianism manifests itself with its own variants in the Russian cycle and its intellectual and popular currents. Cieszkowski, perhaps 'the greatest Polish messianist' according to Berdiaev, formed a link. He announced a Third Age which would be the age of the advent of Christianity in social institutions, and in the founding of which a special role was reserved for the Slavs, 'a race saved by Providence for a high mission', and predestined to this privilege by its many humiliations in the past. This Slav messianism is to be found, according to N. Berdiaev, in *The Russian Idea*, with a long commentary by him in the work of the same name. According to him, 'The Russians are to a degree, consciously or unconsciously different from the millenarians' (p. 205) . . . . 'The Russians are maximalists, and whatever presents itself as a utopia has the greatest chances of being realised in Russia' (p. 255). A personal hypothesis of the author's is: 'The messianic idea of Marxism resting on the idea of the mission of the proletariat has been identified and confused with the Russian messianic idea' (p. 256).

Soloviev 'expounds his utopia which he calls the free theocracy. He believed that the Kingdom of God could also be achieved on earth, and sought for the means to achieve it' (p. 133). 'He was imbued with the messianic idea.' And even 'Bakunin's anarchism rests on Russian messianism' (p. 156). More generally, there is 'something essential to the Russian revolutionary: revolutionaries, anarchists, and socialists were unconscious millenarians. The myth of the Revolution is a millenarian myth' (p. 208). This 'Russian idea' is taken to the limit by the autodidact Fedorov with his dazzling utopian plan for 'a permanent revival', in other words 'an active participation of man in the work of the universal re-establishment of life' (p. 217).

Even at the beginning of the twentieth century, philosophico-religious reunions between ecclesiastics and intellectuals 'reflected the Russian expectation of the era of the Holy Spirit' (p. 235).

Finally, 'An historic Christianity, an historic Church, mean that the Kingdom of God has not come, *signify a failure*, an adaptation of the Christian revelation to the Kingdom of this world. There remains for Christianity a messianic hope, an eschatological expectation, which is stronger in Russian Christianity than in western Christianity' (p. 203).

This hope was particularly ardent in the growth of religious dissidences that come from the Raskol, that is to say the movement of the Old Believers. N. Berdiaev tells of his own contacts with 'these representatives of the most varied sects' (p. 206). 'What a lesson these popular seekers of God are for official orthodoxy.' One of the best known movements, because of the interest that Tolstoy took in it, is that of the Doukhobors, a sizeable contingent of whom emigrated to Canada. As recently as 1912, in a Canadian village, more than six hundred of them, bare foot and with no belongings, sometimes completely naked, marched in the name of the Lord, whose imminent return they believed in. The mounted police had to intervene to put an end to this strange procession. Other Raskolniks succeeded in Russia itself, in creating something of a counter-society in the form of a network of mixed monasticisms, that practised a religious communism, and indeed sometimes achieved a fairly extraordinary economic prosperity. Some of these communities, of Baptist faith, continued in the form of 'religious communes' right up to the 1920s. One of them, which became a Soviet agrotown, bore a name borrowed from Campanella: *the City of the Sun.*

Thus on a parallel scale and without much contact – apart from the correspondence of Leo Tolstoy with the Shakers, or the migrations of the Doukhobors and Hutterites – two ethnic millenarianisms developed or existed in North America and Russia since the eighteenth century, combined on both sides with communitarisms, and founded on both sides on a desire for an exodus, in other words a plan to go out in space and/or time from a society and a religion that were both equally contested.

## 9 The cycle of the French Revolution

While this contestation was growing in the west and in the east, in the USA and in Russia, it exploded in the French Revolution, ridding itself of the eschatological clothing that was obligatory in its predecessor, the English Revolution, but not without retaining the odd shred here and there. A *Prophetic journal* published by the constitutional bishop, Pontard, calls for one to go from the temporal sovereign, 'to the successor of Peter'. The conflicts of the Revolution and the Papacy indeed took on a millenarian aspect in the eyes of many, well before Joseph de Maistre and the meaning of great judgment which he thought he read retrospectively in the events of the French Revolution. In particular a whole Anglo-Saxon public did not cease to interpret 'the signs of the times' in it. It has been possible to catalogue several dozen papers which read in that 'earthquake' the signs that announced, according to them, the inauguration of the new era, and more specifically the fall of 'Babylon the Great', the Papacy. On a middle road between this vindictive puritanism and Joseph de Maistre, Pontard's *Prophetic journal* did indeed argue in favour of the providentialism of the French Revolution, but it also did not despair of rallying the Papacy to it, not the Papacy of the 'temporal sovereign' but of the 'successor of Peter'. Thus it supported the odyssey of a prophetess, Suzette Labrousse, launched by the famous Dom Gerle, who in 1790, defended her in the National Assembly, maintaining that eleven years earlier she had predicted the convening of that Assembly, the end of monastic vows, the reform of abuses, the recalling of the clergy to its primitive purity . . . . The same Dom Gerle was the supporter of Catherine Theot, who was almost a messiah, who said she was the 'Mother of God'; and was thought of as such by the circle of her followers. Was Robespierre part of that circle? His enemies accused him of it, and Vadier made much of a letter addressed to Robespierre by the Mother, in which she assured him that 'his mission was predicted by Ezekiel'. Even if the letter were 'discovered' to suit the cause and the accusation, Robespierre was not antipathetic to the said circle and could well have been a sympathiser. He had given Dom Gerle a certificate of good citizenship, and a declaration was found in a manuscript of Suzette Labrousse's according to which she was 'strongly encouraged along this path by our friend Robespierre' . . . . The path that she followed was the one that led her to Rome to justify the religious politics of the Revolution to the Pope. Did she hope to rally him to it by proving to him 'that he himself should give up all temporal power in order to concern himself undividedly with spiritual power'? The path led her to the Castel Santangelo where she was imprisoned. Several years later, when the French troops entered Rome, a representative of the Directoire came to set her free. He considered her to be mad, saying: 'It is doubtless madness to believe that the Roman clergy, and especially its leader, would give up temporal power and confine itself to spiritual power'.

It was also during the decline of the Revolution that occurred the short-lived group of theophilanthropists, some of whose reminiscences were inscribed in the new Saint-Simonian Christianity. It was still during the Revolution, in 1795, that an enthusiastic descendant of Jansenism was inaugurated at Fareins, in Ain, a 'Republic of Jesus Christ'. The 'Fareinists' sold all their possessions to go 'into the desert', probably to Mont Pilat, near Lyons . . . . They had all

65

taken the name of *Bonjour* with Jewish first names. They were awaiting a visit from the prophet Elijah. They got a visit from the police who suspected them of counter-revolutionary conspiracy, which did not prevent their effervescence from turning into a peaceful millenarianism; the two sons of the founder shared the titles of John the Baptist and Elijah the Prophet.[6] Finally, the great post- and counter-revolutionary messianisms developed consecutively to the Revolution. The messianism of Joseph de Maistre: 'The Jacobins were merely the instruments of a force that knew more than they did . . . either a new religion would be formed, or else Christianity would be rejuvenated in some extraordinary way . . . . We must be prepared for an immense event.' Especially the messianism or messianisms that intermingled through the negotiations or dealings of the Holy Alliance. Mme Krudener, who was prepared by Oberlin and supported by Nicolas Bergasse, was involved in the intrigues, and more specifically gave Tsar Alexander I the conviction that through this 'holy alliance' . . . 'the reign of the Saviour would come'. Metternich acknowledged it: 'The conception of the Holy Alliance developed under the influence of Mme Krudener and M. Bergasse . . . . No-one knows better than I do everything that is connected with that empty, hollow movement'.

## 10 The post-revolutionary European cycle

In this cycle there emerges, and sometimes sparks, the implicit or explicit millenarianism of European socialism, which proposes to 'complete' the Revolution: in France, with Saint-Simon and his messianic *New Christianity*, with Fourier and his Eden-like religion, with Cabet and the Icarian *True Christianity*; in England with Robert Owen and his anti-ecclesiastical *Millennialism*; in Germany with Weitling and his *Gospel of the poor fisherman*; almost everywhere, with the crossroads that were established among these threads of the *European triarchy*, considered by Moses Hess to be the cradle of a New Jerusalem. Slav messianisms, Polish in particular, were not without their interventions, as is shown by the assiduous role of M. Charles, alias Krolikowski, with Cabet. There was also a Saint-Simonian and Fourierist wave in Great Britain, and conversely an Owenite penetration in France. The young Engels wrote in the *New Moral World*, and French utopism, through a Fourierised Lamennais, reached Weitling, who translated his *Book of the people* for the League of the Just, the matrix of the future league of communists. Lamennais had written elsewhere a *Hymn to Poland*, which accused him of opposing pontifical politics, and Montalembert, his disciple, joined Mickiewicz in praising Poland, 'the Christ of nations' . . . .

But besides this utopian maelstrom one also sees another millenarianism develop: that of the powerful Monarch, of the hidden predestined Prince. Vintras claimed that St Joseph appeared to him and announced the reign of the Holy Spirit and the joint advent of 'a Pontiff Saint and a powerful Monarch'. Two popes condemned this claim of Vintras's followers, which 'announced a third reign of the Holy Spirit'. The message was taken up by others: the priest Boullan, to whom Huysmans, according to Massignon, owed his return to the faith; Joseph Vercruysse-Burneel, who was linked to Tardif de Moidrey so dear to Claudel, the defender of La Salette (La Salette's secret, according to him, was his announcement of the birth of Satan, in 1846), and Léon Bloy's initiator. Léon Bloy himself, a great converter to the eternal, found the millenarian impetus of his passionate Expectation in these predecessors:

> I am made to wait for ever . . . I have not been able to do anything else for more than half a century . . . . The sudden burning devouring desire for the Third Reign has taken hold of me . . . *I have such a raging hunger and thirst for the glory of God on earth, that I count the days like a madman . . . someone must come*, someone unheard of, whom I can hear galloping across the abysses . . . *I am awaiting the* Cossacks and the Holy Spirit.

Ernest Hello shared this same expectation, which was both totalising and nihilist. 'It is probable that an event is near. This event must be the Advent or all is lost.' During the Exhibition in 1867, he confided to Henri Lasserre: 'I have just walked past the Tuileries and they are not yet burning. The barbarians are a long time coming. What is Attila doing?' Hello may even have gone so far as to identify himself with the awaited 'Great Monarch'.

Thus a whole millenarianism was the cradle, not only of contemporary socialism, but also of a literary catholicism of modern times.

## 11 A Judeo-Christian cycle of radical Jansenism

It is mentioned here as a reminder. It is to be found strangely linked to the triple theme of the conversion of the Jews, their return to Judea, and the rebuilding of the Temple. We saw the symptoms in the messianism of the Year XIII, which was that of the Fareinists. But there are other examples. Agier (1748–1823) was influenced by the discovery of a great Chilean Jesuit, Lacunza, author of *The coming of Christ in glory and majesty*. Like him, Agier links the millennium to a rectification of the terrestrial axis; the re-establishment of Israel was predicted for 1849. J.-B. Etémare, in 1666, had the same thoughts: 'There is a reign of God in this world. Under this reign the Jews will replace the Gentiles and restore Jerusalem.' A century later, in 1733, in Utrecht, Fernanville wrote an *Idea of a spiritual Babylon, predicted in the Holy Scriptures, in which it is demonstrated, contrary to the Protestants and the constitutionaries, that this Babylon can only be the Catholic Church, and that it will be found in the bosom of this same Church*. Houbigant, an Oratorian, predicted in 1753 that the appearance of the Antichrist and his defeat by Elijah would occur in 1932; he predicted a reign of Christ, coinciding with 'a flourishing State and a temporal reign of the Jews, which will occur after their conversion and before the end of the world'. Merault, another ecclesiastical Jansenist, collaborated with Etémare and Nicolas Legros on a millenarian manuscript, which was seized in Geneva, according to which 'it is necessary to await a new fulfilment'. J.-J. Du Guet (1649–1753), another Oratorian, the confidant of Amand and Nicole; a little later the priest Pilé, author of millenarian services (1778); Michel Pinel, also an Oratorian, author of a alternativist *Horoscope* of 1749; Marc-Antoine Noe, bishop of Troyes (1726–1801), author of a 'Discourse on the future state of the Church, which should have been presented to the Assembly of the Clergy in 1785'; all developed the same themes of a radicalised Jansenism.

Finally we know 'the strange story of the convulsionaries of St Médard', an off-shoot of Jansenism from 1731. Among the better known, many maintained they were Enoch and especially Elijah. This effervescence gradually crystallised into 'revolutionary prophetism'. According to Mousset, in foreseeing the French Revolution 'in a fog of the Apocalypse', these convulsionaries and their descendants were 'a link in the chain that goes from the "leapers" of St Médard . . . to the fanatics and the mystics of the end of the century'.

## 12 The cycles of the third world

They really merit a special chapter of their own for two reasons: because of their breadth and their number; and also because of the determinative influence of acquaintance with them on the recognition of earlier millenarianisms. It was in fact their discovery, their observation, their study, and the inductions obtained from this observation and study, that on the rebound attracted attention to the analogous phenomena of another history and geography, leading to their re-exhumation or re-interpretation. Just as in the sixteenth century the missiology of the Noble Savage was determinative in the emergence of the utopian literary genre, so in the twentieth century the anthropology of exotic Messiahs has been decisive in the formation of that scientific field which could become a messialogy. That is why these cycles of the third world could have been, and perhaps should have been, put at the head of this list.

It will be enough here to note and connote the main cultural regions which appear or have appeared in the 'third world' as the great reservoirs of relatively recent messianisms.

### A The South Sea Islands region
This is the region of the famous 'cargo cults'. A collection of popular messianic movements recently aroused in different

69

parts of the South Sea Islands come under this name. Their origin lies in the regular arrival of cargo ships, whose loads were almost exclusively intended for the Whites. The reaction of the natives, guided by local prophets, was to interpret these cargo ships as being sent by their ancestors, but seized by the Whites. Their expectation was fixed on the arrival of cargo ships which would finally reach their true destination: the local population, who consequently, on the invitation of their new religious leaders, not only abandoned the religion of western missionaries, but also brought about an awakening of the cult of their ancestors, in actively preparing for the event to the point of building quays and warehouses in order to receive the saviour cargo ships. The development of these cults was further fired by the events of the Second World War: the Japanese invasion, the American reconquest, massive disembarkations of troops, the contact of native people with western populations and techniques, etc. These cults seemed to have reached the whole of the South Sea archipelago in one form or another. Here are some examples.

One of the oldest ones is the so-called Mansren movement, from the name of an ancient divinity in Dutch New Guinea. Towards 1857, the natives thought they were 'Konors', messengers and prophets of Mansren. They announced the return of the ancient God and the ancient King, on condition that the Whites leave. In the same area, in 1893, Tokeriu, a native of Milne Bay, announced a devastating tidal wave which would occur before the arrival of a cargo ship bringing back the spirits of the dead; only those who destroyed the producer or consumer goods imported by the Whites would survive the disaster and be able to welcome the cargo ship . . . . An analogous movement, the Koreri, re-appeared in 1939–47 in New Guinea: an old Christian woman prophesied the return of Mansren and the installation of the Koreri (utopia, golden age). The movement distinguished itself by its rites, its trances, its glossolalia, its refusal to pay taxes, its squandering of agriculture and stock, its xenophobia. The arrival of the Japanese set off an increase of effervescence. A prophet predicted the birth of a Papuan empire. Hope reached its paroxysm with the American disembarkation, before being destroyed by disappointment.

In the twentieth century, cargo cults can be counted in their dozens. Prophets mix with adventurers, violence with pacifism, spiritual callings with protest and social subversions. Generally they imply a triple strike: of the missionary *cult* and its gods; of European *culture* and its methods of organisation and administration; of the imported *economy*, as much in its methods and techniques of production as in its consumer goods and methods (clothing, food). This strike is combined with a return to the cult, the culture and the economy, and above all, the gods of the native tradition. In the extreme form there would be no more work; the Blacks would become white and command their old masters, who would become black. In the movement of John Frum, a half-real half-imaginary person who 'appeared' in Tanna (New Hebrides), it occurred as follows: rehabilitation of the cult of their ancestors or of certain pre-Christian rites; ostracism of the Whites and their missionaries; tumultuous expectation of American miracle planes which would bring riches to the natives; the coming of a new Messiah who would unite Tanna 'without the presence of Whites'. Jean Guiart comments: 'A new myth which *replaced the myth of Christ from which they no longer hoped for anything* . . . John Frum would introduce the Golden Age, the Millennium'. The density of such phenomena, although unco-ordinated, appeared in such a way in the South Sea Islands area in the last decades, that it has already been possible to draw up a geography of these cults.

## B The sub-Saharan region

In a recent work D. Barrett was able to list 6000 churches or religious movements that dissent from the Christianity imported by the European missions. They are not all concerned with millenarianism, even less with messianism, but many of them are related to it.

One of the oldest movements listed is the Anthonian movement, revived by the Joan of Arc of the Congo, Donna Beatrice. She believed she was possessed by St Anthony, preached the end of the world, and invited the princes to gather in San Salvador in order to 'restore the Kingdom'. She died at the stake in 1706, but although there has recently been an audience to extol her, there has not been until now any

Church in independent Angola to ask for, if not to obtain, her canonisation, notwithstanding a series of a good dozen Angolese messianisms that followed.

In the nineteenth century, Molageni maintained he was the Kafir Messiah in Basutoland. After resurrecting him from the dead, God gave him the mission of freeing his people from the yoke of the English and the evangelical missions.

> The representatives of the English government and all the Whites without exception will be expelled beyond the seas. The Presbyterians and the churches will be carried off by a hurricane during an earthquake, and all the Blacks who obstinately profess to the doctrines of Christianity will be changed into birds and animals.

In northern Rhodesia, Alice Lenshina also claimed to have been resurrected and went as far as to proclaim that Christ had returned in her person. Her movement, which initially was messianic (1954), evolved into an independent and separate church, whose nationalist accent reached, attracted and 'converted' even the followers of missionary churches.

Isaiah Shembe (1870–1935), from Natal, moved away from the Baptist church to found the Nazaretha Church, which had 80,000 followers. To them, Shembe was a new Christ. 'Jesus Christ is the god of the whites. Now Shembe has come, the god of the Blacks.'

The messianic movements seemed to be more dense in Central Africa. There have been a dozen Angolan messianisms since Donna Beatrice. And the two Congos (ex-Belgian and ex-French) have been the stage of a series of religious effervescences which have succeeded each other, intersected, diversified, been reinterpreted, grown stronger or weaker, increased or been assimilated.

The most well-known is the one that was started, during his time in public life in 1921, by the prophet Simon Kimbangu,[7] whose Gospel was found, but was then seized by the police and locked up in their archives. Arrested in November 1921 and accused of social subversion, Kimbangu did not die until 1951, in the prison in Elizabethville where he spent thirty years after his death sentence was commuted to life imprisonment. But the dispersal of his disciples had made so many itinerant missionaries that the movement was resurrected and became the CJCSK, the Church of Jesus Christ according to Simon Kimbangu . . . . Fifty years earlier, the prophet of Nkamba, who was considered to be a messiah at least by some of his followers, incarnated a double protest: that of the political powers of the colonial administration and that of the religious powers of the congregations or the missionary agencies; and it was reciprocally condemned by these two powers. Fifty years later, the Church that was born of this prophecy and its messianic halo was recognised both by the colonial and later the independent Congolese civil powers, and by the religious powers, in the shape of its acceptance as a Christian church by the World Council of Churches in Geneva. As far as such powers were concerned, the movement was no longer protesting nor protested against. It passed into the phase of peaceful co-existence.

These cases are mentioned here as examples. As in the case of the South Sea Islands, one could also draw up a geography of 'Black Christs' in the sub-Saharan region.[8]

## C The Latin-American region

The north east of Brazil is without doubt a reservoir that is blessed or cursed with messianic effervescences. The Canudos movement is one of the more spectacular ones. Canudos was the name of the holy city built in Sertao by Anthony the Counsellor, an itinerant preacher whose message announced the end of the world in 1900. Taking up the surviving themes of a Portuguese messianism (sebastianism), Anthony promised the return of the magic King, which would put an end to the secular republic and coincide with the arrival of a golden age. The holy city of Canudos was a centre of refuge, a high place of contemplation, and a base for raids. A strict theocratic organisation surrounded the believers, who were familiar with the guerillas and eventually allied to the underground of 'cangaceiros'. Their bands were hardened enough to break up three successive punitive expeditions sent against them. But the fourth, which included a long siege, an artillery attack and a bloody street battle, ended in their extermination.

In the same part of Brazil, Father Cicero was, on the contrary, and despite his differences with the authorities, at the origin of a pacifist messianism. It was only after his death that the peasants, who counted on his resurrection, formed a messianic belief around him. Analogous pacifist messianisms are still observable and observed in contemporary Brazil.

As for violent messianisms, the adventure of Canudos is not the only one of its kind, and Maria de Queiroz has recently been able to assemble the facts concerning another holy war, that of the Contestado. It occurred under a double and ambiguous calling: that of a 'holy' precursor and *pacifist monk*, João Maria, and that of a 'holy' *secular warrior*, José Maria, who channelled in his deeds the devotion incurred by João, whose brother he maintained he was. In his way, José reactivated the medieval myth of the Emperor of the final days. Like Anthony the Counsellor, he was in fact an anti-republican monarchist, and had even been acclaimed an emperor. Furthermore, he himself was escorted by the 'dozen peers of France', for he knew the story of Charlemagne and his Peers, which was part of the literature of colportage. Nevertheless the holy war ended with the rout of the 'Caboclos', who were already decimated by illness, impoverishment and famine. There was an admirable epilogue, described by M. de Queiroz: 'Whereas the belief in José Maria grew weaker and tended to disappear after the holy war, the belief in João Maria, his antecedent, the "saint of Sertao", revived and came into the foreground. The "Caboclos" of the Contestado still keep to this day a photograph of the former in their chapel and continue to wait for him: "he will return one day to bring terrestrial happiness, whose first coming was a precursory sign".' Thus João was 'a kind of John the Baptist'; José 'was the Messiah', a military messiah, a zealot rather than an Essene, a Bar Kochba rather than a Christ. But in the collective memory it is João, the John the Baptist, who is made sublime and even messianised, whereas José, the Bar Kochba, or the Spartacus, is, on the contrary, pushed into the background.

These messianisms were not the only ones in Brazil, nor were the Brazilian messianisms the only ones in Latin-America. One naturally thinks of the earlier pathetic Indian expeditions in search of the Land with no Evil. And Latin-American messianisms are not the only ones in America. We have already mentioned the Indian messianisms of North America: for example, that of Wovoka, who was told in a revelation that he was the precursor of an imminent Kingdom under the aegis of Jesus Christ, a Kingdom in which the Indians would regain their lands which were stolen by the Whites, and would be able to lead the life of buffalo hunters on this land. This pacifist messianism also resulted in bloody expeditions (1890–1) before reverting to forms of passive or evasive resistance.

Further north, in Canada, at the end of the nineteenth century, there was the unforgettable and unforgotten hybrid messianism of Louis Riel.

Even further north, there were probably about half a dozen Eskimo messiahs.


From this long, too long, journey – which however is so cruelly brief and incomplete[9] – there should at least emerge the quasi-universality of this messianic-millenarian phenomenon, and the determination with which collectivities imagine or re-imagine *their* gods of salvation, who are the gods of *their* salvation. In its way, this gallery of phenomena, is according to the saying of Marx: 'The summary of the theoretical struggles of humanity'.

It would not be enough to say that *certain* religious phenomena reflect *certain* social struggles. Not only do they reflect them, they also make them last, and reciprocally it is because of them that they last. In the double frustration, economic-political on the one hand and socio-cultural on the other, the latter is just as determinative, and often more so, than the former. The frustrated collectivities complain: 'You have taken our land, you have taken our gods . . . .' But the commentaries are rarely as follows: 'It is because we want to take back our land that we want to take back our gods'. It is rather that: 'It is because we are taking back our gods that we shall be able to take back our land', or even: 'It is because we are not only taking back our god, but also yours, that, because of our strength and your weakness, our land will be returned to us' . . . or even still: 'You have taken our land, but we have taken your god, and in the long run this god will help us to take back what you have taken . . . .' There are so many subtle variations with which to encircle the irreducibility of this collective psychological force – the god – without which neither resistance nor victory would be possible.

For everywhere there is the rebirth, the renewing, or the birth of a god, the god of a society which does not succeed in being, or which is threatened by nothingness; but a god such that he saves society from nothingness and introduces it to or maintains it in being. A god from nowhere, since everything is disappearing, who starts to be a god from somewhere. A utopian god who becomes local. To be sure, this god would not arise thus if the consciousness of the prophet who is its spark, or that of the collectivity which is its receptacle, had not had to go through the fire of the great historical pressures which are its laboratory: plagues, famines, oppressions, segregations, humiliations, cultural or religious alienations, enforced labour, captivities, deportations, slavery, occupations, colonialisms, defeats, in short *regimes of despair*. But these necessary conditions are not on any account sufficient conditions, and these same causes are not such that they always produce the same effects. These regimes of despair can just as well lead to – and have led to – collective euthanasias, silent genocides, prolonged conditions of misery, prosaic compromises, or even underhand and manipulated collaborations. For the burst of hope, which is the hope of the hopeless, to come from these regimes of despair, it is certainly necessary for these regimes, in their very thread, to nourish the *forces* of revolt and transcendence; but yet such forces have to become operational, these *wishing wills* have to become *wished wills*. These forces of the 'not yet' are still only possibilities draped in the folds of the society that has arrived; *possibilities*, that is to say undetermined about being or not being. How can this indetermination itself determine what it is awaiting in order to be determined itself? The messianic-millenarian phenomenon is precisely a special forum of this self-ignition, or, if one wishes, this self-transcendence: the operation in which a god that is in some way superhumanly dreamed of, determines a collective consciousness and/or an individual consciousness, like a rider mounting, in this stable of possibles, the wild horses which will carry him off, leaving behind the domesticated horses which would jib at the ride. *To be sure, they are the horses that carry him and carry him off, but they would not carry him or carry him off if he had not mounted them.* We shall see a little further on that this image of the rider and his mount is not a random image, and that it even implies more than an image.

One final remark. Besides the human sciences, the phenomena of utopising millenarianism could not fail to captivate the reflection of the two great modes of thought which were nourished by them before moving away from them: on the one hand the dialectical thought of Marxism, and on the other hand the theological thought of Christianity. The treatment has been particularly severe, because in the first case these phenomena are interpreted as an evasive epiphenomenon, and in the second as a fatal deviation . . . . If we look at it closer, however, Marxist dialectic and Christian theologies announce, according to certain symptoms, a reconsideration of summary interpretations.

The Marxism of E. Bloch had already rehabilitated the specificity of this imaginary in his examination of the millenarianism of Thomas Münzer,[10] during the great war of the German peasants. There is, according to him, in the *attraction* thus exercised by a collective religious imagination, something other than a simple resultant of a parallelogram of the forces of economic *pressures*:

> Beyond their economic aspects, one should consider the peasant revolutionaries *in their deepest roots.* If one really wants to grasp the circumstances and potentialities of the time, one must necessarily take into account, *besides the economic factors, another need and another appeal.* For if economic appetites are the most substantial and constant, they are not the only ones nor, in the long run, are they the most powerful; nor do they constitute the most specific motivations of the human soul, especially in times when religious emotion dominates. Contrary to economic events, or parallel to them, one always sees taking effect, not only voluntary free decisions, but also spiritual structures of an absolutely universal importance,

to which one cannot deny at least a sociological reality (p. 72).

Marx himself, who said: 'in spite of the positivist spirit in which it has snatched communism from the theological domain, in order to limit it to the one and only terrain of political economy, thus depriving it of all of its millenarian aspects', offers an opening with which to treat other than 'by reduction to pure ideology, the deepest *contents* of this human history in full seething, this waking dream of the anti-wolf, of a kingdom that is at last brotherly' (p. 73). So for millenarianism in general, as well as for the millenarianism of the war of the peasants in particular, it is impossible –

> besides the economic factors which conditioned the outbreak of the conflict and the choice of its objectives – not to consider in itself that which constitutes its essential and primitive element: *the familiarity with the oldest of dreams, the breakthrough and expansion of the old heretical movement, the ecstatic will – impatient, rebellious and serious to the highest degree – of a march that leads straight to Paradise* (p. 73).

And finally:

> the inclinations, the dreams, the most serious and pure emotions, the enthusiasms directed towards ends, are fed by a need other than the one that immediately comes to mind, and *yet they are never a hollow ideology*; they do not disappear and they leave their mark over a long period of time; *they spring up in the soul from an original point, which gives birth to and defines values*; they survive all empirical catastrophes and keep their full strength, prolonging millenarianism in a constant present . . . (p. 74).

More recently, P. Ansart[11] attempted to explore the possible opening in Marxist premisses to such a sociology of the imaginary.

As for the mode of theological thought of the various Christian faiths, it was probably too advanced in ideology, in the sense of Mannheim, not to turn out to be allergic to the obvious element of utopism in the protests of the millenarians.

Besides, the very fact that they were protesting would have been enough to harden those theologies which are more typically attesting. Yet it is with the signature of Pope Paul VI[12] that, with the generalised failure of ideologies, a very official document, with a new tone, records 'the renaissance *of what are commonly called "utopias"* which pretend to solve the political problem of modern societies better than the ideologies'. The reserve is even more formal in that the said utopias are treated at the level of their most summary significance.[13] Furthermore the text deals more with social utopias than with religious utopias. Finally, the plan to retrieve utopia in Christianity, a plan which is formally admitted, does not correspond at all to the opposite plan of retrieving Christianity or Christianities in utopia. However one can see in the final part of the text hints of a movement from intolerance towards an opening: 'One must admit, this form of (utopian) criticism of the existing society *often provokes the prospective imagination* both in order to *perceive in the present the ignored possible* and to move towards a new future; thus it supports social change *by the confidence it gives to the inventive powers of the human mind and heart* . . . .' The final saving clause: 'and if it does not refuse any opening, it can also meet the Christian call'.

The fact that utopia, or 'utheism', has merited neither this excess of honour, nor this indignity, is another question which will be suggested in the following pages.

# Chapter 3

# Exile and the kingdom in eternal return

> Religion is the greatest utopia to have appeared in history.
>
> A. Gramsci

As we have already indicated, we would now like to look at some non-theological interpretations. Why 'non-theological'? First of all to avoid self-interpretation, second to put in perspective the plurality and diversity, or even the antagonisms, of self-interpretations. This theological ex-territoriality is needed, moreover, in order to get rid of the latent axiologies that too often preside at premature marriages between theology and 'messialogy': either this theology argues from the undeniable extravagances of messianic phenomena, in order to disqualify them polemically to the advantage of *its* ecclesiastical system, or at best, in order to under-qualify them as marginal seethings, obliterated echoes, forerunning outbursts, allusive or illusory repercussions, in short as *membra disjecta*; or on the contrary a theology (or a phenomenological ideology) argues from the no less undeniable sumptuousness of the same phenomena, in order to over-qualify them apologetically to the advantage of its own eschatological exaltation or its pretended *aggiornamentos*, idealising the facts, concealing evil, altering actors' appearances, making the stories legendary, giving a theme to situations, in short valorising as absolute values phenomena which are, however, very relative, so as to escape surreptitiously from the relativisation of its own values: in so doing, in fact, if one desacralises a dogmatic of confirmation, one resacralises a dogmatic of protest, and one only demythologises a theology of tradition to remythologise in a theology of hope.

Even for what should be a simple sociology of hope, it is difficult not to succumb to the temptation of modifying the analysis and even the treatise by either demythologising or remythologising. One only has to draw up a few index-cards and weigh up the terms in order to experience this. For the millenarian phenomenon, with or without its messianic component, is such that it presents itself simultaneously as being *fascinating* enough to induce exaltation and *formidable* enough to set off repression, even in one who claims to be studying it *sine ira ac studio*, without any *a priori* either for or against it. Indeed that is why it is the same in this case as it is in the case of utopia: pinning this label – millenarianism, messianism, utopia – on some phenomenon or other, is, according to the mentalities of those who write it or read it, pointing out that this phenomenon is either particularly precious or particularly depreciated, setting it aside as a reproach or annexing it as a prestige. The common conviction is that one is certainly dealing with an exceptional dynamism, but to some it is good and even honourable, and to others it is evil and erratic.

It is better to admit that the imagination at work is both the fairy and the madwoman. Sometimes one, sometimes the other, and more often both together: a fairy although she is mad, a madwoman although she is a fairy. Unless it is: a fairy because she is mad, or mad because she is a fairy . . . . To ignore this interaction would be taking the risk of not being able to reach the comprehension, or even quite simply the apprehension, of such complex phenomena.

We do not pretend to reach it here, but simply to mark the way on the psychology, typology, and scenario of these phenomena.


## I The psychology

The preceding panorama did not end gratuitously on images of riding. These images are indeed imposed by the anthropological analysis of socio-religious phenomena that are close to messianic phenomena: those of the *cults of possession* and their excited seances, during which the initiates, who are in a trance, are *mounted* by the gods or the spirits, as a horse is

81

mounted by a rider. They themselves turn to this image in order to describe their state. Here are two examples:

The first is the example of Voodoo, which is well-known through the analyses of Métraux[1] among others.

> Communication between men and the gods is achieved through the mechanism of possession or the trance, a phenomenon which constitutes both the most spectacular aspect of Voodoo and its most disturbing mystery. . . . It is nothing other than the *descent* of a god or a genie who has come to possess the person of his choice, after having driven out one of his two souls. The god *borrows the body* of a man or a woman . . . . The possessed person then becomes not only the receptacle of the god but also his instrument. He is expressing *the personality of the god, not his own*, in his behaviour and words . . . . The relationship that is then created between the god and the man whom he has taken over is comparable to *the one that unites a rider and his horse. That is why the possessed person is considered to be 'the horse of the god'* ('choual' in Haitian Creole), a term that allows one the use of a mystical vocabulary of equestrian character. One readily says of a god that he 'mounts' a person, that he 'saddles' him, or that he 'rides' him, and he is asked not to mistreat his 'mount' . . . . the individual 'mounted' by a god loses his identity.

The second example is that of 'the mares of the gods' in the rites of possession in Hawa in Niger.[2] The analogy with Haitian Voodoo is *Bori*, a word which designates both the state of possession and the god or gods who are the possessors. Here, in order to manifest themselves to the collectivity, the gods take as *mounts* women who become their *mares* (*gwaddin bori*). Bori may have come from Carthage. In any case a form of it already existed in the traditional religion, in which 'at the moment of their marriage, the girls were possessed by the god or gods that protected their family' (p. 21). Today, as in Voodoo, 'the initiation is a training that prepares the faithful for divine mounting'. This initiation is a long one: seven days during which the initiate 'must learn the gestures, characteristics and attributes of her own gods' (p. 37). Officiating men or women 'will show her every day the gestures that she must accomplish when the gods mount her'. The cult of possession itself is accompanied by ritual musicians who are usually blind.

> The god, solicited by the sacred instrument playing his name, announces his arrival *in the body of his mare* by creating in her a state of trance, characterized by twitchings and tremblings of her whole body. Covered in sweat, she pants, her eyes turn up, her head twists from left to right. This preliminary period usually lasts for several minutes, then her head is covered with a cloth. At this moment she no longer exists as a person. Under the cloth, the god invades this vacant body, to which one immediately attributes equivalent powers . . . . The metamorphosis has occurred (p. 41).

Some commentary from both authors explains this occurrence further. These cults certainly answer a need of a society. But it is not necessarily a need to escape or to escape from oneself.

> We do not think that Bori is a solution of escape. It answers a need of a non-traditional society that is no more nor less disturbed than any other. *But like any human society, it is also realised in part in the world of the imaginary.* It creates for itself a pantheon in its image, although it is endowed with a power that finally dominates it and is used by it (ibid., p. 45).

Métraux underlines the need for dramatisation: *'Every crisis of possession thus has a theatrical side.'* Yet, in a way, it is not theatre:

> These (similarities) between possession and dramatic representation must not let us forget that in the eyes of the public, the possessed person is not really an actor. He *does not play the role* of a person, he *is* that person throughout the whole trance.

And yet, in another way, it is theatre, even if it is theatre in the round:

The behaviour of the 'god' is observed with interest or amusement by the public. Spectators come up to talk to the god, who gives them advice or, on the contrary, utters threats against them (p. 88).

Sometimes it is theatre improvised from 'impromptu happenings that the possessed organise spontaneously when several divinities manifest themselves simultaneously in different people' (ibid.). At the same time, it is controlled and even ritualised theatre: *'The priests and priestesses would be prepared to call the god to order if his excesses should go beyond the accepted limits'* (p. 90). So are we dealing with oneirically *dual* personalities or with artificially *simulated* personalities? Neither one nor the other, concludes Métraux. We are dealing with *imagined* personalities, this imagination being here a *constituent* part of a second state. *The belief carries a god who carries on this belief,* just as a horse carries the rider who carries on riding.

When one observes certain possessed people, one is tempted to compare them to a child who imagines he is an Indian or an animal, and who helps his flight of fancy with a piece of clothing or an object. The adults contribute to this *waking dream* by going along with the fiction and by giving him the disguises that will help it. The possessed evolve in an even more favourable atmosphere: the public do not pretend to believe in the reality of the action, they sincerely believe in it. In the working class the existence of *loas* and their incarnations are articles of faith. Naturally the possessed person shares this conviction. In the state of tension he is in after submitting to or simulating a nervous crisis, *it is not easy for him to distinguish clearly between his self and the person he represented.* The possessed person improvises as an actor; the ease with which he enters into the skin of the person, proves, if he needs to, that he has *become* that person himself. He plays his role in good faith, attributing it to the will of a god or a spirit who, in some mysterious way, has penetrated him. In short, it would seem that the simple fact of believing one is possessed is enough to cause in the subject the behaviour of the possessed, without there being in any way any intention on his part to deceive (p. 90).

These images, which as Durkheim would say, are also 'emblems', are indeed part of a whole spiritual tradition that goes from the Psalms to Luther via St Augustine. This is shown in the Lutheran text, *De Servo Arbitrio*, which concerns the competition between two possessions – possession by gods and possession by demons, *which are so difficult to distinguish between*.[3] Here is Luther's text, which a Mennonite friend aptly reminded me of:

> Thus the human will is placed between two forces; it is like a mount; if God mounts it, it will wish and go where God wishes, as the Psalm says:[4] 'I was a mere beast in thy sight, O God. Yet I am always with thee.' But if Satan mounts it, it will wish and go where Satan wishes: and it does not choose between the one and the other, to determine which one will mount it, under which one it will run and search: they themselves, the riders in the saddle, fight to obtain and hold its choice.[5]

These most suggestive analyses of possessed personalities can offer a departure point to analogous analyses of messianic, messianised or messianosed personalities. The same images are valid in appreciating such personalities, and the gods that 'ride' them, as a rider rides his mount. Social history itself, with its cruelties or nostalgias, is the ritual laboratory of their initiation. In both cases, there is the same impossibility of distinguishing between duality and simulation. In both cases, there is the same second state, nourished by the intersecting beliefs of the person and the audience. In both cases, there are analogous dramatisations: *it is* a theatre, a sacred theatre, and *it is not* a theatre, because the personalities involved have the person too much under their skin; they are not acting him, *they are him* . . . . In both cases, there is something quite different from a too easy escapism, and even events that become a theophany. In both cases, there is the same contagion, the same sacred and frantic expectation, and even the same liberating and theurgical catharsis.

Thus a whole part of the messianic phenomenon seems to

superimpose itself on to a whole part of the phenomenon of possession. Indeed sometimes the traditional cults have provided the mould for millenarianisms that came after them: it is the same spirits of the gods or of ancestors who came in the one case and who returned in the other. So one can now relate the messianic phenomenon to the phenomenon of those 'exuberant social milieus', in which Durkheim saw the elementary forms of natural religions, and in which one can see the central beginnings of historical religions. In both cases, in a dramatised social life, the personalities concerned are 'mounted' by a sacred personification. Mounted, led, possessed, seized, en-tranced. The messianic tradition is not saying anything different when it says they are *anointed*, according to the etymological meaning of the Greek and Hebrew word. Anointed, in other words penetrated, impregnated, rubbed, steeped, as well as beautified, softened, strengthened, made admirable or athletic, prepared for the victories of beauty or of strength. In this sense, a 'Messiah' is a man seized by the god, like skin soaked in oil, massaged and rubbed in by a patient and inexorable hand: and this god, who is both the oil and the hand, is also *the sacred in its natural state*. But unlike the cults of possession which are appeased in the instantaneousness of individual or collective transports, the messianic phenomenon *lasts throughout time*. It lasts with time. It counts on time. Time stretches from the expectation to its fulfilment. The fulfilment itself takes time. For messianism, although it is the fact of an expectant humanity, is also in a complementary way, the fact of an expected humanity, and in both cases this humanity is that of a man mounted by the god. In this configuration, time is merely *the space between the expectant and the expected*: the space of a creation, the space of a non-repetitive cycle, the space of the limited and unlimited millenarian, who may be the archetype of a time in which not only do things last, but in which they enter *into evolution*, indeed *into revolution*. Who knows whether the cults of possession are not something like an *immediate* messianism of *undeveloped* societies, whereas messianisms are and will be cults of possession – *whose fruition is always delayed* – of *developing* societies? Who knows even whether, between the projected development and its concern on the one hand, and a certain shared messianic or paramessianic consciousness on the other, there is not a kind of connivance analogous to the one that Max Weber noted – and it would thus be merely a particular variable – between the professional Protestant ethnic – the occupation as a *mission* – and the project of the capitalist *venture*? Be that as it may, messianism does not 'catch' – as a fire 'catches' – until that expectation and that fulfilment, that expecting and that expected, draw near to each other in social density, to the point of forming negative and positive poles between which the spark strikes. When it strikes, a man-god becomes a god of men, an expectation of men is fulfilled in the coming of the god. For he *comes*, just as the spring 'comes'. And even if he does not come, he is imminent, and this imminence is hastened by the entreaty: 'Thy Kingdom come on *Earth* as it is in Heaven.' Not that man ceases to be man to become the god, but rather that the god ceases to be the god of the hereafter of men, in order to anoint man, his earth and his kingdoms now, here below. *Heaven on Earth*. May the God come. May the god come to *us*. And may he be a god of men.

## 11 The typology

On the basis of the cycles that we have examined all too quickly, we have at least been able to note the three elements that make up the phenomenon:

*The Person*, who pleads a messianic consciousness, which is sometimes accepted, sometimes rejected by his audience, unless, in some cases, this consciousness is conferred or even superimposed on him by his audience or its successor.

*The Kingdom*, in other words the millennium, the plan of which is described, assigned and sometimes recorded; the millennium, the constant of which is that it presents itself as the reign of god on earth for an indefinite period (a thousand years) between the Millennial Day, which is usually imminent and in any case immanent, and the distant day of its evanescence.

Finally between the Person (messianic) and the Kingdom

(millenarian) there is a strategy of computations that unite the first to the second.

Thus a typology of messianism-millenarianism represents a combination of three typologies: the typology of persons, the typology of kingdoms, the typology of computations.

## 1 The typology of persons

There are three cases to distinguish between: the historically present person, the historically absent person, the person with a vicarious presence.

### *The historically present person*

He may be claiming to be a messiah, or claimed as a messiah. If *claiming*, he usually maintains he has a native link with the supreme divine power, the master of universal history. He is father, mother, son, wife etc., or even, in the form of a *redivivus* being, God himself or the divine Ancestor. In every case a personal claim to messiahship is accompanied by a certain self-deification. This claim may be explosive (following a dream or a revelation); it is most often *progressive*: one is first of all a messenger, a representative, a prophet of the god, and the consciousness of the mission only changes gradually into the consciousness of the messiahship. This claim may be *exclusive* (messiahship of an individual) or *shared* (messiahship of an issue, an ethnic group, or an *ecclesiola* . . .).

The *claimed* Messiah does not give himself the title of Messiah. This title is *attributed* to him either by the circle of his followers or their succeeding generations. In the extreme case, not only do they attribute to him the title of Messiah, they also confer on him or invent for him his historiography or his historialisation. More often, however, this subsequent attribution is made to an historically present person, whose consciousness is merely that of a person with a divine *mission*, who is not claiming himself to have a truly *messianic* consciousness. The collective consciousness thus precedes and catalyses the claim of the individual consciousness to messiahship. The individual is at first a *claimed* messiah before being a *claiming* messiah. In the end the messianic claim is shared, the collective attribution being individually confirmed by the person. Before reaching that stage, there can be many different cases: that of the claim *in suspense* ('you say I am the messiah, that is your affair, do not expect me to confirm or deny it'[6]). There is the case of the *cultivated* claim, as is shown in the relations between Tanchelm and the Tanchelmites. There is the case of the *provoked* claim: from this point of view, there are essential elements for the study of different 'personality cults' to be found in messianisms.

### The historically absent person
These are the cases in which the messianic phenomenon rests either on a subsequent historicisation or on a perspective or retroactive exaltation. Certain constants can be found. The most frequent is the following: the messianic person only allows himself to be defined and described by the presence of the anti-person or anti-Messiah (antichrist), or even by the imminence and super-abundance of events that constitute an anti-type of the messianic Kingdom (the theme of the 'over-flowing cup'). But one also finds other relatively frequent 'formulas' according to the types of messianic messages. One could say that they represent a calculus of the degrees of absence. Here are some of them:

1 The person has come, but no-one has recognised him. In the limiting case he does not recognise himself.
2 He has come, but he remains hidden, only a few recognise him.
3 He has not yet come, but he is imminent (expectation and calculations concerning the mother).
4 He has come, but he has gone again and he is waiting to re-appear (theme of the resurrection).
5 He is here, waiting, but those for whom he came do not want to recognise him.
6 He is definitely elsewhere, but his place must remain vacant, no-one should take it . . . etc.

### The vicarious presence of the person
As we have seen, there is room for many intermediate solutions between the radically differentiated historical presence or absence. They can be grouped around the concept of a vicarious, previous, concomitant or subsequent presence. The types of persons that one most frequently comes across in

these categories are as follows: the wandering ascetic preacher (this person often raises himself or is raised to messianic consciousness, under pressure from the collective consciousness and effervescence); the prophet, or quite simply prophecy; the precursor (not to mention the 'postcursor' claimed by Charles Fourier); the consenting ally (most often a lieutenant entitled to be the secular arm of the messianic proceedings); the ally despite himself (the scourge of God); finally the theocratic pontiff.[7]

## 2 The typology of messianic reigns or kingdoms

Even if these new reigns always imply a link between *religious* factors and *social* factors, which are equally new, their accent can be placed at various different levels. Here are some of them:

### Religious or ecclesiological

Messianism is dominated by a plan of religious or cultural reform, but this plan is accompanied by a socio-religious strike, which is more or less radical in relation to the existing world. At the very least, strike of the dominating 'cults'. At the most, sale of all possessions and refusal to work as we see in primitive adventist expectation. Most often, commitment to a life 'out of the world' by the foundation of conventicles.

### Political

The establishment of dynasties, the advent of regimes, or even the birth of nationalities, are often accompanied by messianic or paramessianic speculations and dissensions. They can be observed, for example, in the history of France, Germany, Italy, Poland or Russia. This fact ties up with and prepares the phenomenon of divine rights accorded to political authority, phenomena which are so often studied by the history of religions.

### Socio-economic

Like the history of nationalities, the history of revolts often suggests a messianic theme. It has even been claimed[8] that the Russian Revolution itself could have rested on a theme of this kind. In any case this fact is particularly obvious when social revolt is joined with the struggle for national independence, as it is in contemporary messianisms in underdeveloped South Sea or African countries.[9]

### Sexual and familial

The new reign is often thought of as being one where there will no longer be 'men nor women'. This conception in its turn gives rise to variants in the proposed regimes: monastic or neo-Manichean asceticism, libertarian affinitarianism, or combinations mixed with variable prescriptions relating to endogamy, exogamy, polygamy (Mormons), or plural marriage (Oneidists); at the outside, themes on androgyny.[10]

### Naturist

The ambition of the new reign may go still further and wish to affect more fundamental regimes: regimes of food consumption (taboos or anti-taboos of certain foods), or of clothing (Adamites, Doukhobors, naked cults); the regime of reproduction (frequency of the theme of Virgin Mothers); or even the regime of death and immortality (metempsychosis, successive resurrections, authority of the *redivivus* person or anti-person).

### Cosmic

The new reign may finally extend to the vegetable, animal and astral world, and tie up with poetic, profane or sacred predictions of the Golden Age: economy of plenty, universal peace, modification of the climate, righting of the terrestrial axis, new relations between the living and the dead . . . etc. At this stage, the sociology of messianism runs into the sociology of utopia.

There is, however, a fairly constant theme in this diversity of levels: that of return or repetition. The new messianic reign is a *future* repetition of a more or less identical *past* regime. This reference may be one of a previous foundation: that of so-called *primitive* Christianity; that of a socio-economical period before the lamented catastrophes, that of an original world (Paradise lost); that of a world, submerged by colonisation or wars, of virtuous and independent ancestors . . . . It is rare that in its very newness, the messianic reign does not appeal from the *present* to a distant, unknown, forgotten or unconscious *past*, in order to found its plan for the *future*. This is shown, among other things, by A. Métraux in his analysis of South American messiahs: 'The subjugated people, whose cultures and beliefs are crushed by the conquest of the invaders, tend to transform their nostalgia for a happy past into dynamic dreams oriented towards a future which will restore their former glory and confound their enemies.' M. Eliade has opportunely systematised this theme of repetition, which is also that of the coincidence between an omega point and the alpha point.[11]

## 3 The typology of computations

The two preceding typologies are found and redistributed in some classifications common to the 'persons' and the 'kingdoms'. Here follows a rudimentary description:

### Messianisms and millenarianisms

A. H. Silver in *A History of Messianic Speculation in Israel* remarks:[12]

> One must remember that it is not the Messiah who introduces the millennium. It is the inevitable advent of the millennium that brings with it the Messiah and his corresponding activities. The Messiah was expected around the second quarter of the first century because the millennium was imminent. He was not expected before that time, because according to the chronology of that period, the millennium was very distant.

It is possible that this determination is confirmed in the period examined by Hillel, and even afterwards in many chronosophic calculations of the patristic era (sabbatical typology of the millennium and millenarian typology of the week). However, one should not insist too much on this dependence which subordinates the person (Messiah) to his era (millennium). It is true that the messianic consciousness often arises in the historical and social *milieu* before crystallising on a *person*, and *a fortiori* before being confirmed or denied by this person himself (it often, as we have said, remains at the stage of a posthumous gratuitous attribution); and there are so many ways of being a divine person (a messenger from God, a man of God, a descendant or ascendant of God), that often, by an ambiguous connivance, the same title may include completely different meanings as used by the initiator and as used by his followers. But two facts are also confirmed. On the one hand the millenarian context may remain on this side of messianism: sometimes the person does not appear, and sometimes, if he does appear, he is either himself an obstruction against the messianic qualification, or he obtains its transfer to a super-historic entity, thus blocking himself in the role of precursor. On the other hand the appearance of the person may *precede* the millennial nostalgia, indeed deliberately provoke it or not, and in thus doing, find an audience or not, and even if he finds an audience, founder because there is a distortion between the emission and the reception of the messages.[13] The determinations between the person and the kingdom do not obey a unilateral logic: they are complex, variable, and most of the time reciprocal.

## Pre- and post-millenarianism
The distinction gave rise to many controversies. It approximately connotes two characteristics which respectively touch a social process of intervention and a theological conception of grace.

*Pre-millenarianism:* 1 The kingdom of God intervenes *ex abrupto* by a revolutionary process, breaking the chain of natural and historical causalities, coming to the world with violence in order to destroy it, and re-create it or not, at a level that is more or less close to the here-below or the here-after.

2 This intervention is the issue of an initiative characterised by an otherworldness (mercy or anger); without it, the action of man can do nothing for the millennial kingdom; it comes before (*pre-*) it, and it alone makes it possible.

*Post-millenarianism:* 1 The kingdom of God is progressively installed by an *evolutive* process, integrating itself in the succession of historical facts (social and ecclesiastical), and directing the world, by the internal logic of its social and religious evolution, towards the point of maturity where it will bear the millennial or messianic kingdom as a tree bears fruit.

2 The religiously motivated and controlled action of man is not only not opposed to this final advent, it is such that it speeds up its rhythm: in any case the millennium comes after (*post-*) this collective human effort, and this is one of its prerequisite conditions.

One could also add: what pre-millenarianism expects from a descent *from high to low in space*, post-millenarianism expects from a progression *from high to low in time*. There is, however, a dimension common to both of them: the Golden Age is *in the future*.

It was no doubt in considering their common dimension – the millennium as an Eden in the future of human history – that Tuveson[14] came to discern a theological source – prior to acculturation – of the philosophies or theosophies of progress.

One should distinguish between the two threads of acculturation and ask oneself: if the optimistic linear theories of continuous progress do indeed have their background, as Tuveson suggests, in the gradually secularised post-millenarianisms, could not the pre-millenarianisms also provide a background, depending on their own secularisation, to certain pessimistic clear-out practices of a discontinuous revolution? Did not W. Weitling, who attained a quasi-messianic consciousness, refuse to accept Thomas Münzer as a precursor, in whom Mannheim thought he discerned the link between the medieval chiliast and the modern revolutionary? . . .

## Immanence and imminence

According to the messianisms in question, the announced or proposed kingdom could put the accent on one or the other. In some cases, one may be tempted to think that the pre-eminence of one tends even to exclude the other. The adventist *imminence* of the Second Coming implies an assumption that makes the whole system here-below obsolete and superfluous. At the extreme, the *Heaven on Earth* changes into *Earth in Heaven*. Time vanishes into space and the 'world' is a site that at best seeks only to be liquidated. Finally the perspective of imminence is willingly thaumaturgical: the coming of the miraculous person or persons, the mobilisation of natural or historical disasters for the selection of the saints and the damned, promises of immortality or resurrection, etc.

*Immanence*, on the contrary, takes time. It is usually post-millenarian, precisely to the extent that in order to prove itself, it mobilises the rhythms of times, events, seasons. And finally is not the optimism of its chronosophic computations the fact that it shows the unexpected gratuitousness of the advent as a *necessity*, that in spite of everything, is expected by the stars? The kingdom that it wishes to demonstrate does not, for all that, demand resignation to the established fact. It does not demand that one be absent from this world, but on the contrary, that one may be present in it, albeit in terms of Max Weber's well-known inner-worldly asceticism with dimensions at which classical puritanism could eventually take fright.

Imminence without immanence gives the background to a mystical adventism. Immanence without imminence gives the background to an evolutionist doctrine. When immanence and imminence are joined together, the background is, according to the pre-eminence of one or the other, either that of a revolutionary praxis of a chiliastic type, or that of a coexistence held by the impatience of the victory of the messianic kingdom over the resistances of the global society.

## Micro- and macro-millenarianism

The specific 'new heavens and new earths' of the messianic reign could oppose or offer themselves to the established socio-religious regime in two ways. They can either, in acting to the maximum on the *whole* regime and eventually from *within* this regime, transform it itself into the kingdom of God, using as a *macro*-millenarianism violent or non-violent means. Or, on the contrary, in distinguishing itself to the maximum from the said regime, it can form *outside* the regime a *micro*-society which, although it is small, does not pretend to be any the less global. To take an old example, one can think of cases such as the one formed by the macro-millenarianism of Münzerian theology on the one hand, and the micro-millenarianism of the Shaker societies on the other. In both cases, it is certainly a matter of a 'Kingdom of God' in the category of immanence, *but in one case it is a matter of transforming society itself into a theocracy, and in the other, of a theocratic society outside of a society which is judged to be inherently incapable of*

95

*transformation*. This opposition may have been the one that differentiated between Essenian messianism and Zealot messianism, the Pauline Christian messianism and the Bar Kochba Jewish messianism, or latterly, the millenarian characteristics of Manicheism and the Manichean characteristics in Mazdakite messianism . . . .

## Violence and non-violence

It is fairly rare not to find, even in *micro*-millenarianisms, an intention to absorb finally – by the very logic of non-co-operation – the society in the margins of which they deliberately install themselves. And, reciprocally, it is not rare to find in a *macro*-millenarianism the establishment of a selected minority body, submitted to a special discipline (guard, fraternity, league) and destined to instigate or control the proposed transformation: Joseph Smith, that apostle of what one can consider to be a macro-millenarianism (Mormons, Latter Day Saints), had for example, an apostolic body, a guard, and even a secret police. Thomas Münzer also created a league of this kind.

Just as the principle of the *active minority* is found in several cases, an added distinction may be found in the nature of the *methods* used by one minority or another: violent or non-violent.

The millenarian tradition of *violent* methods can claim a long inheritance. Without going back as far as Bar Kochba or the various military messiahs of the Jewish wars, medieval chiliasm provides a good example of messiahs or pseudo-messiahs who preached the inauguration of the Kingdom in a bloodbath as high as 'a horse's breast'; it is true that the antichiliasm represented by the inquisitorial organisation was also not famous for its gentleness. N. Cohn unearthed the undoubtedly millenarian project for a *Fraternity of the Yellow Cross*, that with astonishing analogies, gives a foretaste of its successor, the party of the swastika. Later the *Fifth Monarchy Men* organised riots and conspiracies. And did not W. Weitling, that authentic chiliast, dream of opening the prisons and urging the freed criminals to eradicate the existing disorder?

The *non-violent* tradition is just as ancient and continuous.

Its aim is non-cooperation, a quasi-ontological form of a managing strike which can cut more or less deeply into the biological, moral, religious or cultural systems of the environment. Refusal to use money is one of the most regular forms (including the form of *fater bursarius* in the Fraticelli). But there are others that characterise this tradition: refusal to eat meat, refusal of reproduction, refusal of marriage, refusal of commerce, refusal of medicine, refusal of industrial production or of proximity to towns, refusal of the ecclesiastical cult and a ministerial clergy, refusal of the law courts and taking the oath, refusal of military service, refusal of taxes, refusal of the electorate or eligibility, refusal of alcohol and tobacco, etc.: every one of these refusals is the negative *reverse* side, the positive structure or regime of which constitute the *right* side by the discovery or re-discovery of a way of life that is judged to be Eden-like or primitive Christian.

These are some of the broad classifications suggested by the messianic or messianising population, a population which was roughly outlined in the preceding panorama. One should underline yet again its limits and its relativity. Indeed, despite the intensity of explorations and compilations, there is still an unknown factor, which may be an infringement of the Cartesian rule of whole enumerations. One can never be certain of such an enumeration, not only because of the multitude or the difficulty of the sources, but also because messianic facts are among those which are the most easily *transformed by the collective memory*: for although they can be created or furthered by this collective memory, they can also be rejected or eliminated by it. So when one comes across a cultural region or an historic phase that are apparently *without* messianic facts, as indeed when one comes across the fact of a 'messianic combination' *without* the observation of a corresponding reality, one will always ask oneself whether this 'without' is the fact of an *initially null* reality or of a *finally annulled* reality.

## III The scenario

Doubtless one distinguishes this scenario according to whether one reads it face up or face down: face up, that is to say how it is conceived seen from the inside; face down, that is to say how it unfolds seen from the outside.

The same phenomenon can thus be interpreted in two ways. I applied this experiment to one of the phenomena that I know best: that of Shaker messianism.[15]

Seen from the outside, it is a religious phenomenon in four stages: the stage of the *Kingdom*, dreamed of in the mystical crisis and 'revelation' of the imprisoned little proletarian, Ann Lee; the stage of a *Church* (the Millennial Church), which attempted to establish itself and propagate itself through the exodus to America and the three great revivals of the first decades; the stage of an *Order* that aimed to be the great religious order of American Protestantism; and finally the stage of a declining and decaying *sect* . . . .

Each of these stages can be dated, detailed and noted by its correlations with social, economic or political phenomena as varied as the proletarian condition in a Manchester suburb, the migratory movements to the United States, the American War of Independence, the thrust towards the West and its agricultural colonisations, the beginning of industrialisation and its first social movements, the Civil War and its economic consequences, the acceleration of industrialisation, the break-up of closed economies, etc.

But the same sequence was interpreted from the inside in terms of religious meanings, and this interpretation was effected successively and diversely:

in *mystical* terms by the founder;

in *kerygmatic* terms by the circle of the first illiterate followers;

in *theological* or theologico-historical terms by the promotion of newly 'converted' clerics or pastors;

in *catechetic* or *apologetic* terms by the propagandists and popularisers;

in *commemorative* and *historialising* terms by the annalists of the movement;

in terms of *aggiornamento* and of dialogue with the world, therefore in terms of the theology of terrestrial realities or even of revolution, when the great Elder Evans, a brilliant converted Owenite, played the role of Eusebius of Caesarea;

in terms of *jeremiads*, under the pen of some old surviving
Eldress, or the final meetings of little groups that had
become witnessing organs . . . .

Each of these thousand and one messianic-millenarian
movements could thus be interpreted in two ways: self-
interpretation and other interpretation. And indeed in each
case the results would be very varied. Taken as a whole, one
can however see the double scenario, which is perceptible in
each case.

## 1 The scenario as it is conceived

The millenarian tradition, as we have seen, can be cumulative. Not that an earlier millenarianism determines a later
millenarianism as the cause preceding its subsequent effect.
But very often, at least, the later millenarianism identifies
itself with an earlier millenarianism in order to justify its
procedure. There is no natural affiliation, there is paternity
by adoption. But that is enough for a retroactive recovery in
which memory is forged by strokes of imagination. Semi-
mythical, semi-historical material is thus transmitted from
stage to stage, gradually shaped to form the archetype of a
scenario upon which each phenomenon embroiders its
variables.

If one follows the threads, at least in the Christian era, back
to their quoted sources, the source of sources is obviously the
Bible, with priorities, preferences or emphases, according to
the case, in one or other book, or even one or other passage
from the Old and New Testaments. One can see a dozen texts
emerge, from the frequency of the quotations, which will be
eternally invoked, commented, questioned, debated, interpreted and re-interpreted.

The most important text is the one in which the millennium
has its etymological source, that is to say the twentieth
chapter of the Revelation of John in which the theme of a
thousand years is emphasised in the sequence of half a dozen
verses: *a thousand years* between the first and second resurrection for the reign of the saints on earth; the Angel chains up
the Dragon for *a thousand years* (verse 2); the souls of the
martyrs come to life and reign with Christ for *a thousand years*
(verse 4); the rest of the dead do not come to life until the

99

*thousand years* are over (verse 6); only when the *thousand years* are over, will the final great conflagration occur (verse 7) . . . .

As we can see, it is only then, on the *last* day of those thousand years that the end of *the* world will occur; but from the *first* day of those same thousand years, the end of *a* world and the inauguration of *another* world occur, an interim world, which although it is a world of transition, is no less a triumphal world in a *here-below* visited by the hereafter. We have already seen to how many hopes this text has served as an emblem.

But it is not the only one. In the same Apocalypse, a good half dozen other texts are there to offer other emblems to other variants of the same hope:

Chapter VII, verses 1–4. The *hundred and forty-four thousand* from all the tribes of Israel who must be found and gathered together in a safe place before the four Angels unleash the exterminating winds.

Chapter XI, verses 1–7. *The witnesses in sackcloth*, who before being killed, will prophesy for 1260 days, while the Gentiles trample the Holy city underfoot for forty-two months.

Chapter XII, verses 1–14. *The woman in the wilderness*, so dear to the American micro-millenarianisms, who took that name.

Chapter XIII, verses 1–18. *The number of the Beast*, 'his number is 666'. The image of the Beast, or rather of the two Beasts, the second one being in the service of the first, represents the ominous relations between Church and State, with regard to which the scenario is conceived as the great Resistance 'for 42 months'.

Chapter XVI, verses 17–20. *The seventh bowl* and the destruction of Babylon the great, whom God made drink the cup 'which was filled with the fierce wine of his vengeance'.

Chapter XVIII, verses 1–4. *The leaving of Babylon*, at the edge of the abyss: 'Come out of her . . .' Sacralisation of schisms, exoduses, migrations, undergrounds.

Chapter XVII, verses 1–6. *The whore in purple and scarlet*, another name for the same 'Babylon the great'. The colour of her clothes, the sumptuousness of her ornaments, the cruelty of her actions make it easy to identify the Roman Court and the Inquisition with her . . . .

After the author of the Apocalypse, the next most important author is the prophet Daniel. He evokes the famous statue with feet of clay whose destruction is accompanied by the unassailable founding of the Fifth Monarchy (Chapter II, verses 31–44). This Fifth Monarchy was the emblem of the Fifth Monarchy Men under Cromwell. Several other evocations of Daniel's are often cited:

The triumph of the Fourth Beast, but also the revenge of the saints: 'And the time came when the saints gained possession of the kingly power' (Chapter VII, verses 7–26).

Treading down the Holy Place for 2300 evenings and mornings (Chapter VIII, verses 3–14).

The confusion of weeks during which a Messiah Prince restores and rebuilds Jerusalem (Chapter IV, verses 24–7), a theme which is dear to the millenarianism of the radicalised Jansenists.

The 1290 days and 1335 days (Chapter XII, verses 11–12), the duration of the 'abomination of desolation' or of the necessary hope.

In the New Testament, apart from the Apocalypse, the texts on the Last Judgment do not give a topical reference to the scenario. They aim at the end of *the* world, and that is not what we are dealing with. On the other hand, the text of Paul (Romans, Chapter XI, verses 7–28) on the reconciliation of Israel, or even the text of Peter (2 Peter, Chapter III, verses 7–10) on the 'day of the Lord which will come like a thief', offer better examples to millenarian speculation. Finally, last but not least, the reference in the Acts of the Apostles to the apostolic community (Acts, Chapter II, verses 44–7) had a vast influence on the praxis of micromillenarianism and its monastic,[16] semi-monastic or meta-monastic religious communisms.

These are the most important texts, or in any case the ones that are the most frequently quoted in the messianic tradition. Despite the disparity of their images and their esoteric calculations, one can see the pattern of the millenarian scenario and its three successive stages.

*1 The stage of Oppression*
An oppression that becomes *more and more serious*. The silver

Kingdom follows the golden Kingdom, then the bronze
Kingdom, then the 'iron and clay' Kingdom (Daniel, Chapter
II). The fourth Beast is worse than the three preceding ones:
'. . . It trampled underfoot all that was left' (Daniel, Chapter
VII). The King who 'works havoc upon a holy people' will
come 'when sin is at its height' (Daniel, Chapter VIII, verses
23–4). The Dragon who was conquered in Heaven comes *to
Earth* to pursue the Woman in the Wilderness (Revelation,
Chapter XII, verse 13). The ravages of the first Beast are
taken to a subtle paroxysm by the second Beast, who has the
body of a lamb and the speech of a dragon; everyone is
branded with his number (Revelation, Chapter XIII, verses
11–16). Oppression must thus go to the limits of oppressivity,
slavery and alienation, not only political, but also spiritual:
'The saints themselves are delivered into the hands' of this
anti-messianic Kingdom: 'The abomination of desolation'.

## 2 The stage of Resistance

Angels brand the foreheads of the servants of God. Witnesses
prophesy in sackcloth. Victories are won 'in Heaven'. Battles
occur on earth, but still without success. The first bowls of the
wrath of God are already passed round. Refuges – one is
tempted to call them maquis – are set up in 'the Wilderness'.
It is the time of martyrs. The time of silences or suppressed
prophecies. The time of heroic and rare refusal. The time of
solitude. The time of disgust at the profligacies of the
dominating Beasts. The time of impatience. 'Until when? . . . .'
said the saints. And as this time grew longer, the time of
exoduses: 'Come out of her, my people, lest you take part in
her sins and share in her plagues . . . .' The time finally for the
gathering together of the 144,000 who will be spared.

## 3 The stage of Liberation

The small stone shatters the giant statue (Daniel, Chapter
II). The Ancient gives judgment in favour of the saints and
the saints gain possession of the kingly power (Daniel,
Chapter VII, verse 22). A messiah prince presides over the
rebuilding of Jerusalem (Daniel, Chapter IX, verse 25). A
miraculous time in which the Day of the Lord will come like a
thief (2 Peter, Chapter III, verse 10). Time of the reappear-

ance in the light of day of the slaughtered witnesses (Revelation, Chapter XI, verse 11). Time of the seventh bowl of the wrath of God (Revelation, Chapter XVI, verses 17–18). Time of the destruction of Babylon the great, the whore in purple and scarlet. Time of victory: the Angel conquers the Dragon and chains it up for a thousand years. Time of the *first* resurrection for those who died during and for the Resistance: 'these came to life again and reigned . . . .' (Revelation, Chapter XX, verse 4). Time of the millennium for a people of priests and kings: 'They shall be priests of God and of Christ and shall reign with him for the thousand years . . . .' (Revelation, Chapter XX, verse 6).

As we can see from the scenario, we are dealing with the prospective of a battle, a hopeless battle. The principle of Hope implied in messianism-millenarianism is indeed that: *spes contra spem*, a hope of the hopeless. A cry from the depths of despair. A cry as a last resort because all other resorts have failed; even perhaps *so that* all other resorts fail; so that no other alliance should tarnish the supreme alliance with the Ally, beyond all possible allies, beyond all false collaboration. An epic poem wrought for the use henceforth of all the movements of the world under the evil of oppression, the struggle of resistance, the hope of liberation. From then on, it would serve churches, sects, orders, kingdoms, nations, social groups, active minorities, social classes, communities in the throes of establishing themselves, emigrants in the vicissitudes of their emigration, political protests as well as theological protests . . . . It would serve them all, whenever global liberation is opposed to global alienation, each one aggravating the other.

In short, the scenario *as it is conceived* comes into the category of *victory*, and even victory taken as far as *apotheosis*, in other words not only to a theism culminating in theurgy, but to a theurgy superlatively celebrated in an irreversible cosmic festivity.

As we shall see, the scenario *as it unfolds*, on the contrary, comes into the category of *failure*.

## 2 The scenario as it unfolds

'All those who have attempted to define messianism and to

discover the factors or conditions of its appearance, have naturally first studied the messianic movements that *succeeded*. One may wonder whether it would not be a good method henceforth to bring one's research to bear on the movements that *failed*.'[17] This statement of Roger Bastide's, which he made fifteen years ago, is worth considering when exploring the social meanings of messianic phenomena. One question arises from this, which we believe to be of increasing importance: can one insist on the distinction between 'successful messianisms' and 'failed messianisms'? Or rather is it not the essence of *all* messianism to be more or less a failed messianism? And if messianism (or its corollary, millenarianism) is a fundamental religious category, is this category not also fundamentally a category of failure? It is a hypothesis, and only a hypothesis. We shall explore it here for heuristic reasons.

At first one notices a contrast. On the one hand messianism rests on an *integral* humanism, something like 'all religion in all life'. From this fact there comes a cultural matrix – symbolic not logical – of exceptional richness, as much for the processes of evolution as for the processes of revolution in social history. Indeed evolution and revolution from all sides, for this matrix can nourish the claims of a royal dynasty as well as the plans of a republican regime, the legitimation of an 'upper upper' social class as well as the demands of another 'lower lower' class, and finally the mythical halo of a rational theory as well as the practical ideation of a wild spontaneity . . . . But whatever the variable, the matrix brings about an axiology, in other words *a collection of reasons for living or dying at a level where enthusiasm has its reasons which reason does not know*. Hence this apparent success, this air of being the goose that laid the golden egg, thanks to which the messianic-millenarian currents unfold their cycles of eternal return, throughout which they list in turn, with their various convolutions, religions, churches, states, dynasties, movements, currents of thought or of action . . . .

But equally on the other hand, messianism, if it went as far as the fulfilment of its success, in other words the realisation of its dream, would represent at the limit a *triumphalist* humanism. And from then on, its very success would be its failure. It would not be viable. The Republic of Saints has always been either a morose republic or else a traumatising republic. Sometimes both at once. But in each case, whether too little happens, or too much, the regime becomes or will become *unviable* at the level of daily life, for a *duration*. Durkheim has already remarked on it as far as cults of possession are concerned, and his remark is valid for the messianic phenomena: the super-society to which such cults or such phenomena would give access, cannot be an everyday society.[18]

In this need to open the paths to or from these experiences of the sacred, Durkheim was not far from noticing the justification for this 'administration of the sacred', in which the Durkheimian school defines real religion . . . . Similarly, the messianic-millenarian experience does not prolong itself, and cannot prolong itself *over time* other than *by its viable residues*. Or else, to express it in another way, it is the propelling force that puts the systems of thought or action in their orbits, but which itself, like a spent rocket, *falls back down*, and cannot not fall back down, whereas henceforth these systems revolve on the orbit of their tradition. *And yet they would not revolve in this way if they had not been put there.*

Such is the messialogical dilemma for the successors of the messianic movements:

Either commemorate or even reactivate the driving and matrix energy of the original current, in order to increase the exaltation of an integral humanism; but the other side of this success would be the danger of a tedious, dulling, even penitentiary, humanism.

Or cast off the rocket, control the acculturation, in other words the *relaxation* that follows this irritant *tension*, and, for all that, make triumphalist humanism viable and livable, *given certain accommodations;* but the other side of this success would be the great risk of demoralisation, what Maxime Rodinson so rightly calls the 'demobilisation of truths and values', and its horizon would be the entrance into a world without dreams, without ideology, without utopia, without myths, the technical world of 'thingness', of 'Sachlichkeit', the Balzacian world of mediocracy.

These first remarks, added to the all too rapid preceding

notes on the meanings and cycles of messianism, do at least enable one to return to the question put by Roger Bastide: that of the category of failure. Why are there failed messianisms? And even, why do all messianisms fail in a way? And how is one to judge this failure?

One has observed that the messianic operation (millenarianising messianisms or messianising millenarianisms) is a process of interaction:

(1) Between a Person (Messiah) and a Kingdom (Millennium), the said Kingdom implying an identification of religion and daily social life, of the reign of god on earth as in heaven, let us say an identification of religious society and political society.

(2) But this plan runs out of steam or is brought up short. One had set off towards the Kingdom, but one calls a halt:

a  either in a religious society that is distinct from the political society; to be brief we shall call this religious society 'Church', and a second kind of interaction will follow between this Person and this Church.

b  or on the contrary, one calls a halt in a political society, let us say merely society itself, and a third kind of interaction will follow between the Person and this Society.

If we combine these different kinds of interaction we can show them in something like a messianic circle, which would be as follows:

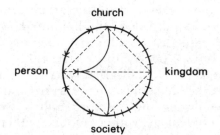

(3) The movement towards the Kingdom therefore splits – at a certain stage in its development – to produce either a new form of religious society (Church), or a new form of political society. It does, however, keep some of its initial impulse in this division, and this momentum is expressed either by a religious plan of political intervention or by a social plan in religious terms. Besides, in repercussion, the Person is historialised or re-historialised according to the perception (image) that henceforth either the Church or Society will have of him; Church and Society that have come from him as they are, although his plan was to bring about something quite different – the Kingdom – from what they end up being. Hence the possibility of messianic re-appearances in the very name of the distance between the intention of the plan and the result of the operation; there is, for all that, a new interaction between the society (or the Church) *in statu renascendi* and a new messianic person.

a The interaction of type 1 *between the person and the kingdom* brings up again the question of Silver's that we have already mentioned. How does the current pass from a personal messianic consciousness to a collective millenarian consciousness and vice versa?

Naturally the answer will vary according to whether one practises oneself one kind of philosophy of history or another, and according to whether, for example, one believes with Carlyle that this history is merely the 'biography of great men'; or, on the contrary, according to whether one deplores the fact with Saint-Simon that it is too often reduced to the 'biography of powers'. But disregarding all *a priori*, consultation of the records usually exacts a subtle answer and leads to a reciprocal putting in perspective.

For on the one hand it is true, as Silver reminds us, that a messiah emerges when the millennium is ripe: one seeks the former because the latter is coming to its end. 'Are you the one who will come or should we expect another?' At this moment of extreme expectation, he who will come can no longer not come. And if he does not come in person, he will come by proxy, if only as a dreamed person, a literary hero, a story, a song: *his essence will be stronger than his non-existence*, and even if, at the outside, he is a purely *constructed* messiah, he will be no less efficient in his thaumaturgy or his theurgies.

But on the other hand, it is no less true that messianism is a phenomenon favourable to the development of great personalities, or more exactly personalities who are open to a second state, capable of sinking their *self* in the *person*, and once they have identified the former with the latter, of living on the double register of society and super-society, nature and supernature. Indeed this is what dogma confirmed when it spoke of Christ as a Person of two Natures, but dogma extrapolates in a field which cannot be verified, when it speaks of a *divine* person. The messiahs one can observe are human persons. They belong to what is human, too human, and in observing them one can see this attraction of their humanity towards the super-human, never knowing whether this is the kingdom of the sacred or of folly, the kingdom of god or of delirium, the kingdom of a challenge to be taken up or of the impossible in which body and *soul* are engulfed. *Soul.* For the messiahs only become messiahs in changing their souls. Their organisms hesitate, resist this change which bores into them, reject it. That is doubtless why the operation only occurs in the theatre of great historical pressures: catastrophes, plagues, oppressions, wars, slaveries, violent frustrations . . . all of them conditions which are the noviciate of the messiah, a noviciate which is often later obscured in the brilliance of his public appearance. Albeit that this appearance occurs little by little, dream after dream, journey after journey, manifestation after manifestation.

That is when the relationship of the messiah to the kingdom is affected by the rhythm of his *audience*. For if the messiah gradually *broadcasts* the message of the Kingdom (the Good News), and if he broadcasts it in his own rhythm, the *audience receives* this message in their own rhythm. And these rhythms rarely coincide.

The rhythm of the audience can be *too fast*: then it *rushes* the messianic consciousness, it calls upon the messiah to become messiah faster than he would wish to himself; it attributes to him a power that he himself however knows that he does not have; it takes decisions from him that he knows to be null and void. It was in thinking of this shift that Proudhon spoke of 'messianosis' . . . .

Or else, on the contrary, the rhythm of the audience is *too slow*: collective consciousness does not follow; what it *receives* is short of what was *broadcast* . . . distortions intervene, fadings, interferences that take on an unexpected importance. The message is shifted, 'prosaicised', as Saint-Simon said, dulled, deadened, bastardised. It was in becoming aware of this shift that Friedrich Engels, in the work that we have already quoted, dealt with the ambiguous relations between the millenarian message of Thomas Münzer and his *audience*, 'the hard heads of the great mass of his followers'; Engels diagnosed an insoluble dilemma, because a given person put in a given situation is torn between what he 'should do' in the name of his kingdom, and what he 'can do', taking into account his circle of followers. 'He who falls into this false situation,' concluded Engels, 'is irremediably lost.' Let us add that there can be a double shift: the audience being both *too slow* on one level and *too fast* on another. So many reasons for a messianism to fail.

b The interaction of type 2 (which has the Church as its pole) was surrounded, as it has been noted, by the subtle problem raised by Loisy – 'Jesus announced the Kingdom and it was the Church that came' – and by its way of organically combining the failure of an eschatologisation and the success of an acculturation. In the same way, other authors such as Ernst Troeltsch, attempted to show elsewhere a line of sects as a re-eschatologisation of the Church, and on the contrary, a series of religious orders as a re-ecclesification of sects.

Despite the manifold refutations and objections levelled at the Loisyist hypothesis, one cannot help but remark – apart from truly theological considerations – that they turn around the allegation of a sociological impossibility: it is impossible that such a hope should come from such an alleged disappointment, *that such an alleged success should come from such an alleged failure*. This eventuality is so possible that it seems to have occurred or re-occurred dozens of times in comparative history, and one may even ask oneself whether it did not represent something like a certain law of its kind.

L. Festinger[19] found many examples of this 'increase of proselyting following unequivocal disconfirmation of a belief'. He found it in the Montanists: 'Nor did the delay of the second advent put an end to the movement. *On the contrary*, it gave it new life and form . . .' (p. 6). In the Anabaptists: 'From all accounts it would seem that instead of dampening the ardour of the Anabaptists, the *disconfirmation* of the predicted Second Coming *increased* their enthusiasm and activity' (p. 8). In the Sabbataian movement (Sabbatai Zevi): 'The Sabbataian movement strikingly illustrates the phenomenon we are concerned with: when people are committed to a belief and a course of action, clear *disconfirming* evidence may simply result in deepened conviction and *increased* proselyting' (p. 12). In the millenarian movement (W. Miller): 'Here once again we note the appearance of *increased* enthusiasm and conviction after a disconfirmation' (p. 16). He applies himself to the dissection of a witnessing group and confirms his hypothesis, according to which the 'dissonance' itself, which develops at an *intensive* level when the prophecy fails, *can* give the group in question the determination to appeal to a different level, an extensive level, where this disappointment will be overcome: in this way, the disappointment is not a discouragement but an encouragement for proselytism: 'If the proselyting proves successful, then by gathering more adherents and effectively surrounding himself with supporters, the believer reduces dissonance to the point where he can live with it. In the light of this explanation of the phenomenon *proselyting increases as a result of a disconfirmation* . . .' (p. 28). It does not follow – even for Festinger – that that is a *necessary* issue or *the only* issue. But it does follow that this issue is far from being impossible. *Ab actu ad posse valet consecutio.* And there is something in this that could lead one to re-evaluate or reconsider the Loisyist hypothesis, not as a theological hypothesis, but at least as a sociological hypothesis.

If the Durkheimian school has suggested that: 'Religion is the administration of the sacred', the present hypothesis can suggest in its turn that the Church or any other assimilated ecclesiastical body would be the substitute of the Kingdom, in other words simultaneously something like the kingdom which is *refused* by occultation and *obtained* by proxy.

c The interaction that the sociologists have studied the most is without doubt the third one, which has society as its pole. The emergence of messianism or of the messiah is usually noted as the *involution* of a political, economical or social programme of emancipation, in other words, to use Comtian terminology, something like the 'theological state' coming from what would be the 'political state' represented by this programme. At the basis of such a demand for emancipation is a noticeable frustration, and even a double frustration: economic and social frustration, certainly, since most of the time, in societies where persons appeared, conditions were needy if not wretched, and in any case, the object of harassment, persecution or oppression; but also, and the much missed E. G. Leonard would probably have added *but especially*, global religious frustration: beyond denominational dissidence, there develops, in candidates for emancipation, the aspiration to a god who will at last be *their* god, without proxy of alienation, be it the stateless god of a country that is not even or not yet a country, the god *of the wilderness*, who may also be the god of silence or of 'speech in unknown tongues'. This dimension can be seen in the very fact that *foreign* oppression, domination and occupation come to play a fundamental role through questions of languages, lineage, native land, national independence or dignity, briefly, through all the conditions that imply truly *cultural* alienation or disalienation.

It is the tight interaction of this double frustration, experienced as a total social phenomenon, which leads to a simultaneous elaboration of the milieu of life and the milieu of cult, by interiorising the remedy for this frustration in the organisations and patterns of daily life.

The unilateral tendency to consider the messianist or millenarian *messages* as being merely politico-economic *programmes* which are *still involuted*, ignores what Georges Duveau called 'the man of Utopia' as opposed to 'the man of History'. In his *Ultima verba*,[20] Duveau emphatically denounces this under-estimation of the former and over-estimation of the latter. For indeed, if the former can be the 'repressed in action', the latter can equally be 'repressed . . . in art' (p.100). 'an artist . . . who has literally lost his way, living the novel that he was unable to write' (p. 124). For all that messianism, by the unfolding of a sacred imagination, comes from the logics of utopia (as Duveau repeatedly suggests), one cannot decide *a priori* whether it is itself a *still involuted* substitute of historic action in which it seems to find its outlet, or if, on the contrary, this historic action is an *already derived* sub-product in relation to the message in which it apparently has its source.

In this final hypothesis, the relations between the message (religious) and the programme (political) should be put in reciprocal perspectives: for if, in one way, the message is the involution of the programme, in another way, could not the programme be like the sociological spin-off of the message?

The phases and intricacies of this circumvolution make it clear perhaps that the messianic fact is faced less with a dilemma (to succeed *or* to fail) than with a destiny (to succeed *and* to fail). Its dialectic is not circular, as though its essence required it to *loop* round itself; rather it is spiral, as this essence implies congenitally the failure represented by the fact that it *escapes from itself* in a loop that is considered, according to the axiology, to be the inferior or superior loop of the spiral.

Perhaps there are *only* failed messianisms in socio-religious history. This hypothesis has at least a question as its counterpart: does not this messianism, whose success cannot be located anywhere, reveal itself elsewhere, and by its very failure, *to be latent almost everywhere* in the genesis of what is considered elsewhere to be a success? One could even at the limit ask oneself whether historical development in all its dimensions is finally nothing other than a failed messianism. A trick of History! Everything occurred as it did in the voyages of discovery of the Renaissance: the ships set off to discover the location of the lost Paradise. Naturally they did not find this Paradise: therefore they had failed. They did, however, come to a new continent, therefore they had succeeded. *Their very success had as a reason a plan which was doomed to failure.*

## The Kingdom and the Exile

Thus messianism is a plan for a Kingdom, conceived in the lands of Exile. One must assuredly say that collectivities nourish it *because they* are in Exile. But one must also say:

1 *In a reciprocal way:* these collectivities become aware that these lands are lands of Exile because they conceive the plan for the Kingdom there.
2 *In a complementary way:* the very fact of conceiving this plan, albeit imaginary, already makes these lands of Exile into a starting point for the Kingdom.

## Exile and Kingdom in circumincession

And finally one must add: the plan is such that even if the Kingdom comes, *either it will be too much like itself to be livable, or it will become too livable to remain like itself.* The Kingdom that has 'come' is already a new Exile in which to feed nostalgia for another Kingdom.

## Exile and Kingdom in eternal return

A recent study on the functions of utopian language[21] rightly underlines the bankruptcy of the treatment which consists in gauging utopias according to their effectiveness in having proposed their own achievements. Indeed according to such a criterion, utopias would be hardly anything more than fanciful prospects, fallacious 'horoscopes', or a deceptive 'social astrology'. However utopias may have another function, a function of destroying reality, in which their effectiveness is not measured in terms of bringing one *into* reality but in taking one *out* of reality, even if in so doing the tricks of history unexpectedly bring one back into reality, which is not in the programme of the utopia itself: 'It seems that another function of the utopia appears here: social imagination is practised in the utopia'.[22]

If one transposes this analysis, one could make the following comment: equally the social function of messianisms-millenarianisms is not so much to prepare their own realisation. Gauged in this way, there can only be failed messianisms: whether its outlet is in the tribulations of a suffering church or in the vulgarity of a triumphant church, the Kingdom is such that it can and should always repeat after the poet, 'I am the promise that cannot be kept. And my grace consists in that itself'. But it seems that another function of these phenomena in which hope is exposed appears here too: religious imagination is practised in them, something like a logic of 'permanent resuscitation', to take up the utopian theme and expression of Federov's. This logic consists of allergies to the here-belows clothed in the hereafters, and of empathies for the hereafters veiled in the here-belows; it is sensitive to the nostalgia for Kingdoms in the greyness of exile, without, however, becoming insensitive to the discomforts of exile in the syndromes of an established Kingdom. Its disturbances are haunted by the gods of elsewhere, gods such as they could be, such as they have never been, and even perhaps such as they will never be.

That is why hope as a human phenomenon and even as a religious phenomenon cannot be satisfied by an ecclesiastically repressed millenarianism. But nor can it identify itself with an ideologically exalted millenarianism. This 'but' serves as an introduction to the thoughts that follow.

# Chapter 4

# Revolutionary ideologies and religious messianisms

> Let us not make ourselves the leaders of a new religion,
> even if this religion is the religion of reason . . . .
> 
> P.-J. Proudhon (letter to Karl Marx)

There is sometimes a craze for examining titles. Let us give in to this craze once more, as far as the title proposed here is concerned.

First: the title is in the plural. This is meaningful in itself. Twenty-five years ago I contributed one of my first articles to *Economie et Humanisme*: 'Marxism as a prophetic humanism'. I have discovered, *post factum*, that in effect this article treated the same theme, but in the singular, in confronting *a* revolutionary ideology – Marxism – and *a* religious messianism – Christianity – both of them pushed to the foreground of archetypes. It is probable that the pluralisations that intervened afterwards – *the* religious messianisms, *the* revolutionary ideologies – lead one to extend, certainly, but also to reconsider this initial confrontation.

Second: one would probably not be saying the same thing if one swapped the nouns and adjectives, and announced, for example, in the singular or in the plural: 'Ideological revolution(s) and messianic religion(s)'. One would be saying something else again if one swapped only the adjectives: 'Religious ideologies and revolutionary messianisms', etc.

Indeed each of the terms, be they noun or adjective, is worth examining in itself.

*Ideologies:* they balance us between blind and blinding themes on the one hand, and on the other, ideas, ideals or 'ideations'[1] which can be enlightened or enlightening.

*Revolutionary:* they balance us between radical social changes which are sometimes deplored as unfortunate traps and

sometimes glorified as the *magnificent* moments of history.[2]
*Messianisms*, including millenarianisms, balance us between
the magnificence and teratology of the 'kingdoms of God' and
the 'heavens on earth'.[3]
*Religious*, in other words where the sacred has been made
viable; but this very act of making it viable causes us to
waver, according to whether, for some, it is *active* in taming
the sacred, or, for others, it remains *passive* in obtaining this
taming of the sacred only by locking it up in a cage.[4]

Finally, one naturally asks oneself, *a priori*, whether the four
terms of this title are not linked by an interior logic, something like a genealogy. Such a genesis is apparent in binary
groups: a messianism engenders a religion; a revolution
engenders an ideology. And even, in a sense, a religion is often
the sociological spin-off of a messianism, in the way that an
ideology is often the epistemological spin-off of a revolution.
On the other hand, the genealogy is less obvious, from group
to group: there is a re-arrangement in the engendering:
sometimes A (religious messianisms) engenders B (revolutionary ideologies), and sometimes B (revolutionary ideologies) engenders A (religious messianisms). Most often another
process replaces the 'sometimes – sometimes': the same effervescence, which initially is undifferentiated (revolutionary
messianisms), in activating and re-activating A and B, the
one by the other, comes to a fork from which currents, which
are henceforth differentiated, each one according to its own
way and its own thread, convey the initial flow through the
political and/or religious meanderings of acculturation,
deculturation, transculturation or counter-acculturation.

From these first terminological attempts one can at least
make some comments, starting with the proposed title. After
a cursory remark about its background, one can pinpoint
three problems. Two of them concern the reciprocal relationship between revolutionary ideologies and religious messianisms: the relationship of their reciprocal geneses, their
amalgamations, their conflicts. The third problem is the
problem of the process of breaking with the closed field
constituted by this system of relationships, in whatever
combination. Let us say that, according to these three
approaches, the messianic-revolutionary global phenomenon

is successively: espoused in an *epic* way; filtered in a *critical* way, rejected in a *sceptical* and *stoical* way.


# I Backgrounds

If one looks at the path taken over the last twenty-five years by this problematic, it seems that one can note three major changes.

## 1 From monism to pluralism

As we have already indicated, this confrontation was somewhat arbitrarily blocked for rather a long time in facing two prototypes: the 'messianic' prototype which proposed Christianity, and the 'revolutionary' prototype which imposed Marxism.

On the one hand, research (anthropological, ethnological, sociological, historical) has led to a plurality of messianisms, not only of Christian messianisms – there are already so many Christianities – not only of syncretist messianisms infected by the Christian missions, but also of messianisms-millenarianisms that, in other traditions, be they religious or not, have had other names. There is however a recurrent structure under the diversity of labels. If one amplified it, one could today confirm the old work of Wallis's: *Messiahs, their role in civilization* (1943). The messianic phenomenon is a constant whose variables animate almost the whole panorama of historical societies, notwithstanding the animation, by cults of possession, of societies that do not come into history, or that, by means of a collective memory, do not ask for the imagination which is offered to them.

As for Marxism, not only theoretical research, but also historical development have undertaken to pluralise it. Henceforth, the constellation of Marxism*s*, and furthermore, the aura of socialism*s*, offer the wherewithal to compose the book of the thousand and one manifestations of an essence or a pseudo-essence, which will come henceforth – in the manner of what occurred to 'the essence of Christianity' – from a process of demythologisation up to and including 'Marx is dead', which henceforth will be a pair to 'God is dead'. This panorama is even more pluralised in that it is contributed to elsewhere by the exhumations of what – rightly or wrongly – K. Kautsky called the *Vorläufer*, the forerunners, while waiting for the examinations to give us what – rightly or wrongly – Fourier would have called the 'postcursors'. The whole of this pluralisation suggests a generalised *aggiornamento*. René Dumont had the strength to break the taboo by putting forward such a suggestion in his plan for a non-ideological socialism 'knowing itself to be imperfect'.[5]

So today we are faced with a double population of both 'revolutionary ideologies' and 'religious messianisms'. In the plural. A condition propitious for stepping back and looking at them in perspective.

## 2 From altercation to alternative

Axiom of revolutionary ideology: religion is 'the opium of the people'. Axiom of the messianic religion which is Christianity: communism is 'intrinsically perverse'. Altercation in the past tense, and doubly so.

At first the ideologists of the revolution and the clerics of messianism met in order to 'hold a dialogue'. From apparatchik to apparatchik, of course, and with all the risks of eventual disowning of the apparatchik by his 'apparatus'. Sometimes there were negotiations – with great support from reciprocal references to the 'scriptures' and to 'traditions' – between the official delegations of the Most Christian King and the Great Turk. Sometimes there were muffled discussions or ardent controversies on matters that future historians found to be as minor and yet as important as the dialectical subtleties of the ancient councils on the nature of divine beings, on sufficient grace or on the *Filioque*. And sometimes, here and there, there were bottles thrown into the sea by those whom Kropotkin once named 'lost sentries', such as the messages of a Dietrich Bonhoeffer or an Ernst Bloch . . . . Even if the dialogue was still an altercation, it already revealed an alternative.

But there was also and perhaps especially, a double emergence from the accolades or skirmishes between apparatuses or their representatives: the emergence of the permanent element of revolution in ideology on the one hand;

and the emergence of the reappearance of messianism in religion on the other. For all that, *the apparatuses* were questioned by *the networks*. They found their resources in this meta-religion or meta-ideology which is *the imaginary*, as opposed to rationalisations or institutionalisations. More precisely still, they found their resources in common branches of *both* messianism *and* revolution. There was an exploration of kinship, reciprocal reactivations of the messianic spirit and the revolutionary spirit. The ecclesiastical institutions and the political institutions were turned away, back to back: 'Neither Marx, nor Jesus'. There was the experience of the sacred in the social *in statu nascendi*, and the experience of this sacred *in its natural state*. The Saint-Simonians had had an experience of this kind under a sign that was both socialist and 'messiacal'. Later, others, according to Saint-Simon, 'thought they had imagination: they only had reminiscences'. And so it was again!

The alternative was thus divided. In the first stage the opposition between revolutionary ideology and religious messianism resulted in a *mediation*. In the second stage it postulated a *change*: henceforth the alternative implied or re-implied a double altercation against the double form – religious and political – of what the contestants used to call Church and State, and against the negotiators between the Church, whatever its messianic alibi, and the State, whatever its revolutionary alibi. The double altercation related precisely to this double alibi.[6] In its matrix, a messianism *without religion* wishes to join a revolution *without ideology*: a social procedure that has analogues in pure poetry, concrete music or non-figurative art . . . .[7]

### 3 From a closed system to its break

The games that are played between revolutionary ideologies and religious messianisms are impressive for their splendour, albeit illusory. It all occurs as though all men should be partner to them. All men and all of man. Do not all the parties propose the salvation of the world by the end of a world and the advent of a kingdom? Should one not mobilise in the militant city in order to reach the triumphant era? Is it not a matter of salvation for one and for all?

But is it not also a brain-washing operation? A clever and

cunningly held obsession? A psychological intoxication or self-intoxication? A 'messianosis', as Proudhon said? A confusion between 'communism and communion', as Marx said? Effervescences which in the long run are 'unviable', Durkheim remarked . . . . The announcer is in his scenario when, according to him, man does not live by bread alone, but by words that speak of the kingdom of god. But should the scenario not be coupled with the reverse scenario? For man does not live by words alone, but also by bread, by the work that gives him this bread, by the tools of this work, by days and nights in the vastness and moderation of a daily life, with children being born, old people dying, adolescents joining together, generations following each other, bodies, minds, hearts, crossing one by one the oases of their joys and the desert of their wounds. Work and days which are just as heavy as, and heavier than, the theogonies . . . .

In weighing this weight, in measuring this thickness, in multiplying it by the millions of men over whom rolled the chariots of triumph or the chariots of flight of the revolutionary or messianic epics, does not this prosaic history overshadow its epic legends? This is what Bakunin, who was not susceptible to the prosaic, nevertheless noted:[8]

> The millions of individuals who have provided the living and suffering matrix in this history, which is both triumphant and dire, triumphant because of the vast slaughter of human victims crushed under its chariot, these millions of obscure individuals, without whom none of the great abstract results of history would have been obtained, are not given the slightest mention in its annals. They came. They were sacrificed for the good of abstract humanity, that is all.

A pure coincidence: as I wrote these lines, I was reading two words: one about the dreams of Eldorado, because of which the Spanish Conquistadors attacked and destroyed the native cultures and civilisations of the New World in epic wars both odious and prestigious;[9] the other about the recent evaluation, drawn up by an ethnologist missionary, of a large Indian ethnic group which has survived: not only has its cultural universe resisted, more or less unharmed, four centuries of subversion, it has also turned round the dialectic of the messages: those whom it was planned to make servants of Christian religions, on the contrary made their missionaries ministers of a non-Christian religion.[10] The chariots rolled across moving sands which engulfed them.

Finally there is the point of view of the human sciences, which are neither ideological nor religious, even when they are applied to the social phenomena which are ideology or religion. Let us not join these millions of men, said G. Le Bras, 'until they are armed, and then in order to establish the action of a leader, the effect of a propaganda' . . . . It would be thus if one considered messianism and revolution in a closed circuit. Doubtless they belong to the *visible* part of the iceberg. They come on stage and act out their adventures, including the one in which the audience participates in order to accomplish an integral dramatisation of social life. Until now social life has turned down the invitation, and even when it allowed itself to be enrolled for a time, the recruits were like all soldiers confined to barracks: they awaited another time, the time of 'liberation', as they called it.

Perhaps that is why the human sciences, both because they are human and because they are sciences, revolt at being enclosed in this dramatisation, be it the ideological drama-tisation of the Revolution or the religious dramatisation of a messianism. Neither re-theologisation nor re-ideologisation. To be sure, we know that a certain anthropologist devoted to observing the voodoo cult was unable to resist: she stopped observing and took part in the dance. This *sollicitatio ad sublimia*, which exists in the closed circle where the only question is that of the proportion between messianism and revolution or the transfer from one to the other, has never ceased to exist, nor does it cease to exist. Is not this circle, one argues, the source of the 'meaning' or 'values' and of 'final reasons', as it has shown so many times in unwinding its spirals century after century?

And yet thorough knowledge of it comes from a centre of reflection situated outside it: that is enough for the circle to be called on to open and for the phenomenon to remain a phenomenon and to cease being a noumenon. In this approach, which becomes more general, revolutionary ideologies and religious messianisms are not opposed; they are joined even, in that they come from the same kind of behaviour. But if another approach once joined them (cf. *supra* 2), in order to place itself *inside* them at their epicentre – participation winning over keeping at a distance – here, on the contrary, if one detects an analogous structure in them, it is in order to place itself *outside* them, beyond their hold or influence, their distinctions or contagions: keeping at a distance wins over participation.

For such a view from a distance and from outside, there is a human phenomenon which corresponds to the squaring of the title, a phenomenon which in a way is 'ideologico-revolutionary – messianico-religious'. But on the one hand it is a human phenomenon, the reoccurrences of which have many variables: its unity demands to be pluralised. And on the other hand this plurality does not make it count more as *one* human phenomenon among others, and in a way as one person among many persons susceptible to being acted by an individual or collective personality: without its eventual claim to dominate or mobilise the scene, being anything but an *act*: without its declarations of being everything, being anything but a way of acting *its* part; without its ambitions of having a leading role, being able to fake situations in which it certainly is not the last instance.

## II Geneses and amalgamations: or the relationship seen in an epic way

Let us take an example. In 1949, a Moslem messiah, Moussa Aminou, was crushed with his seventy followers in a mosque in black Africa: the revolutionary outcome of a long religious path narrated in the originator's diary. His para-messianic consciousness began in a visionary dream: 'The Prophet (Mohammed) was on a ship and I was with him. The ship was sailing across the sea with no captain. On the shore a dog was barking at us; it was standing in the setting sun and it was yellow. The Prophet prayed: "O Lord, Master, I beg You to free my people from this sea . . . ."' The commentator explains the dream as follows: 'the ship on the sea is the

Moslem community, the yellow dog in the setting sun is the Europeans who forbid the ship to come into shore'. This coming into shore will be obtained by a liberator: Moussa Aminou. The final revelation: 'You are the Mahdi in this world and in the next'. And this final confirmation leads to a holy way: 'Do not fear the Christians . . . God will bring you victory . . . Moussa, you are my true son. Your religion must win over all other religions, and the authority of the Christians must cease so that only the authority of Islam remains'.[11] This is the genesis of a revolutionary ideology in a religious messianism, or at least an example of such a genesis.

There are also examples of a reverse genesis: the revolutionary who becomes the claiming or claimed messiah, or more precisely, the violent revolution which becomes a non-violent messianism, correspond to the messiah who becomes a revolutionary. I have already[12] mentioned the moving figure of a woman messiah, Ann Lee, the mother of the Shaker communal network; her messianism which is paroxysmal, is the result of a triple revolution: the English political revolution in the background, the Manchester industrial revolution, the American revolution and the war of Independence. It is no less non-violent and no less of a conscientious objector. Similarly, the Indian Ghost Dance, with its motifs of armed revolt, gradually ends up as peyotism, a messianism of peaceful coexistence with the American nation. One could thus examine most of the great European revolutions, the worker uprising in 1381, the Hussite war in the fifteenth century, the war of the German peasants in the sixteenth century, the English political revolution in the seventeenth century. If one sees in each of them grafts on to a messianism-millenarianism, conversely, one sees suckers of messianism, which originate from that revolution, flourish from each of them.[13] Even the French Revolution, which Engels did not wish to be touched by such a reference, offers as many seeds from within itself, its *Journal prophétique* (of Pontard's), its distinguished prophetess, Suzette Labrousse[14]; its millenarianised echo in the Anglo-Saxon countries . . . .[15]

As for the interchanges of these two geneses, one could study them at will in the genesis of the Two Greats: the United States[16] or the Soviet Union.[17]

But obviously it was with this revolution of the twentieth century which is the accession of the third-world countries to independence or quite simply to notoriety, that this problematic got across. The works are too well-known and too numerous to be quoted. One can even draw up a geography of what is alternately called 'religious movements of the oppressed people',[18] 'revolutionary messianisms of the third world',[19] 'revolutions in traditional societies',[20] . . . names which after all are better than 'fanatics of the Apocalypse', which the French edition gave to the rather precious work of Norman Cohn's on the Middle Ages.[21] This geography has even been drawn up on cultural regions such as the ones of the Cargo cults, the rest of the classification of the ecumenical factors being pursued elsewhere in current research for a collective second edition of the dictionary already mentioned.

The main geographical reservoirs of this recent cycle are now known; we have already mentioned them (cf. *supra.* ch. 2). In the foreground come the South Sea Islands populations of the Cargo cults, the reciprocal reinterpretation of the traditional cults of the dead and of imported missionary messages: the whole culminating in a religious and subversive contestation, pre-revolutionary even, of white power, and an aspiration to retrieve it.

The second area is doubtless that of sub-Saharan black Africa in the manifestations of its black Christs; these Christian dissidences, with a millenarianising and messianising form, have been deciphered and interpreted by Balandier, Anderson, Bengt Sundkler and others.[22] On the one hand the proliferation of south African prophetisms (see Sundkler) is apparent, as are on the other hand, the well-known personalities of the Congolese area, from Doña Beatrice[23] to the Kimbangu-Lumumba couple, who, henceforth we are assured, will be celebrated together in the collective memory.

A third area is without doubt that of the messianic quasi-Jacqueries of South America and of Brazil in particular, whose highly colourful personalities still share the favours of a literature of colportage (the literature of 'Cordel') with the Cangaceiros, and whose messages were perhaps reactivated in the millenarian plans of certain agrarian leagues of Francisco Juliao. M. I. Pereira de Queiroz devoted himself to

the study of this catalogue; the old contributions of A.
Métraux remain classic, and R. Bastide, with his usual
penetration, is untiring in forwarding its analysis.[24]

These areas are not limited. The North American region
had its Indian messiahs. Recently in Canada, an ethnologist
offered half a dozen examples of Eskimo messianisms, while a
young sociologist proposed the exhumation of the half-caste
messianism of Louis Riel. H. Fuchs brought back a group of
'rebellious prophets' from India. J. Chesneaux drew our
attention to the millenarianisms of Chinese sects; others to the
millenarianisms of the social peasant revolts in Indonesia.[25]
North African Islam added to this collection with the
important tradition of its mahdisms.[26] Even social revolts in
modern Europe turned out to be connected with a 'primitive'
fund of millenarianism.[27] And one wonders more and more
whether such a 'primitive fund' is not present in the genesis of
modern socialisms.[28] Of course these are only the first signs.

In the context of eventual links between ancient religious
millenarianisms and recent social millenarianisms, I have
quoted elsewhere a typical fragment of Francisco Juliao's
*ABC of the peasant*. I was even able to suggest to Juliao that he
was reproducing the themes and the accent of Gerrard
Winstanley, whose Diggers practised in seventeenth-century
England a strategy analogous to that of the Leagues in the
State of Pernambouc. Here is an extract from this *ABC*,
whose fervent and ardent style is so characteristic of this
literary genre.

What is the path? To change the law. But how can one
change the law? By everyone uniting. By a mass movement. By pressure. That is why the League exists. That
is why the Union must exist. If the violence of the
servant and the pressure of the police do not make you
give in because you have a drop of light in your consciousness and you are ready to die for your freedom, the
'latifundio' then uses the name of God. In what way? Let
me explain. The 'latifundio' says: 'The punishment of
God falls on those who revolt against him. If the one is
rich and the other poor, if the one owns the land and the
other not, if the one must put his pickaxe on his shoulder

and work and the other grows rich from the fruits of this work, if the one lives in a palace and the other in a slum, it is because God wishes it. He who revolts against this revolts against God. He will bring punishments from heaven: plague, war, famine. And when he dies, he will go to hell. The poor man must be poor so that the rich man can be rich. The world has always been thus. And it will always be thus. God wishes it.' Those are the words of a land owner. He invokes the name of God to frighten you. Because you believe in God. But this God of the owner is not your God. Your God is as gentle as a lamb. He is called Jesus Christ. He was born in a stable. He lived among the poor. He was surrounded by fishermen, peasants, workers, beggars. He wanted freedom for all of them. He said that the land should belong to the man that worked it. And that the results should belong to everyone. These are His words: 'It is easier for a camel to pass through the eye of a needle than for a rich man to enter the Kingdom of heaven'. And because he said that and many other things he was crucified by the 'latifundiarios' of his time. Today he would have been shot. Or locked up in a lunatic asylum. Or put in prison as a communist. Listen carefully to what I'm saying, peasant. If a priest or a pastor speaks to you of a God who threatens the people with war, with plague, with famine, with lightning and storms, and the fires of hell as well, you can be sure that that priest or pastor is the servant of ownership. He is not a minister of God. He is a false priest. He is a pastor who is worth nothing. The true priest or the good pastor is the one who has the courage to say: 'God made the earth for all of us, but the more evil have seized hold of it. You will earn your bread by the sweat of your brow, not by the sweat of your neighbour's brow. No one should be the slave of anyone. Nor of a people. Nor a man of another man. Because all are equal before the law. And before nature. And in front of God. If that is communism then God is communist. Because that is what is written in the Holy Scriptures. And what is in the mouth of Christ. And in the mouths of all his apostles.'

Sometimes the genesis goes from religious messianism to revolutionary ideology. And sometimes on the contrary from revolutionary ideology to religious messianism. The amalgamation itself occurs sometimes with one stress – religious messianism amalgamating *with* a revolutionary ideology – sometimes with another – religious messianism amalgamating such an ideology *to itself*. But to say that, is to say too much or not enough. For, as we have already underlined, these pairs are involuted, the one in the other. If one conceives that 'messianism' and 'revolution' are *both* included in the category of radical social change, which is *also* economic and cultural, the radical *cultural* change which is messianism will initiate the *economic* change which is revolution. And vice versa. They tend to be postulated or to overlap each other through lateral operations which are precisely the nature of the amalgamation.

'The coincidence of value judgments and judgments of reality is a constant of all the ideological movements based on an active optimism – *be they religious or atheist*, universalist or ethnico-national. The militants of all these movements could always have adhered to the proclamation addressed to the proletariat by the Marxist song, the *Varsorienne*: "Your cause is just and your inspiration is powerful", with the following detail added in the case of religious movements: "Your inspiration is powerful because it comes from God." . . .'[29]

The messianic impetus found itself lieutenants, secular arms, historical executors of its plan. The revolutionary impetus armed itself with a historico-worldwide myth, and thus conferred on the bearers of such a myth and those to whom it was attributed, a ritual or cultural hieratism: the process went from the cult of Charlemagne, beneficiary of the myth of the 'Emperor of the final days', to the 'personality cults', which were repetitions of the nineteenth-century millenarian themes of the 'strong Monarch'.

The amalgamation has an even more fascinating attraction[30] in that messianic plans and revolutionary plans reveal an indisputable connivance. In different ways they obey the same scenario in three stages:

(1) The stage of *oppression* which is taken to the limits of oppressiveness. In revolutionary terms: 'alienation'. In messianic terms: 'the abomination of desolation'. It is the

black stage: the blacker it is, the more it enters into the scenario. And even if it is not black enough, the scenario demands that it be blackened either by a short-cut to any 'revisionist' improvement, or by making this blackness into a fixed idea.

(2) The stage of *resistance*: the stage of impatience, of the last square, of the 'desert' or of the underground, of *spes contra spem*, of the hope of the hopeless, of the suppression of the elites and the elected of the counter-society, of the accumulation – a maximum of density in a minimum of volume[31] – of the explosive charge, of the concentration of this charge on a person who is chosen as or chooses himself to be the totem – 'the -ism makes the man' of the movement.

(3) The stage of *liberation* with the event – the inaugural advent of its D-Day, the millennial Day, the Great Day or the Great Night coming unexpectedly, breaking in 'like a thief', yet obeying the inexorable determinism of what could not come. After that the Reign would begin: the 'reign of freedom', or the reign of the Saints. The reign of 'Heavens on Earth, Heavens below', in a kingdom where each living man will be like an unchained glory.

And not only is there the same visionary scenario, but also the same transformations: these *militant* epics, which are messianisms as well as revolutions, end up only as failures: failed messianisms or failed revolutions. The failure can differ according to whether the epic turns into an *ailing* issue or onto a *triumphant* path. It does not fail any the less in both cases: in one because of the repression and liquidation that follow, in the other because of the tricks and hoaxes that accompany it. From that point of view the ecclesiastical institutions which are the heirs of adventisms are no more important than the 'institutionalised revolutionary parties'. No less important either: do they not both attempt to make the unviable viable? For, to the extent that either revolutions or messianisms succeed in making the unviable viable, the same final transformation occurs in both cases: the one that frustrates the securing of the catch by the pursuit of the chase, causes the de-seizing of what has already been seized after the re-seizing of the unseizable, disputes the established, questions real socialities with possible socialities, cracks the 'here and now' with the 'not yet', saps the apparent solidity of reality by the effectual resistance of the imaginary, or more simply and more elementarily, denounces the purgatory in what called itself paradise: as one used to say, the 'critical period' fixes itself in the heart of the 'organic period' . . . . As Pascal said: 'We do not ever search for things, but for the search of things'.

Finally there is the same paradox. This scenario, which seems pre-eminently to reject all structure in the name of anti-structure, which seems to empty all institutions in the uprush of perpetual event, does not any the less appear devoid of tendential regularities, reoccurrences, analogies or homologies such that its repetitions reveal something like a matrix: not an essence or a type whose manifestations would be specific accidents, but a table of elementary factors liable to enter into a thousand and one combinations, which would put the same *constant* list of fundamental elements in a variable order, with variable signs (of presence or absence) and in variable intensities. The genesis of this structure always corresponds with the structure of this genesis: like a volcanic eruption foretold withal in the unalterable system of the stars. But as this correspondence is always skewed, it only holds good on condition that it gets a push from this astrology, which is what the amalgamation is.

## III Conflicts: or the relationship seen in a critical way

To account for both this reoccurrence and this instability, each of which is as congenital as the other, one is surprised to resort to Sartre's hypothesis of reality as 'an aborted effort', of 'a failed God', and of 'perpetual failure'.[32]

Such a sociological disintegration fixes itself, and cannot but fix itself, in the conflicts or tensions that come to confront one or the other of our four terms: messianisms, religions, revolutions, ideologies. In reality there should be six, for if 'messianism' corresponds relatively to 'revolution', 'religions' corresponds to something lacking *between* revolutions and ideology, whereas 'ideologies', as J. Wach suggested, would correspond more to 'theology', beneath and this side of 'religions' (cf. the complex diagram) . . . . But restricting ourselves to the four terms (cf. the simplified diagram), one can distinguish several sociological areas of conflict: the unitary areas, the binary areas and the ternary areas.

Indeed if one inscribes these four terms at the four poles of a quadrilateral, giving each of them a letter for the sake of brevity, A, B, C, D, one sees straight away the possible conflicts.

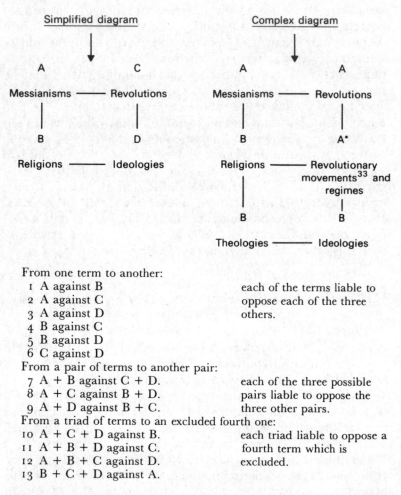

From one term to another:

| | | |
|---|---|---|
| 1 | A against B | each of the terms liable to oppose each of the three others. |
| 2 | A against C | |
| 3 | A against D | |
| 4 | B against C | |
| 5 | B against D | |
| 6 | C against D | |

From a pair of terms to another pair:

| | | |
|---|---|---|
| 7 | A + B against C + D. | each of the three possible pairs liable to oppose the three other pairs. |
| 8 | A + C against B + D. | |
| 9 | A + D against B + C. | |

From a triad of terms to an excluded fourth one:

| | | |
|---|---|---|
| 10 | A + C + D against B. | each triad liable to oppose a fourth term which is excluded. |
| 11 | A + B + D against C. | |
| 12 | A + B + C against D. | |
| 13 | B + C + D against A. | |

This scheme may appear to be sophistical. Not so. It suffers only from the imprecision of the terms. But once this imprecision has been accepted and the terms have been taken for what they convey in the literature of the subject, the scheme may be useful for decoding the often paradoxical, even delusive messages of this literature. What follows does not however go beyond the scope of a simple exemplification.

## 1 A against B Messianisms versus religion

If messianism is an operative eschatology, it is obvious that religion fits into the canalisation of such an eschatology, even as a reasoned diseschatologisation. As far as the moments of messianic-millenarian effervescence are concerned, Durkheim formulated the diagnosis that we have already quoted:[34]

> *The ideal tends to become one with the real: that is why men believe that the time is near when it will become reality itself and when the kingdom of God will be realised on this earth.* But the illusion is never lasting *because this exaltation can never last*: it is too exhausting . . . . *So all that was done . . . during the period of fertile upheaval only survives in the form of memory . . .* in the form of ideals . . . . *Certainly these ideals would quickly be vitiated if they were not periodically revived . . . . That is the purpose of festivals, ceremonies . . .* of Church, or of School . . . . *They are like partial and weakened revivals of the effervescence of creative eras . . . .*

In other equivalent terms Loisy said: 'The Kingdom was expected and it was the Church that came', adding moreover and rightly so . . . '*and which could not come . . .*' lest this messianism did not survive. But if that is the case, it is at the same time the inauguration of the tension between a religion without messianism and a messianism without religion: with, E. Troeltsch added, the possibility of a periodical re-eschatologisation of Christianity in the 'sectarian' or dissident millenarianisms or messianisms (*Sektentypus*), contesting religions of ecclesiastical type (*Kirchentypus*).

## 2 A against C Messianisms versus revolution

One could pinpoint an example of this tension in the conflict between Marx and W. Weitling, that person whom Marx and Engels agreed, in their later correspondence, that he thought himself to be a Jesus Christ *redivivus*. According to Engels,

131

Weitling was nothing less than the founder of German communism, and was even, through the *League of the Just* and his relations with E. Cabet, one of the main pioneers of European communism. In fact Weitling, although he did not take himself to be the Messiah, was nevertheless a chiliast messianist. He quoted previous chiliasms and his revolutionism was amalgamated with their tradition: an amalgamation of 'communism and communion'. He denounced Marx's circular against Kriege, a follower of Weitling.[35] The showdown was stormy: 'Until now ignorance was never of any use to anyone,' Marx finally replied as Weitling slammed the door.

It is a case which has its own nuance. Others have a different nuance: that of the Judeo-Christian messianists who were allergic to the uprising of Bar Kochba, or that of all the pacifist and conscientious objector millenarians who rebelled against any violence whatsoever, even revolutionary.

### 3 A against D Messianisms versus ideologies (revolutionary)

There are many cases of social effervescence with a messianic thread which are out of step with anti-religious post-revolutionary ideologies. They are all part of the general framework according to which, in the west, modern revolutions have been anti-religious, and in the third world countries the native religions, whether they were endowed with millenarian reactivations or not, are pre-revolutionary, in that through them the occupied people save their cultural identity and resist the religion or the missiology of the occupying people. In the same way, H. Lefebvre said: 'Historically one may wonder whether materialism constituted the philosophy of the oppressed, revolting or revolutionary classes; more careful study seems to show that mysticism or heresies stimulated and directed the masses much more and much better than materialism . . . .' This is echoed today in the declaration of a Libyan colonel: 'With their religion and historical heritage, the Arabs can do without Marxism-Leninism and other imported ideologies' (*Le Monde* 14 April 1970).

## 4  B against C  Religions versus revolutions

To be more precise: religions (instituted) against revolutions (emerging). This was the classic case in the nineteenth century: the one which, by repercussion, nourished revolutionary 'atheism' and its plan for a society without churches or gods.

## 5  B against D  Religions versus ideologies

One should also be more precise in this case: already ideologised religions (in theological form) and still revolutionary ideologies (in the form of political philosophies). There are dialogues of conflict or conciliatory polemics between the clerics who self-interpret the messianic origins of their religions, and the intelligentsias of apparatuses who self-interpret the revolutionary residues of their ideology.

## 6  C against D  Revolution versus ideologies

This is the answer to A against B (cf. *supra* 1). Either the ideologists give a theme to the diseschatologisation of the revolution, or the 'revolutionaries' attempt to re-eschatologise the ideology. Here the weight of A* is found wanting in the analysis: that of the established revolutionary movement or 'regime', in relation to which are differentiated the conformist ideologies of justification and the contesting ideologies of reinterpretation, each accusing the other of 'betraying' the Revolution.

## 7  A + B against C + D  Religious messianism versus revolutionary ideology

There is either the relationship of declared opposition: from one conception of the world to another conception of the world, from one strategy to another strategy; or there is an ambiguous relationship made of reciprocal reinterpretation and specious recovery: A + B is infected by ideological revolutionarism or C + D is infected by socio-cultural messianism.

## 8  A + C against B + D  Coalition of messianisms + revolutions versus the joint resistances of religions and ideologies

This is a fundamental category. Messianic-millenarian networks join revolutionary networks in the common plan to question simultaneously instituted religions and ideological acculturations. The acknowledged or latent unity of B + D could answer this coalition of A + C in order to contain, subdue or tame this hold. So a messianism without an instituted religion (yet) is associated with a revolution without an established ideology (yet) and comes up against the connivance, if not the alliance, of a sobered or sobering religious institution and an ideology for which the revolution would only have become viable through its verbal, conceptual or commemorative celebration.

## 9  A + D versus B + C

It is not unusual in matrices of this kind for certain areas to remain blank, or else for their contents to come from a paradox, a utopia. This may be the case here.

## 10  B (isolated) versus A + B + D

That is to say: a religious institution surrounded by a coalition of a messianic leap, a revolutionary explosion, and an ideology tacking the one on to the other. The contemporary situation of what a document already quoted called 'Churches in crisis' could be representative of a combination of this kind.

## 11  C (isolated) versus A + B + D

The opposite situation to the preceding one. C (revolution) is confined to pure revolt. It has against it not only the force of a messianism joined to a religion, but the reinforcement of this force by an ideology for which henceforth the 'construction' of the revolutionary '-ism', or even the presentation alone of what is constructed, comes before any dismantling or questioning.

## 12  D (isolated) versus A + B + C

D (the ideology of the A* regime) does not necessarily lose. It is a question of the relationship of forces. D has its arms and generally even its heavy arms. A + B + C have their harassment, which because of, or in spite of its lightness, is finally not without the power to disarm.

## 13  A (isolated) versus B + C + D

A (messianisms) also does not necessarily lose. It is also a question of the relationship of forces. But here the force comes from the socio-cultural level. In the extreme case, it is the force of the imaginary. The conquering penetration of the great founders, of Buddha, Zoroaster, Mani, Christ, Mohammed, have thus illustrated something like the 'miracle of the rope' in order to get out of such an encirclement and overcome it.

It is easy to continue this exercise, and in so doing, to become aware of its triple complexity.

Indeed, on the one hand, the *versus* implies a reciprocal relationship, in other words a relationship in which each of the terms is in turn liable to be the subject of action or the object of reaction.

Then, whether it has the initiative or not, it can be the winner or the loser of this conflict.

Finally, whatever the issue may be, this issue, in the mind of the observer who notes it, is surreptitiously given a value or deprived of value, ratified or contested, glorified as being fortunate or rejected as being unfortunate.

The pattern is not a grammar. It does not replace language, and even less messages. But perhaps it informs each of the languages or possible messages that it is only one possibility among many others and that even if it tends to turn towards hypostasis or apotheosis, it is nevertheless inscribed in this morphology and syntax: be it reluctantly and in spite of its dissatisfaction. Messianism, religion, revolution, ideology see themselves or are seen as sovereign bodies. And after all, as M. Mauss remarked: 'It may be that sociology does not satisfy sovereign bodies'.[36]

## IV Breaks: or the relationship seen in a sceptical and stoical way

'Magnificence, magnificence, do not celebrate without us.' This was the entreaty of a great Catholic writer of the nineteenth century affected by the fascination of a messianism. Revolutionary fascination is no less intoxicating. Do they not both award membership to the universal history of a salvation of the world or the salvation of a world? Do they not both proudly stride over the thin greyness of reasoning reason's ant-like paths, covered in small steps, counted and dis-counted? In the manner of the mysticism that enables the individual to leap above himself, do their myths not offer to collectivities that ecstatic leap towards achievements by annihilations in which the ultimate plan to 'come by some path towards a state of mind outside of which nothing exists' is reached?

Marcel Mauss, who is solidly immunised against such contagions, for once allows his agitation to show. In his magnificent obituary notice on his old master in Indianism, Sylvain Levy, he in fact remarks: 'He (S.L.) believed that there were other methods of knowledge than the rational discursive paths or even the experimental inductive ones. We often discussed these matters. It was *a deep difference between us*. But, I admit, his enchantment, his charm, his joy, his power of action came from those thoughts . . . *he felt he was a kind of visionary . . . which he was.*'[37] Doubtless this charm was also made of 'that gentle scepticism of he who has been able to stifle within himself all the vulgar thirst for life'[38]: he was made of stoical solitude and of the liberality of men who are sources. Mauss knew this better than anyone. He is no less separated from Sylvain Levy. To Levy's 'yes' to 'other methods of knowledge' is opposed his impenitent 'no': 'It was a difference between us'.

For all that religious messianisms and/or revolutionary ideologies represent other methods of knowledge than the 'rational discursive paths or even the experimental inductive ones', there is indeed in front of this ambition or this claim, a behaviour that is no less human, a type of man and perhaps a dimension of humanity to raise something like an objection of conscience, to testify to a deep difference, and to raise a *sic et non*.

In this 'no', which signifies at least a discontinuity if not a break, Mauss shows himself to be a rather faithful follower of his other master, Durkheim. Durkheim, although he is so attentive to social effervescences – of the primitive cults of possession, of revolutionary exaltations, of those which were contemporaries of socio-Christian revivals or socialisms – is never resigned to admitting them other than in the infra- or meta-, or in any case the extrascientific category of 'collective ideations', reserving all care and attention for the rational investigation of what would be a social science.

In his lecture on Saint-Simonism he takes up a position and asserts:[39]

What do the socio-religious movement and the socialist movement witness to? That if science is a means it is not an end, and as the end to be reached is far, that science can only reach it slowly and laboriously, the passionate and impatient minds endeavour to seize it immediately . . . . One undertakes to find the remedy instinctively, and nothing could be more natural, if one did not make a unique process of this method and if one did not exaggerate its importance to the point of denying science.

And later in *Forms*: 'Science is fragmentary and incomplete, it advances slowly and is never concluded: life, however, cannot wait. Theories that are destined to make one live, to make one act, are therefore obliged to anticipate science and complete it prematurely . . . .'[40]

There is no doubt that in this category of 'practical' and 'premature theories', Durkheim would have placed *both religious messianisms and revolutionary ideologies*, in order to situate himself – life and reasons for living – *outside* of them both, in the *strictness* of a methodical meditation on the whole of these phenomena of *fervour*: all with the hope, albeit hardly adventist, that the essential of a supplement of science would dispense humanity of this artificial supplement of soul.

In fact from this distant point of view, differentiations, amalgamations, antagonisms between the terms or the pairs of our title, fade, are reabsorbed, intermingle to show the fact that this global phenomenon – whatever its variables – is a fruit grown on the tree of life, rather than a flower blossoming on the tree of science. There is a whole part or dimension of humanity which nevertheless prefers such a flower to such a fruit. One fears in the heady fruit of these collective ideations that they hold within themselves neither the criteria nor the logic with which to reflect upon and master themselves. Open hearts in closed minds, in any case incapable henceforth of opening up to anything but themselves and their self-interpretation. They beguile, but their incantation is ambiguous because geniality is mixed with deliriums which are not all ones that Plato thought he should glorify. They Edenise, but their garden of delights has nothing with which to defend itself against its own intoxication. In piling on top of each other the thousand and one manifestations of religious messianisms, the thousand and one vicissitudes of revolutionary ideologies, one certainly builds a fascinating pyramid. It is no less formidable. Heady as the mingled music of organ, brass and woodwind; but when he heard it, Engels fled from the cathedral so as not to fall into the net of its volutes. He preferred to make a break.

Thus Marx preferred to break with Weitling so as not to countenance the confusion between communism and communion. For, he said: 'faith, and more precisely faith in the holy spirit of the community, is the last thing one demands for the realisation of communism'. In not resisting this confusion, not only does one dilute a science of social change into a visionary conviction dispensed by uncontrollable prophets, but this congenitally limited system cannot but fall into its own trap: intolerance.[41]

It is a logical consequence of this new religion, which, like any other, hates and persecutes to death all its enemies. The enemy of the party is transformed by a merciless logic into a heretic, this *enemy* of the party which really exists, in which one *struggles*, is transformed into a *sinner* against an imaginarily existing humanity, a sinner who must be punished.

Thus Proudhon, at about the same time – which is paradoxical – risked breaking with Marx for reasons analogous to those for which Marx broke with Weitling:

> *Let us search together, if you so wish, for the laws of society, the way in which these laws are realised, the progress according to which we succeed in discovering them; but, by God, after having demolished all the dogmatisms 'a priori', let us not dream in our turn of indoctrinating the people. Let us not carve out a new task for humanity with new confusions . . . . Let us give the world the example of wise and far-sighted tolerance, but just because we are at the head of the movement,* let us not make ourselves the leaders of a new religion, albeit the religion of logic, the religion of reason. *Let us welcome, encourage all protests, let us make all that is exclusive,* all the mysticisms *fade away; let us never consider a question to be exhausted, and when we have used our last argument, let us begin again if we must with eloquence and irony . . . .* So much for messianism.

As for revolution:[42]

> You may still be of the opinion that no reform is possible at present without a helping hand, without what was once called a revolution, but which is nothing more than a shake-up. My recent studies have made me completely change this opinion, which I can understand, excuse and willingly discuss, having held it myself for a long time. I believe that we do not need that in order to succeed . . . revolutionary action, as a means of social reform . . . would be quite simply a call to force, to the arbitrary, in short a contradiction . . . I prefer to burn ownership with a small flame rather than give it a new force by having a St Bartholomew's Day Massacre with the owners . . . . Our proletarians have such a great thirst for science that one would receive a very bad welcome from them if one could only offer them blood to drink . . . . In my opinion it would be bad policy on our behalf to talk as exterminators.

In his later works, Proudhon stigmatised any amalgamation in denouncing what he called a *messianosis*, that social illness which mixed 'theology with political economy, or, as

139

the proverb says, the Good Lord with plums'. The anti-theism of Proudhon is thus an obstinacy in exterritorialising his procedure in relation to any procedure that implies sliding into the trap of the pseudo-absolutes, be they messianosed or ideologised.[43] In Saint-Simonian terms: an obstinacy in not placing oneself 'either in the class of believers or in the class of makers of belief'.

One finds this same behaviour – to present yet another case – in another witness, Roger Martin du Gard, in his corres-pondence with André Gide, particularly at the time when the latter was intoxicated by his evangelical flirtation with revolu-tionary ideology, which was then Stalinist:

> *Yes frankly I am embarrassed to see you embrace all that with the touching fervour of a pious little child. In reading this letter, the word 'conversion', which has always seemed to me to be invidious and imprecise, takes on a new meaning. Your tone is that of a neophyte, the tone of a man who has 'submitted'* . . . . *The element of grandeur in abnegation, in voluntary humility – which I know well – does not stop me from thinking that other virtues would suit you better, at your age, with your past history of free and rebellious critical thought, and your influence. I see there the sign of an* intoxication *rather than a development that is really natural to you* (6 July 1935). *It is difficult to keep within the bounds of the appreciation of facts, to take care that the generosity of the heart does not dominate. I always come to the same conclusions:* I am the opposite of a believer. And in this new world, which was born from the war, I come up against faith everywhere. I see only fanatics who defend opposing religions. I cannot but dismiss them all. Thought only begins with doubt. *All education that systematically removes doubt . . . not only fails to give the intelligence healthy nourishment, but also falsifies it from the start; to the extent that any later amendment becomes very difficult, not to say impossible* (18 September 1935).

From this point of view, religious messianisms and revolu-tionary ideologies are therefore 'dismissed'.

This example may be enough to guarantee the hypothesis of a behaviour or of a personality on a basis which is innately allergic to what there is in common in religious messianisms and revolutionary ideologies, henceforth held to be the forms, which are sacred in one case and secular in the other, of a similar type of alienation: the element of *tremendum* in their irrationality is henceforth seen as interwoven with what would have been the element of *fascinosum* in their pretended super-rationality. The two pairs have in common the plan of a society which is at last perfect. They have in common the fact that they enclose themselves in this plan. They have in common their social and historical classification of black and white aspects: the society that one must go beyond must be a black society; the society that goes beyond it can only be a white one; these variations of colour are to be found in the vaticinations of the prophets, the pamphlets of *True Christianity*, the prognostics of medieval messiahs, the announcements of the social millenarianisms of the third world, the phraseologies of the European revolutions . . . . 'And too bad for the facts', as Hegel once would have replied. Let the black be black even if the facts are white; and above all let the white be white even if the facts are black.[44]

Finally the two pairs have in common a paroxysmal voluntarism paradoxically carried by the undertow of a latent determinism. Little does it matter that this determinism is of a providential kind in its religious conception and of a fatalist kind in its ideological conception: one should reread Gramsci,[45] who has already been quoted on these transfers of one kind to the other.

The Kingdom of God and the perfect society are thus nourished, openly or surreptitiously, by the ambiguous logics of an argument of St Anselm: their essence leads to their existence and if that does not come about, the enchantment of their essence mitigates the tribulation of their inexistence . . . Unless the spell is broken and disenchantment intervenes. Milovan Djilas relates such a – rather pathetic – disenchantment in his latest work,[46] in which he explicitly includes among lost beliefs *both* revolutionary ideology *and* religious messianism: 'I was never, nor am I today one of those communists who return to the religion of their ancestors, after being disappointed by the reality of communism, or who, although it is more difficult, invent their own religion.' Here too, religious messianisms and revolutionary ideologies are dismissed, having once been accepted. 'I think that today we are the witnesses of the twilight of all the humanisms that are founded on doctrinaire and theoretical hypotheses about the human being.'

This does not prevent Djilas from finding *his* faith, a sceptical and stoical faith which breaks with any historico-worldwide ideology or speculation, and criticises any messiano-religious or politico-revolutionary utopia. In exchange for his lost faith, is his 'faith' found 'during the night of 7 to 8 December 1953': an antitheist faith, in the Proudhonian sense of the word, that is to say immune to any overtures of an historic commitment towards ideas, ideals, people, and movements which have pretensions towards the perfections of the absolute. For these pretensions are trapped in the very trap of utopia.

> *I am convinced that society cannot be perfect. Men must keep to their ideas and ideals but they must not think that either one or the other are realisable. We must understand the nature of utopia. Once the utopian comes to power he becomes dogmatic and he can easily cause human suffering in the name of his idealism. To talk of an imperfect society is perhaps to imply that it can be perfect, which in truth is impossible. The duty of man in our time is to accept as a reality the imperfection of society, but also to understand that humanism and humanitarian dreams and imaginations are necessary in order to keep reforming society, to improve it and to make it progress* (pp. 16–17).

The path is open only to a perfectible society. The horizon of the perfect society is but a mirage of unreasoning reason. And there are men whose reason for reasoning as well as their reason for living, are precisely those of devoting themselves to or providing courses in detoxification, witness the act of breaking with mirages. Let us add a quotation from Althusser, *and this addition makes one question everything again*, including the mirage of a society without religions or ideologies:[47]

Only an ideological conception of the world could have imagined societies *without ideologies* and have admitted straight away the utopian idea of a world in which the ideology (and not just its historical forms) would disappear without a trace, to be replaced by *science*; this utopia for example, follows the principle of the idea that morals, which in their essence are an ideology, could be replaced by science or become thoroughly scientific; *or the religion which is dispersed by science, which would in a way take its place* . . .

## Are we going round in circles?

It was easy for Montaigne to conclude: 'We are going round in circles . . . .' Trapped in the visionary poetry of perfect societies, for this poetry verges on the excesses of hot societies. But also no less trapped in the prose of ready made societies, for this prose is bait for the paralysis of cold societies. Happiness itself is not a criterion of discrimination: one may be happy through enthusiasm in the exaltation of anomy; one can be just as happy in the equilibrium of impassibility.

More generally still, there may be here a contradictory dialectic: of fervour against rigour, of a warm heart and cold blood, of a universality in which to lose onself and of an intimacy in which to find onself, where a thousand years are like a day, a day like a thousand years. Of '-urgies' against '-logies'.

Doubtless Durkheim was quite right: 'Nothing is any good without moderation.' Doubtless the 'messianico-religio-ideologico-revolutionary' whole is but a part of the human phenomenon, even if it constitutes a prophetic dimension of collective consciousness; in order to fall on their feet, the latter seek to brace themselves against an antagonistic or complementary part of the whole, which is *neither* messianic, nor religious, *nor* ideological, *nor* revolutionary, a part in which occur technical changes or mental changes whose radicalism, although it may be less noisy, is however, no less operative in the long run: 'These peaceful revolutions, whose imperceptible march is led by the slow hand of time', sighed Condorcet. Reciprocal counterbalancing: it is an alternative.

Finally a last alternative: that of reciprocal annihilation.

Divided and as though stretched between these parts of the whole, is man in his individuality or in his collectivities not invited to lean sometimes on one in order to *deny* the other, sometimes on the other in order to deny the one, thus also denying his *reason* by his *inspiration* and reciprocally, his *logical* side (his logos) by his mythical and *pneumatic* side (his pneuma), his *topism* by his *utopism*, his *calculated* verifications by his *visionary* revelations, his dimensions of homo *sapiens* by his dimensions of homo *ludens*, etc.? For if a classical axiom demands that man becomes what he is, another axiom – and Djilas finds it in Camus – offers its alternative: 'Man is the only being who can refuse what he is . . . .'

Paraphrasing Claudel, one should add: 'Man makes man as the sea makes the continents. *In receding*'. Perhaps this is just another mirage . . . . But it does re-open the axiological question underlying this entire investigation. Everything depends on the order each person gives to the answers and the 'buts' that give them their tonality:

'Only the mirages set the caravan in motion; *but* no route has ever led any caravan to reach its mirage . . .', says one, preferring the catch to the hunt.

'No route has ever led any caravan to reach its mirage; *but* only the mirages have set the caravan in motion . . .', says the other preferring the hunt to the catch . . . .[48]

They are both saying the same thing. And yet, as Mauss remarked, there is 'a profound difference'. Even if both of them, the one preferring the *hunt*, the other the *catch*, are two people in search of the same author.

# Chapter 5

# Religious phenomena and collective imagination

> There is therefore an area in nature where the formula of *idealism* is applied almost to the letter: it is the social reign. Here more than anywhere, the idea makes the reality.
>
> E. Durkheim *Elementary Forms*

I have often had the occasion in the past to compare a memorable text of G. Le Bras with a less commemorated text of Marx.

Here is G. Le Bras's text:[1]

> The conditions of life are partly given by nature, but they depend more widely on the society that conquers its habitat, shapes men, establishes relationships, creates its economy, and to a certain extent its gods.

And here is Marx's text:[2]

> The difficult thing is not to understand (*verstehen*) that Greek art and the epic are linked to certain forms of social development (but to understand) that they can still give us aesthetic enjoyment and be considered in some respects (in gewisser Beziehung) as the inaccessible norm and model (als Norm und unerreichbare Muster).

These two sociologists of religion are situated on each side of a demarcation line separating two options: the option of the sociologist who is a believer, claiming a transcendence according to which the gods make man; and the option of the atheist sociologist, according to which men make their gods. The points of comparison are brought to our attention by a double fact. On the one hand it is the sociologist who believes (G. Le Bras) who recognises a certain immanence of a temporal genesis, whereas it is the atheist socialist (Marx) who finds himself acclaiming a certain transcendence of an intemporal attraction. On the other hand, they both seem to be holding themselves back only by nuances: 'to a certain extent' (G. Le Bras), 'in some respects' (Marx). Therefore, *to a certain extent* man creates his gods, but *in some respects* these creations, once they have been made comprehensible by 'certain forms of social development (or under-development)', remain norms and models that transcend their own genesis.

My brief remarks on this provisional sketch of the collective imagination are presented in the no man's land that borders each side of this demarcation line. G. Le Bras invites us there. Having had the occasion to interview him about the quoted text, his reply does in fact direct us to the double phenomenon of the image: the image of the god in the believer of a religion, and the image of the god in the founder of this religion.[3]

The thesis or hypothesis are as follows. A sociological tradition has diagnosed the collective imagination as a system of correlative *representations* of . . . even reducible to a series of *situations*; in this diagnosis the collective imagination is constituted more or less in the last analysis by the constraints of reality. Could there not be another sociological tradition – linked however to the preceding one – in whose terms the phenomena of the collective imagination would assert themselves as phenomena of a *constituent* imagination, in the name of, if not a last analysis, at least a leading role[4] played by it in the constraints which give social *facts* their *meaning*, conferring on reality a surreality without which this reality would not be itself?

This question is formulated from that continuing inquiry into the religious components implied in the phenomena of collective imagination: utopising millenarianisms and millenarianising utopias, the ones intermeshed with the others.[5]

It rests, moreover, on the Durkheimian postulate according to which 'religion is not only a system of *ideas*, it is above all a system of *forces*'.[6]

Henceforth the question is as follows. How does a collective imagination – hanging, it seems, on ideas 'up in the air', judged by reasoning reason as factitious, fantastic, erroneous, empty ideas, indeed even as mumbo-jumbo or as pernicious ideas – how does this imagination exert a *force* of attraction, mobilisation, dynamisation, activation or reactivation, a force such that populations hang on to it themselves, and which holds them, maintains them and supports them? Briefly, how does imagination take power?

It seems, moreover, that that would be an ideal area in which to start examining this logic, according to which men make gods who make men who make gods who make men, etc.

Finally this examination leaves open the metaphysical option which, depending on the case, puts the accent on the intangibility of a *creator creans* or on the omnivalence of a *creatura creatrix*. The theism of the believer and the atheism of the non-believer benefit here from the exterritoriality. Neither one nor the other qualifies or disqualifies for such an analysis. Neither one nor the other is qualified or disqualified by this analysis.

We shall examine in succession:
I   The religious springboards of the collective imagination.
II  The religious outbursts of the collective imagination.

## I The religious springboards of the collective imagination

Hundreds, possibly thousands, of phenomena are available to the observer or annalist who wishes to see the collective imagination in religious confinement through what French nineteenth-century sociology called the *critical* periods, as opposed to the *organic* periods of History. In this field, a quick glance reveals two traits.

The first – upheld implicitly by G. Le Bras – is that, at least as far as *founded* religions are concerned, the image of the god in the believer goes back to the image of the god in the founder or in the foundation. That is a trait, which, it seems, achieves a great unanimity in sociological tradition, since, under diverse patronage, this tradition distinguishes classically two levels in the religious phenomenon: one corresponding to its emergence in the form of an *effervescent* event, the other corresponding to its transmission under the form of an established *institution*: 'first hand' religion and 'second hand' religion, according to William James; 'living religion' and 'preserved religion' acording to Bastide; 'open religion' and 'closed religion' according to Bergson; 'elementary forms' of a 'hot' society and consecutive forms in a 'cold' society according to Durkheim; 'experience' and 'expressions' according to Joachim Wach . . . etc. Everything occurs as though the religious trajectory came from *two* systems of forces: a force of *explosion*, which places the device in orbit; a force of *attraction* which, depending on the secondary accelerations or decelerations, explains the gravitation in orbit . . . . In any case, the second stage goes back to the first, in other words to the explosive stage of the collective consciousness: at that stage the founder founded. The collective imagination is mediated by the intense stage of this collective *consciousness*.

The second trait has also been picked out by many analysts, in particular by Mircea Eliade in his examination of the cargo cults and the fact that in these cults the New Era coincides with an archetypal return of the Ancestors. The future is guaranteed by the past. The Omega point aimed at by the imagination leans against an Alpha point reactivated by memory. This retrospective point of support can vary: it is the time before colonisation, the time of the pentecostal commune before Constantinisation, the time of village consciousness before the grip of feudalities, the time of nomadic life before sedentary agriculture, or even the time of a pacific sedentariness before the ravaging invasion of a nomadism, the time of the earth without evil, the time of free life before slavery, the time of good savages before the time of the mediocrities and evils of a civilisation, the time of Eden before sin and the fall, the time of 'old *gentes*' before the division of society into classes, the time of the lost tribes of Israel, the time of faded innocence and childhood . . . etc. Almost everywhere, the future shows itself to be a 'reviviscence on a superior scale' of all of these lost paradises. The enlargement of the imagination supposes an enlargement of the memory. The collective imagination is back to back with the long time of this collective *memory*.

Collective consciousness and collective memory are thus respectively the hearth and the guarantee of the collective imagination.

## 1 The collective consciousness and the mobilisation of the living

Even if Durkheim allowed a certain ambiguity to hover over what he calls 'elementary forms' of religious life,[7] the self-commentary of his major work broadens out to the whole gamut of religious phenomena the induction based on the Australian cults of possession. One remembers this induction: 'It is therefore in these ebullient social milieus and from this very *effervescence* that the religious idea seems to have been born . . . .' 'By gathering itself almost wholly in these given moments of time, collective life could indeed reach its maximum intensity and efficacy, and therefore give man a keener feeling of the double existence he leads and the double nature he is part of.' *Elementary Forms*. And we know that the self-commentary has broadened this induction to include all religious and even para-religious phenomena: 'Indeed it has been during the moments of effervescence of this kind that the great ideals upon which civilisations rest, have, at all times, been constituted.'[8]

To propose that the collective *existence* determines the collective *consciousness*, or, in other words, that *situations* give rise to *representations*, would be no more than a sociological commonplace threatened moreover with being univocal or equivocal. In the end, do we not see this commonplace govern the laborious and problematic correlations between representations reduced to rates of religious practice and situations reduced to a stratification by socio-economic status? Durkheimian inductions have the merit – apparently unrecognised – of refocusing sociological attention on three points:

(1) Referring this empirical sociology to an historical sociology that relates to the social modalities, according to which, this *conjuncture*, mediated by a *tradition* (familial, regional or national, cultural or other), enters into communication with its 'elementary form', in other words the intense time of foundation, which was the time of the event.

(2) Treating collective existence in *operational* terms, in other words distinguishing it and relating it to the times and places where existence simultaneously collectivises itself and the collectivity existentialises itself. According to Durkheimian terminology, this operationalisation requires for the population concerned an optimum of *volume* combined with an optimum of *density* in order to set off the phenomenon of 'coalescence'. Only in these conditions does the 'dynamogenic influence that religion exerts on consciousnesses' (*La Science sociale et l'action*, p. 309) function, that influence which has to do with this thermodynamic of social *movements*,[9] gaining precisely in volume and in density and producing the heat, alias 'the effervescence', which is characteristic of religious geneses.[10]

(3) Evaluating the collective consciousness in terms of *matrix*. If this consciousness – and the gods that it creates – finds itself to be the *daughter* of a collective existence that is brought to 'ebullition', this same consciousness is no less the mother of such a collectivity where men cease to attend to their individual situation, leap above themselves, transcend themselves in an existence that borders on ecstasy, and reach a lyrical and dramatic representation that is denser than their attention to empirical everyday life. From this point of view:

> So, in a way, the gods owe their existence to man: yet, in another way, man owes his existence to the gods, for once they have reached maturity, it is from the gods that he will borrow the necesssary strength to maintain and repair his spiritual being. Therefore it is he who makes his gods, one could say, or at least it is he who makes them last; *but at the same time it is because of them that he lasts.*

Religion is the form taken by the collective consciousness in an act of mobilisation of living men. The Latin-American works on adult education have created the term 'conscientisation' as a label for the intervention of a pedagogy as the 'practice of freedom' (Paulo Freire), in the animation of a collectivity. In referring to this neologism one could say of religion – at least of the level where it is 'first-hand' religion – certainly it is a social phenomenon but this phenomenon is that of a society in the business of 'super-conscientisation', therefore of a super-society.

This mobilisation is meta-rational as it is meta-moral, as Durkheim tirelessly observes in the cases he presents. Today the list of such cases is unending. Two recent conferences[11] have attempted to draw up typologies, structures or even the geography of what are called 'cults of possession', during which *people* are 'mounted' by the spirits, until they are alienated and find themselves in the skin of the personalities that these spirits make them act out.[12]

*Processes of delirium.* Why not? Plato had already listed four forms of delirium in Phaedra and had attempted to give them some authority.[13] Erasmus was not only thinking of a 'ludibrium' when he wrote *In praise of madness*. And Durkheim himself keeps coming back to it: 'Under the effect of the collective force they are sometimes overtaken by a real delirium which incites them to acts in which they do not recognise themselves' (*La Science sociale et l'action*, p. 308).[14] These 'deliriums' have their own specific logic, that of hot societies, which is different from that of reasoning reasons which function in cold societies or in societies that have grown cold. They belong to ludic rites, to the sacred theatre, to dramatic representation, to surrealist lyricism, to mobilising enthusiasm.

For they do mobilise. Contracted by traditional societies, they even coincide most of the time either with their resistance against the dominating societies of universal history, or with their own entry – their great rite of passage – into this history. But they do not only occur in traditional societies. For if these cults of possession can in a way pass for the millenarianisms of societies that are still without history, prey to the archetypes of eternal return as they are, over against that, are not millenarianisms something like cults of possession of societies that have already entered history and aspire epidemically to get out of it? The models of collective behaviour reveal singular regularities. Historical societies find or find again examples at the cradles of most of the great nations of the west or the east. As for religious societies, for how many of them has this *baptism in the Spirit* and possession by the Spirit not been or is not the motor of their activation or reactivations?

Prophets arise, adorcisms are celebrated, improbable messages are given, rites are carried out in which the spirits and the bodies seize hold of each other and exalt each other, unknown languages are uttered, trances become contagious, marches, processions and parades get under way, dances impose their fascinating improvisations, therapies are hoped for or obtained, fabulous histories tack a re-imagined past into an imaginary future, music and songs deafen assemblies, a sublime and disjointing festival leads to the enjoyment of sacrifices, the sabbath imposes itself, the world becomes other, an old world goes away, a new world envelops one with the magic of its presence.

Images, images! At the best, acted images! Certainly, but these images are not just of the imaginary.[15] This ludism is not just an alibi. For this imagery, this play of the collective consciousness, imply the experience of a collective super-existence, an experience such that whatever precedes it or follows it, henceforth appears only as its prelude or its aftermath. A people, a nation, a religion, a denomination, a sect, an order, a social movement can be constructed like a temple with its columns, its arches, its buttresses; the experience thus lived and eventually relived, remains the keystone. Later festive practices are nothing more, according to Durkheim than 'partial and weakened re-occurrences of the ebullience of the creative eras', the ones which were the mobilising factor of the generation, henceforth the mother of the genealogy. For this exuberant collective consciousness will certainly have been a *constituted* consciousness, but also, if not more so, a *constituting* consciousness.

## 2 Collective memory and the resurrection of the dead

If the collective imagination thus has as a focus and point of reference a theurgical or 'sociurgical' experience endured and enjoyed by a collective consciousness, the link between this *consciousness* and this *imagination* is not however established in a direct circuit. It rebounds off a relay: this relay is memory, a memory which is not limited to recording or even to simply recalling or commemorating. It is a collective memory and it also tends to be a *constituting* memory as much as and more than a *constituted* memory.

A French sociologist, Maurice Halbwachs, applied himself
to finding the ins and outs of it. It is indeed a sign of the times
that the attention of sociologists is focused today on exhuming
from the dungeons the work of this forgotten sociologist.[16]
Without doubt he made the distinction between a *universal
memory of the human kind*', the one through which the
aseptic pictures of events are transmitted, and the *collective
memory*, or rather memories, through which *forces* are com-
municated.[17] Writings are filed or refiled in the first category.
A tradition is lived or relived in the second category. Indeed it
goes without saying that 'universal memory, the typical ideal
of history and historians, is secured by a certain collective
memory', if, as Sartre emphasised, the historian being
himself more or less historialised, 'the past is continually
being adjourned'.[18] Reciprocally, it goes without saying that
a collective memory tends to present itself as a universal
memory which is transcendent and preferable to *other* collective memories: what national history does not suppose it is the
history of a universally predestinated nation? *Gesta Dei per
Francos, Gott mit uns*, 'God save the Queen', etc. 'Redeemer
Nation',[19] 'crucified Poland',[20] 'Russian idea',[21] etc. Let us
add: what history of a church does not claim to be *the* History
of *the* Church, the axis of a universal history of religious
phenomena redistributed henceforth in its anticipations (Old
Testament, Chain of Witnesses), its fringes (sects, dissidences,
'separated brothers') or its exterior dark areas of infidelity or
misbeliefs?

Approaching the implications of *a* collective memory in *the*
universal memory supposedly identified with historical
science, does not come within the bounds of this essay. It has
to do with a historical sociology on which our colleague Jean
Séguy is presently working.[22] On the other hand, some
observations on the implications of *the* universal and univer-
salising memory in *a* collective memory may be made . . . .

M. Halbwachs has already evoked the paradoxical *constituting* power of this symbiosis in analysing the legendary
topography of the Gospels in the Holy Land![23]

Collective memory is essentially a reconstruction of the
past . . . it adapts the image of ancient facts to the beliefs

and spiritual needs of the present . . . (*Topographie*, p. 9).
Therefore the sacred places do not commemorate facts
certified by contemporary witnesses, but beliefs that may
have been born not far from these places, and that have
become stronger in taking root there (p. 175). . . . one
has started from dogmas more than from testimonies . . .
(ibid). It is not to the real places but to the beliefs that
the image must adapt itself. While the places were
vanishing the beliefs were growing stronger (p. 165) . . .
the memory of groups, as much as the memory of
individuals, sometimes transposes into reality what is
merely its element of imagination and dreaming, and
looks for and finds its place in some area of space
(p. 175) . . . Collective memory is distinct from history
(p. 188). The memory of groups . . . only retains the
events that are also teachings (p. 19). The collective
memory reconstructs its memories so that they are in
agreement with contemporary ideas and preoccupations
(p. 192). *Thus the history of holy places is transformed into a
sociology of sacred locations* . . . Thus the era of Constantine,
then the era of the Crusades, mark the two moments
when the Christian memory, the collective memory that
truly represents the whole of the Christian community
during those two eras, sought for the location of
evangelical facts, forced itself to localise its memories,
and, in a way, to situate itself in space, in Jerusalem and
in the Holy Land (p. 203).

It is the universal Christian community that retakes
possession of the holy places and wants them to reproduce the image that it has built up of them at a distance
throughout the centuries (p. 204). Whatever era one
thinks of, one's attention is directed . . . towards the
groups of the faithful. Towards their work of commemoration. *The image of these groups is imprinted in the
physiognomy presented by the holy places in successive eras*
(p. 205).

Therefore are there not only *real* high places honoured by
the collective memory, but also unreal high places *constructed*

or reconstructed in and by the collective memory, to the point that their reality in the memory makes up for their unreality on earth? One could decide on whether the answer provided has a peremptory character or not . . . . One should hesitate even less on the importance of the question that is asked, in that this is the case of other high places, St Besse, for example, analysed by Hertz.[24] An affirmative answer meets with less reticence: there are high places whose sacred consistence relies essentially and only on the fact that this sacred character has been set and settled on it by the collective memory. As Durkheim said: 'The ideal comes to rest where it wishes.'

Recent work by P. Delooz has shown an analogous effectiveness of a collective memory: first in the phenomenon of the canonisation of *real* saints, in other words saints whose existence is confirmed by history; then in the canonisation of *constructed* saints, in other words saints whose lives come either from a historialisation, or even, in the extreme case, from a subsequent historicisation.[25]

Most saints were real people. They existed. They experienced events that enable one to define their historically assured characteristic traits. But, next to them, there also exist saints that one could call 'constructed', in that the traits that characterise them come from a repertory of traditional images assembled according to a particular montage. In other terms, the reputation of saintliness is the collective mental representation of someone as a saint, either from a knowledge of facts which really occurred, or from *constructed* facts which are partly, if not completely, imaginary. But in fact more or less all the saints appear to be *constructed saints* in that, being necessarily saints because of a reputation made by others, and because of the role expected of them by others, they are remodelled at the level of collective mental representations. They can even be remodelled to such a degree that nothing or almost nothing remains of the *real* saint. At the very limit – and the limit has been reached more than once – there are saints *who are only constructed saints*, in that nothing historical is known about them, everything, including *their existence, is the fruit of collective mental representations*.

Indeed let us add in confirmation of our hypothesis on real *forces* coming from the imaginary unreality: the *constructed* saints have been no less thaumaturgical than the others. In some cases one could even add: *on the contrary*, even if an ecclesiastical collective memory sometimes has attacks of bad conscience which makes it cross them out of its calendar.

The present inquiry into messianisms also similarly sometimes brings us into contact with *constructed* messiahs, in other words not only messiahs becoming messiahs *reluctantly* under the pressure of their audiences or their descendants,[26] but, at the limit, messiahs whose very existence has been formed from people who are dreamed of, then made sacred by the collective memory before it glorifies some historical hero or other. The character of the 'Emperor of the last days' thus goes through the Middle Ages at the will of the dynastic groups that memorialised him. John Frum, that parousiacal character of Tanna in the New Hebrides in the 1940s,[27] was initially merely an 'apparition' or a 'white figure' on a 'black night' (op. cit., p. 154), but all the collective memory of a traditional god was unloaded on to this figure, the mobilising memory of the cultural resistance to the god, therefore to white power . . . . If there was no messiah in such cases, there was a 'messianosis', according to the term invented by Proudhon to cover this phenomenon of constructed messianism.

Supplementary and complementary effectiveness of the same collective memory: not only the call to construct a new sacrality, but also the refusal to destroy an old sacrality. Not only does the collective memory conceive virginally, so to say – in other words without marriage or with an unconsummated marriage with reality – high places, saints, messiahs and perhaps unreal *and* surreal gods, it also achieves another miracle: it assures the immortality and in some cases the resurrection of the engulfed pantheons. As Bastide suggests in his commentary on 'the principle of cleavage', it gives life and survival to the *superstructures* whose infrastructures are however dying or even dead. 'Everything occurs as though the driving memory were more coherent and longer lasting than the memorising memory.'[28] The gods of the 'Black Americas' are gods in exile. Not only have the African societies that they have given life to and that have given life to them, been deported or destructured, but the very myths of these societies have often left only minute and troubled traces in the movements of an enslaved and evangelised collectivity. Are the gods dead? Absolutely not: not only do they move in the driving memory of cults but also in the reconstitution of a whole social and cultural tissue, the rampart of a final identity against a supreme alienation. Thanks to their collective memories, Black Americas that apply the 'principle of cleavage' exist in a double range: the infrastructure of a cruel reality, the superstructure of a nostalgic commemoration. Their *deficient* memory is at the same time a restoring and even *constituting* memory.[29]

Memory – ideation of the past – like consciousness – ideation of the present – and even imagination – ideation of the future – are relays through which are passed and re-distributed messages that are addressed to each other by economic situations and cultural representations, both of them being used as receivers and as transmitters. As Halbwachs underlined:[30] 'we must understand that the material forms of society act on it, not because of a physical restraint, as a body would act on another body, but by the *consciousness that we have of it*.' Therefore an economic situation does not *determine* a memory, or perhaps it determines a memory to memorise a past which, once it is memorised, determines the situation, not necessarily to confirm it, but eventually to oppose it, either in a strategy of cleavage, like the one interpreted by R. Bastide, or even in a strategy of radical transformation, like the one analysed by Karl Marx.

Indeed it is in a Marxist analysis of the French Revolution of 1848[31] that the collective memory is celebrated as being charged with a special mission in the revolutionary strategy. A paradoxical mission because it is a 'resurrection of the dead'. A perspicacious remark was made: 'It is when men seem to be busy . . . creating something quite new, it is precisely at those moments of revolutionary crisis, that they invoke . . . the spirits of the past'. Hence the function of a collective memory resurrecting the dead: '*The resurrection of the dead* in these revolutions consequently served to magnify the new struggles, not to parody the old ones, *to exaggerate in the imagination the task to be accomplished, not to avoid their solution in taking refuge in reality* . . . .'[32]

Thus the memory of a former revolution (1789, 1793, 1795) feeds the imagination of a new revolution (1848). And especially: the imagination of the second one reactivates, 'resurrects' the presence of the first one in a reiterated representation. A Marxologist comments: 'modalities of social practice . . . cannot be realised without the specific organisa-tion of a game of fantasies which is both immanent to this practice and *dialectically constitutive*'. And further on he adds: 'In this way, the opposition between the infrastructure and the superstructure ceases to be illuminating because the ideology of the class is not an effect of a practice: it takes roots in this practice and participates in it as a *constitutive form*'.[33] R. Bastide's induction on the 'principle of cleavage' echoes here Ansart's induction on what he himself calls 'points of dis-jointedness'.[34]

Saint-Simon had already discovered this mutual guarantee of collective memory and imagination. The imagination needs a lot of memory as soon as it is a question of 'glimpsing the possibility of carrying out the great moral, poetic and scientific operation which must move the terrestrial paradise and trans-port it from the past to the future'. And memory needs a lot of imagination, because 'in this great undertaking . . . men with imagination will make a start . . . . Let them transport the terrestrial paradise into the future . . . and this system will promptly be constituted'.[35]

Before undertaking the exploration of this constitutive imag-ination and its religious forms, it was necessary to sketch the important roles, which are also constitutive, of both the collec-tive consciousness and the collective memory, which most of the time are intermingled, as is intermingled the collective imagin-ation, already glittering there before bursting into more specific phenomena. All three, in their own way, together or separately, show themselves to be capable of fomenting the sacred, and therefore the gods, or in any case what Durkheim called their collective ideation: the *uprising* of the gods is fomented in the

collective *consciousness*; their *resurrection*, or at least their resistance to death, is fomented in memory; and, as we shall see,
something which borders on their *insurrection* is fomented in
imagination.

## II  The religious eruptions of the collective imagination

There are phenomena of which one could say either that they
are religious phenomena in which a society erupts, or that they
are social phenomena in which a religion erupts. In both cases
there is the *disruption* of an old system and *eruption* of a new.
Phenomena of this category have in common the fact that,
whether they are more or less sacralised or more or less
secularised, they all imply, to different degrees, first the
promotion of an 'eruptive' society in protest against a 'disrupted' society, then the treatment of both these societies as
global societies, both spiritual *and* temporal, religious *and*
political, as Church and State, Heaven and Earth.

The historical manifestation of these phenomena can be
found in a double population: that of utopising millenarianisms
and that of millenarianising utopias. In fact, if one considers
the process in the long term, it is doubtless a question of a
single population accentuated in two ways, the second
probably representing a simple secularisation of the first,
which obviously is not enough to immunise it against religious
complications. A secularised millenarianism is not de-
millenarianised, it has simply gone from its 'sacred form' to
its 'non sacred form', to use Marx's terms. In an old work that
we have already quoted[36] Tuveson brings out the connections
between the sacred forms of apocalypticism and the secular
forms of the philosophy of progress.[37]

One could doubtless go deeper into such connections in
distinguishing those that link the *post*-millenarianisms to the
*evolutionist* phenomenon and those that link the *pre*-millen-
arianisms to the *revolutionary* phenomenon . . . .[38] It will suffice
here to distinguish two groups: the one of utopising millenarianisms, the other of millenarianising utopias, indicating
two social periods which, although successive, may be
chronologically contemporaneous.

## 1 Utopising millenarianisms

Although attempts were made to extend its diffusion,[39] the group of utopising millenarianisms revolves round the three great Abrahamic religions: Judaism and Judeo-Christianity, Christianity, its confessions and sects, and Islam and its mahdisms.

Its *sociological* actuality seems to be increasing because it has fed for some decades on a *social* actuality: actuality based on the emergence of messianising or millenarianising phenomena in the syncretic insurrections of gods dominated until then by the gods of the dominating powers, either in the countries of the Third World, or in the dissidences or resistances offered almost everywhere to societies and/or churches which are seen as alienating. This double actuality has indeed rebounded on the oblivion in which analogous historical phenomena were shrouded, those of the Middle Ages in particular, and has exhumed them from the drawers of heresiology and forced them on the attention of anthropology.[40]

## 2 Millenarianising utopias

It is noticeable in this inventory that the first population, that of utopising millenarianisms (or messianisms) is geared to the second one, that of 'millenarianising utopias'. Some consider that they can and should distinguish between them or even oppose them, in maintaining that the first kind has to do with a group or a mass and the second one with an individuality; or that the first one has to do with a popular movement and the second one with 'bourgeois' escapism; or finally that the first one comes from a subversive *practice*, whereas the second one comes from an accommodating *writing*.

Obviously everything depends on the sample, and one can surely define such a sample so that it corresponds to the required criteria. But even when one has admitted – *dato non concesso* – that the utopian phenomenon is an affair of European consciousness from Thomas More to the present day, and, if one wishes to consider it in the long term, it is not clear how to justify such a discontinuity. Indeed the utopian field is not reducible to the fabrication of a few, albeit illustrious, satires, such as those of Thomas More, Campanella, Bacon.

It covers a vast cultural field in which it can be, and has been, both the affair of groups animated by it *and* of popular movements mobilised in it, *as well as* social practices modelled on it. For *practised* utopias generally correspond to *written* utopias, whether this practice precedes or reactivates the writing, or whether this writing nourishes a practice.[41]

From this point of view, utopian thought is no more a form of *pre-logical* thought than so-called primitive thought. As far as the latter is concerned, Maurice Leenhardt has shown not only that this so-called pre-logicality had its own logic, combining logic and myth, but that the so-called logical thought could well, in different, but after all no more paradoxical, proportions, present an analogous combination or crypto-combination.[42]

Utopia certainly comes from the *imaginary*, but from an imaginary subtly calculated as such for the emission and transmission of a message that conceals its own rationality, which latter has analogies with the effectiveness of millenarian imagination. In both cases, there is the same reference to a collective memory as guarantee of an imagination which seeks a collective audience; sometimes there is the same kind of popular movement.[43]

And very often, let us add, there is the same embodiment in a social practice: that of the practised utopia or that of a practice derived from the utopia. History makes utopias and utopias make history, as Morgan said.[44] For there is a practised Cabetism or Icarianism; a practised Fourierism,[45] a practised Saint-Simonism,[46] a practised Owenism,[47] a practised Weitlingism (that of the League of the Just),[48] and if one looks carefully, is there not a 'practice' of More (in Vasco de Quiroga and its villages of regroupings), of Campanella (if only in the Soviet Agroville which bore the name of the City of the Sun), of Bacon (in the Royal Society) and in the many Colleges,[49] of Winstanley in the adventure of the Diggers,[50] etc.?

## 3 Meeting points

The separation is even more unsafe in that there are meeting points. The millenarian message and the utopian message are thus joined. Saint-Simon announced 'a great messianic era, an era in which religious doctrine would be presented with all the generality to which it lends itself' . . . Fourier does not jib at the title of 'post-cursor prophet' or even of 'Messiah of reason' . . . Owen published *The Millennium in Practice* (1835) and a *Millennial Gazette* . . . . Weitling referred back to Thomas Münzer . . . Cabet identified his Icarianism with a re-millenarianised *True Christianity* . . . Engels found the guarantee of his still utopian communism in the micro-millenarianism of the North American 'communities'[51] . . . . Even the contemporary utopian communities of California have a millenarian slogan: 'Paradise now'[52] . . . .

Indeed, even with explicit references, is not utopia, like millenarianism, the promotion of an *eruptive* society in the protest against a *disrupted* society? Finally in the thousand utopias already known and catalogued,[53] does one not distinguish the imagination and creation of a god: Thomas More's god Mythra, Campanella's solar god, the Baconian god of the magi in the Temple of Solomon or the College of the Work of the six days, the god of the development and glory of the ecumenical in Saint-Simon, the Owenite god of the 'rational religionists' and of their fiery missions, the Fourierist god of the new world in love: 'god the mechanic, the acrobat, enemy of intemperance and deprivation, who knows how to establish the balance between all joys and guarantee them from excess by their very abundance' . . . Weitling's subversive and putschist god, the conventual and soldier-like god of Cabet . . . as many dreamed of gods, spare-part gods: in continuity *ex parte ante* with these spare dreams,[54] authoritarian or libertarian gods, thought of by millenarian dissidences as so many gods of the opposition facing gods of power; in continuity perhaps *ex parte post* with, if not the new gods, at least the new theologies or anti-theologies, the ones of hope, of terrestrial realities, of liberation, of development, of revolution, of the death or the absence of gods. For the imagination, or if one prefers the 'imaginaction',[55] of the gods has not ceased to live among us.

And among the theologies; and among the sociologies; and even among those sociologies which are considered to be latently allergic to the 'imaginary'.

## 4 Constitutive imagination

This vast contingent of joined millenarianisms and utopisms presents a sociological problem: that of a *sociology of hope*,[56] the problem of the problem being precisely that of *constitutive imagination*. So many gods with or without *their* societies, so many societies with or without *their* gods have simmered in its furnace! So many movements have hung on to it, and yet itself it seems to hang on a fallacious, illusory and inconsistent position! How can fullness rest on emptiness? How can a path be sought in what looks to be a mirage? How can a reality be supported by a dream? How can the force of an experienced conviction draw from the slenderness of a hallucinogenic image? How can such a creation operate *ex nihilo*, as it were? These questions are all the more crucial in that not only do they address themselves to the religious imagination in its 'eruptive' forms, but that through them their demand concerns any religion as imagination creative or recreative of its gods. And what religion escapes this theurgy?

This paradox can perhaps be explained if one considers the constituting force of the imaginary comparatively.

E. Morin distinguishes it in an inquiry on 'the rumour of Orleans'.[57] There was a rumour in Orleans according to which Jewish tradesmen had kidnapped, drugged and locked up young girls from the town, and handed them over to the white slave market. It was only a *rumour* and one that was shown by inquiries by the police and the press to be entirely without foundation. Nevertheless this rumour swelled and put the whole town in turmoil, in effervescence, which in earlier times could have started a pogrom. *Constitutive imagination*.

In the sixteenth century another rumour set off an 'undertaking of visionaries which obsessed European adventurers for more than a century'.[58] The rumour of Eldorado: somewhere in the north of the North American subcontinent, a fabulous King, covered with gold dust and precious stones, bathed every year in a no less fabulous lake. *El dorado*, the golden man, could only reign over a kingdom of gold. Decade after decade, ships' crews, gangs and armies swarmed in search of this imaginary kingdom. *Constitutive imagination*.

In a conference to celebrate the centenary of *Capital*,[59] the discussion turned to Freud. He was consulted by hysterical young girls who invariably gave as the origin of their problems the fact that they had been raped by their fathers. After analysis Freud discovered that there had been no rapes; the rapes were imagined, and this imagination was enough to set off the crisis; at the same time the crisis fed this imagination. 'To tell the truth, it all turns around nothing.'[60] 'The power of ideas,' diagnosed Freud. *Constitutive imagination*.

## 5 Gods of insurrection. Insurrection of the gods

Millenarianisms and utopias have thus been and are phenomena of the collective imagination which becomes a constitutive imagination. The imagination of a Kingdom and/or a society of Elsewhere or of 'Not yet'. They are provoked, certainly, either by a combination of social and historical pressures and oppressions which make the *hic et nunc* untenable, or by a system of mutually aggravating representations according to which such a combination is seen as such. But this horror of the contested combination, although it is a condition necessary for the hope of a projected society, is not a sufficient condition for the success of this project. The same combination can produce half a dozen different typical developments. As Sartre wrote: 'Valéry is a *petit-bourgeois* intellectual. Every *petit-bourgeois* intellectual is not Valéry'. Millenarianisms and utopias are a form of collective imagination for oppressed societies, but oppression does not necessarily express itself uniquely in this form. The modelisation of this diversity can be found in an account that can be here considered as involuntarily archetypal: Steiner's account of the horrors of Treblinka,[61] the concentration camp where a thousand Jews, under the whip of the S.S. and their Ukrainian henchmen, had to send fifteen thousand of their brothers to the ovens every day. This story shows the half-dozen different types of behaviour in each case elaborated in a religious image:

1 Betrayal in cooperating with the executioners to whom

Genns, the president of the *Judenrat*, decided to deliver the body of a rebel whom he had beaten to death.[62]

2 The deaf and dumb, dazed indifference of the *Hoffjuden*. 'They neither commit suicide nor seek to escape. They ignore everything, they act as though death did not exist. *On Friday evenings they light the candles* . . . .'[63]

3 The exalted resignation of the *Hassid* . . . 'Our wise men have taught us to serve the Lord, blessed be His name, whether he grants us comfort or deals out retribution.'[64]

4 Suicide in order to keep *'one's own* right to die', the hanging accompanied by prayers.[65]

5 Individual escapes or escapes in small groups in order to join the underground in their struggle. 'To get out so that one can tell the living, warn them . . . . Think of all those who sin unconsciously . . . . Think of all those who seal their *eternal unhappiness* with a light heart.'

6 Finally revolt, at first in improvised and individual attempts, then in planned, collective uprisings, followed by a general break-out by those who survived (4 per cent).

One could comment on how these last three types of behaviour correspond precisely to a range of millenarianising or utopising sequences which actually take place, including suicidal behaviour, for conducts of self-annihilation by fire, hunger or 'mortification' are not lacking in the records any more than the form of collective escape exemplified by self-managing strikes in disputed societies and manifested in the countless violent or pacifist micro-communities; any more than the insurrectional forms: peasant risings, holy wars, uprisings, counter-offensives to repression, crusades, putschist or revolutionary undertakings. Gods have been or are the *emblems* of all these types of behaviour. Furthermore they become the sociological locus for the uprising of a god when the collective imagination calls upon him and ad-orcises (neologism: antonym of 'exorcise') him. An emblem! In other words these gods are not just ideas, or indeed irrational ideas. Even if and *especially* if these ideas appear to be irrational, it is these gods that give strength, the strength of dream gods.

## 6 Identity and alterity

Because it leads to this uprising of the gods, the collective imagination rediscovers in its eruption both the collective consciousness and the collective memory. It offers the collective consciousness an inner reviviscence because it unfolds like a quasi cult of possession: holy marches towards an earth without evil, uprisings, trances, sacrifices, extenuating or exterminating ecstasies, exalting and iconoclastic festivities, general and sometimes biological strikes of societies that are too well-established, all-or-nothing risks, the joys of a holocaust, ritual procedures of spells and magic, departures, journeys, exoduses, crusades, exits from space and time . . . . It offers the collective memory the reactivation of its guarantee, because if it links up with this memory, it creates or recreates its own frame of reference, it appeals from a less profound tradition to a more profound tradition, reviving a hidden or dead past and restoring its light or life; its plan for an 'after' validates its memory of the 'before'.

Ultimately, the collective memory, the collective consciousness and the collective imagination culminate and merge, triple constituents of an ideal super-society,[66] the seed of a collective new identity and alterity.

Identity *and* alterity. A new way of being both the *same* and *other*. It would remarkably flatten, impoverish and weaken this function of the collective imagination if one were to confine it to ephemeral prelogical fantasies which soon crumble on the arrival, with its arms full of flowers, of a reason that is finally logical and a logic that is finally reasoning. Euphoria of the rationaliser who thinks he had lost his taste for climbing because his cable-car is functioning. Certainly the imagination can be hallucinatory, alienating, delirious, in the pejorative meaning of such terms. But everything occurs in this unilateral blockage as though the criticism were surreptitiously polarised itself by the crypto-utopia of a society that is so scientific or so rationalised, that it becomes a society without imagination or even a society without dreams: the republic where poets are forbidden. The classical experiment of depriving an individual of dreams has been tried; the result is the onset of neurosis. 'Nothing is good without moderation,' said Durkheim, observing that people commit suicide either because of too much or too little individualisation or socialisation. The possible inductions on

the phenomena of the collective imagination – utopising and/
or millenarianising – all lead to a double alienation, an
alienation of 'too much', but also an alienation of 'too little'
collective imagination. Societies become suicidal when they
show *too much* or *too little* imagination.

## 7 Religion and lived theatre

This 'too much' or 'too little' are perhaps more precise in the
counter-balancing of the functions of alterity (being other),
that have already been distinguished (cf. *supra* ch. I), and the
functions of aseity (being oneself), which are complementarily
discernible.

| *Functions of alterity* | *Functions of aseity* |
|---|---|
| 1 Alternance | Oneiric |
| 2 Altercation | Prospective |
| 3 Alternative | Theatrical |

(1) The function of alternance: first a function of strangeness
presents itself; the one which enables one to become strange
or a stranger; the one that brings up from the depths the
nocturnal being that comes to the level of the diurnal being:
'that stranger in black who could be my brother'. That is
probably why this function of alternance goes with or is
prolonged in a function of aseity: the oneiric and perhaps
oneirotherapeutic function, the one which legitimises a
dreamed existence or counter-existence, a dreamed society or
counter-society, and which eventually incorporates this
existence or this society in the waking dream of a lived
experience, the safety valve of an everyday life that would be
less liveable or even unliveable without it. The experience of
the 'world upside down' in the sabbath, the carnival, or the
festival of fools.[67] The experience of admitting the inadmis-
sible, of the likeliness of the unlikely, the possibilities of the
impossible. A waking dream with no other function but to be
dysfunctional, no other result than the decompression that is
thus obtained, the halt that is thus secured, the school that is
thus played truant from, the challenge that is thus made, the
uselessness that is thus introduced, the fable that is thus
fictionalised, the delirium that is thus courted, the festivity

that is thus interposed, the game that is thus played, the potlatch that is thus squandered.

(2) Another function of alterity is the function of *altercation*. The imagination ceases to be a plan of escape. It becomes a plan of protest. The society that it imagines, including its imaginary gods, enters into conflict with the dominating society and its gods. Various states can be seen: the ideal dream thrown like a bottle into the sea, or thrown incognito over the walls; the critical literature seeking an audience; the plan or even the specification of a project which is a testing ground; the pilot experiment and its diffusion; the anti-conformist network; finally the bridgehead of a counter-society and/or a counter-church . . . . This function of altercation thus hinges naturally on a function of *prospective*, which is to aseity what altercation is to alterity. Furthermore the latter is the exploration of *being oneself* combined with the necessity of *being other*.

(3) Finally a function of *alternative*. For utopia and millenarianism can be simultaneously defined as *imaginary plans of an alternative society*. They are essentially the plan of an Else-where, or an Other: *another* regime of human relations, *another* regime of economics, *another* regime of work or leisure, *another* regime of authority, *another* regime of cultural or spiritual life, *another* earth, *another* heaven, *other* men, *other* gods. The alternative is at first hesitant, nostalgic, uncertain, but it becomes consistent, persistent, convinced. It was merely a mental representation, it becomes an *idée-force*, operationalised in a social *dramatisation*, no other than the millennium, where for a thousand years the just and the saints will reign *on the stage* of the world, at last holding the leading roles in a society that is at last perfect. Here too the function of alterity – which opens up this alternative – hinges on a function of aseity, a theatrical function. From this latter point of view, if religion appears as the sacred theatre of possessions by the spirits of yesterday,[68] the theatre appears as the religion of possessions by the spirits of tomorrow. The ultimate millenarian utopia is that of Antonin Artaud: 'Knowing whether, in this world which is slipping by and committing suicide without realising it, there

can be found a nucleus of men who are capable of imposing this superior notion of the theatre, which will return to us all the natural and magic equivalent of the dogmas that we no longer believe in'.[69] Does it not echo the Fourierist utopia of a generalised opera, 'a branch of religion', 'a branch of religious memory', 'an axis of cult', 'a religious exercise as sacred as the parish services', 'an operation that God wants to carry out on all our functions of work and leisure' . . . ?

To support thus the constitutive function of the collective consciousness, memory and imagination, and the impregnation of religious phenomena by such functions, is surely to remove oneself from a sociology whose entire ambition is reduced, according to the consecrated formula, to finding 'the non-theological factors of theological phenomena'. It would even be rather to do the opposite and, if not subordinate, at least coordinate the famous determination of the infrastructures with a self-determination of a superstructure. Social determinisms do not induce the religious man to anything but self-determination, and this self-determination coincides with a strange self-construction, in which he constructs gods who construct him. Men of god perpetually make gods of men, and gods of men make men of god, whereas in the crucible of this circumincession men become men and gods become gods. 'To a certain extent' . . . 'in some respects', collective consciousness, memory or imagination carry out acts that are a double creation: an adoration creating its gods and gods creating adoration.

But this paradox connects both the religious phenomenon and the human phenomenon to other aspects of the human phenomenon which show themselves through this same constitutive force. The phenomenon of *love*: the lover loves the loved one, certainly because the loved one is good-looking but also and above all, the loved one is good-looking because the lover loves him or her. The phenomenon of *action*, the phenomenon of *freedom* . . . for – the aphorism is repeated from Aristotle to Bergson – one does not choose an act because one finds it preferable, one finds it preferable because one has chosen it. The phenomenon of *conviction*, lost or won.

Durkheim states: 'A preconception does not disappear because it is irrational, but one discovers that it was irrational because it is disappearing'. One could reverse the proposition: a conviction, including a religious one, is not held because one found it to be rational, one finds that it becomes rational because one is holding it. Above and below the systems of *ideas* that seem to come from a religious phenomenon, a system of *forces* and of constitutive creative forces inserts itself, as it does in love, action and liberty. The constructive energy of the religious phenomenon resides in the illogical logic of these forces which make societies, and without which, or without the equivalent of which, societies, including religious ones, are unmade.

One advantage of religious phenomena linked to the imagination, and therefore to the collective consciousness and memory, is to circumscribe the historical and social laboratory in which such forces manifest themselves, and furthermore to show up the gods, in some miraculous way,[70] as receivers of the imaginary.

Another advantage is analogous to the one that Renouvier sought in writing his *Uchronie*, 'or history as it could have been and as it has never been'. It would lead, beyond the variables or the conflicts between theisms or atheisms, to something like a 'utheism', in other words a perception of the gods and the non-gods as they could have been and as they have never been.

# Conclusion

# The sociology of hope and
# the hopes of sociology

Just a simple pause on a long path that stretches towards
who knows what horizon, for it is a horizon that retreats
with every step we make towards it, towards its promise
of light and clarity.

Roger Bastide

When one presents some fragments of this sociology of hope
to one's theologian colleagues, one obviously exposes oneself
to refusal. This is what occurred with J. Moltmann[1] at a
meeting we both attended. He expressed his reserve as
follows:[2]

> Is there not a messianism in sociology? Is sociology in
> itself not a great messianic undertaking? In Auguste
> Comte's law of three states, one finally finds the three
> ages of Joachim de Flore . . . Is the historical scheme not
> an expression of a trinitarian doctrine reduced to history,
> introduced into history? It is the scheme of a great
> *evolution* which makes sociological rationalisation a
> messianic undertaking . . . .

This suspicion can finally lead to three suggestions, if not to
three answers.

(1) The suspicion is topical and it is quite remarkable that
one can at the outset bring an additional stream to this
theological mill. Indeed there are, or in any case there were,
religiously invested sociological hopes. Auguste Comte's is
one of them, even if his evocation in Joachimite terms is
arguable, as is the said law of the three stages. P. Arbousse-
Bastide has demonstrated it: the Comte who acknowledges
himself to be religious, is the Comte of a *fourth* stage, in

171

comparison with which the other three are merely preambles: 'In fact true science is just as preliminary as theology and metaphysics, and should finally be wholly eliminated by the universal religion to which these three preambles are provisory, transitory and preparatory'.[3] Therefore one could not count Comte as a messianic champion of a 'sociological rationalisation', and more generally of a science that he rejects and that he even accuses of 'aspiring to perpetuate its spiritual interregnum' . . . This being so, it is obvious that a 'Treatise of Sociology instituting the Religion of Humanity' – such was the subtitle of the *System of Positive Polity* – could not be free of a crypto-messianism.

It is not the only case, and we find two others in a predecessor and successor of Auguste Comte. The predecessor is Saint-Simon: not only in committing the final libel of New Christianity which was explicitly 'Messiacal', but also in his avowal in his earlier writings, which proposed the 'social physiology' destined later, according to G. Gurvitch, to become sociology. From these writings Durkheim was able to make the following diagnosis: 'It is the *faith* he had in the omnipotence of science that *inspired* the conception of social science'.[4]

As for Durkheim, Auguste Comte's successor, did he not often nourish a quasi-adventist nostalgia? 'The old ideals and the divinities that incarnated them are dying because they do not satisfactorily answer the new aspirations which have arisen, and the new ideals which are necessary to direct our lives have not yet arisen . . . .' But '*the day will come* when our societies will once again know moments of creative exuberance during which new ideas will arise . . . . There are no immortal gospels, and there is no reason to believe that henceforth humanity is incapable of conceiving of new ones.'[5]

This triptych does not pretend to be a restrictive list, and it is most likely that a deep analysis of many a sociologist – including contemporary ones and including the sociologists of hope – would find not only a hope – why should a sociologist be deprived or free of it? – but a hope that is openly or surreptitiously endowed with a legitimating and/or subversive religious reference . . . .

But this *endowed* hope is not the only one.

(2) Another discernible logic is – conversely – antiseptic hope. In the areas that he observes, a sociologist hears so many gods speak to so many men in order to give so many messages, which are as peremptory as they are antagonistic, as captivating in their convictions as they are all too often penitentiary in their consequences! He becomes reserved himself on the literary genre of 'revelations', especially when they intend or pretend to monopolise *the* Revelation. Amazed by hope when it emerges and throws the rope, how can he not fear tricks, traps, exaltations or occultations, self-suggestions or even impostures? And if, enveloped in the folds of his own science, he distinguishes something as being *his* revelation – his inner devil or angel, and they are both indistinguishable – it is as if he were vaccinated against possible incantations by necessary disincantations. In this way, how can a sociology of religions not be a critical sociology?

On the other hand, sociology knows that science alone is not contagious. But it also knows that to be contagious it must be contaminated. Marx, of course, could be bewitched by a presumed contagion of science: 'Religious enthusiasm consumes itself at its supreme moment in ecstasy, whereas philosophical enthusiasm transmits itself to science as a pure and ideal flame. That is why the former has merely gently warmed a few souls, whereas the latter has become the animating spirit of universal historical evolutions.'[6] In saying this, he is doubly mistaken. On the one hand, religious enthusiasm did inspire 'universal historical evolutions', and this is recognised by a Marxist: 'Historically one may wonder whether materialism represented the philosophy of the oppressed classes . . . . A more attentive study seems to show that mysticisms and heresies have stimulated and guided the masses much more and much better.'[7] And on the other hand, if social science, especially the social science of 'scientific socialism', has also animated a 'universal historical evolution', does this animation not come from a *theme* more equivalent to a *kerygmatic* theme than from its *informed variations*? Another Marxist suggests so,[8] even if others refute it.[9]

In any case, sociology, even if it is not Marxist, will tend to recall the young philosopher Marx's challenge to the theologies of his time, and reiterate it, especially if they are Marxist-inclined, to the theologies of our time:[10]

> Philosophy speaks of religious subjects differently from the way you have spoken of them. You speak without having studied, it speaks after having studied. You address yourself to passion, it addresses itself to intelligence. You insult, it teaches. You promise heaven and earth, it only promises truth. You insist that one has faith in your faith, it does not insist that one believes in its results, it insists on examination from doubt . . . . Who can decide the limits of scientific research if not scientific research itself?

Hope, certainly, but an *antiseptic* hope, *religiös unmusikalisch*, insensitive to the music of religions.

(3) We know that Max Weber wished it to be so. But on looking closely at his own declarations, the intermeshing is complex between the thread of this antiseptic hope and the chain of this hope, which despite all, is endowed. Exorcism and adorcism intermingle. Exorcism, certainly:

> Nothing has yet come from fervour and expectation alone. One must go about it in a different way, set to work, answer the demands of each day in one's life as a man, but also in one's working life.

Yet adorcism also:[11]

> Work would be simple and easy if each man found *the demon who holds the threads of his life and obeyed him*.

Jean Séguy, who quotes and comments on these texts, goes so far as to ask: 'Is this attention to daily professional tasks in the conviction of obeying a transcendent duty not the *manifestation of an inner expectation*, the model of which was first drawn by the prophets in the Old Testament?'[12]

Therefore it is probable that something like a hope, which is both hopeless and unhoped for, emerges along the scholar's path. A *spes contra spem*, like the one celebrated by L. Leprince-

Ringuet in his final lecture at the Collège de France in May 1972. A certain hopelessness:

> The inquirer asks himself the formidable question: what have I got from my work, from my twenty years of hard and strenuous labour? Sometimes he is overwhelmed by a feeling of disappointment . . . . The results seem disappointing . . . . So he may ask himself if all his life has been a success . . . . He risks being disheartened, even if, and especially if, he put all his energy, all his intelligence and all his heart into his work . . . .

And yet there is an unhoped for hope:[13]

> Science is knocking down barriers, enabling one to cross frontiers, establishing currents of brotherhood between men. In its rational method, its language, its way of approaching problems and solving them, it establishes a universal intellectual and spiritual attitude. This universal language is an instrument of brotherhood, and furthermore, the ethics of science, with its virtues, its spirits of welcome, *its hope*, and the joy of progressing further in the knowledge of truth, is a ferment of liberation, an element of transcendence . . . .

Science is therefore a receiver of both hope and hopelessness. The hopes are comparable to trances, especially in the fever that accompanies a miracle of the rope. To use Roger Bastide's terms, they have 'aspects of wild outbursts, of a contagious epidemic, of the spell of nocturnal abysses' . . . . Spectacular trances of revolutionary dramas in which 'men and things are caught in the sparkle of diamonds' (Marx); secret trance of the 'demon' who does not inhabit scientific ataraxy without being something like a 'nocturnal abyss'. But Roger Bastide also shows the ambiguity of attitudes and even traditional rites in relation to this phenomenon of the trance: 'The whole of African and Afro-American religion is thus directed against the uncontrolled trance. It is almost an "anti-trance".'[14] If there is an 'original matrix from which came shamanisms, cults of possession, messianisms or prophetic movements',[15] the analogy between trance and hope should be taken further, and if the trance postulates an 'anti-trance', then hope postulates a 'counter-hope'.

Finally one comes back to Max Weber and his dialectic of an ethic of conviction opposed to an ethic of responsibility, other labels of the opposition of '-urgies' and '-logies'. He knows that if politics 'are made in the mind', 'they are not made only in the mind', and 'on this point, the proponents of the ethic of conviction are absolutely right'. But he prefers to appeal to an inner dialectic in which hope would certainly be the enthusiasm of a conviction, but balanced by a calculation of responsibilities. Failing this 'inner balance' of the 'proponents of the ethic of conviction':[16]

> I have the impression that nine times out of ten, I find myself in the presence of windbags who are not really conscious of the responsibilities they take on, but who, on the contrary, are carried away by romantic feelings. This does not interest me from a human point of view and does not move me in any way whatsoever. On the other hand I feel deeply overwhelmed by the attitude of a mature man – whether he is young or old – who considers himself to be really and wholeheartedly responsible for his actions, and who, in practising the ethic of responsibility, comes to the point where he declares: 'I cannot do otherwise. I stop there!' Such an attitude is genuinely human and moving. Each of us could find ourselves in a similar situation one day, if our souls are not completely dead. One can see it now: the ethic of conviction and the ethic of responsibility are not contradictory, they complement each other, and together they constitute the authentic man . . .

This sociological counter-hope can only be – in this way and at that level – an anti-theology, even if, and perhaps especially if, it is secularised. An anti-theology that is equivalent to something like a fundamental reticence towards any *Weltgeschichte*, identified or erected as *Weltgericht*. Indeed there is a no less fundamental allergy to any last judgment. Is it not, in the case of science, and therefore in the case of sociology, its way of espousing a hope in the teeth of everything, even hope itself? Hope as it is drawn by Kafka:

> The Messiah will come only when he is no longer
> needed. He will only come one day after his advent. He
> will not come on the day of the last judgment, but on the
> day after.

# Notes

### Introduction: The miracle of the rope

1 M. Eliade, *Méphistophélès et l'Androgyne*, ch. IV, 'Ropes and puppets', Gallimard, Paris, 1962.
2 Ibid., p. 237.
3 Die Hoffnung ist ein Seil; könnt ein Verdammter hoffen Gott zog ihn aus dem Pfuhl, in deum er ist ersoffen.
(Hope is a rope; and God would pull a condemned man from a swamp if he had hope.)
Cf. Angelus Silesius, *Le Pèlerin Chérubique*, ed. E. Susini, P.U.F., Paris, 1964.
4 Cf. *infra*, ch. 2 and 3 with a background of our *Dictionnaire des Messies*, cf. bibl. H.D. VI.
5 Cf. a fragment of this approach in H.D. XVI (cf. bibl.).
6 Cf. H.D. III and *infra*, ch. 4.
7 Cf. *infra*, ch. 5.
8 Cf. *infra*, ch. 1.
9 E. Morin, 'Le retour de l'événement', in *Communications*, 18, 1972 (Special issue in 'the event').
10 M. Weber, *Le Judaïsme antique*, p. 284, Plon, Paris, 1971. (Our emphasis.) (*Ancient Judaism*, trs. and ed. H. H. Gerth and D. Martindale, Collier-Macmillan, London, 1967.)

### Chapter 1: Religious hope: its peaks and troughs. An anthological approach

1 R. Bastide, *Le rêve, la transe et la folie*, Flammarion, Paris, 1972. He adds: 'In a very different register, but one that can help one to understand better the action of the Africans, Jean Baruzi told us of the effort made by the Jesuits to mould the mysticism of St Theresa in the framework of Catholic tradition.'
2 A. Dumas: 'If imagination reigns, it risks reigning only over itself. If it holds all power, it risks wielding it over nothing. In the depths of imagination there is an irresistible tendency towards schizophrenia . . . the image is too free to be really so . . . .' 'Stades sur le chemin de la foi' in *Christus*, 73, p. 106.

179

3 Cf. H.D., I.
4 Extracts of three documents by this Pope, all dated 28 December 1878.
5 Encyclical letter on the Third Order of St Francis, 17 September 1882.
6 P. Haubtmann, *P.-J. Proudhon. Genèse d'un antithéiste*, p. 173, Mame, Paris, 1969.
7 Discussed in W. D. Morris, *The Christian Origins of Social Revolt*.
8 My friend and colleague, A. Gauthier, states: 'This phrase is one of the countless phrases that figure in Greek compilations, which are sometimes anonymous, sometimes attributed to one author, sometimes to another. When this one is not anonymous, it is attributed to Pindarus (Stobaeus), to Plato (Aelianus, beginning of the third century A.D.), to Aristotle (Diogenes Laertius same period). None of these attributions has any authority. For example, according to Aelianus, *Plato dicebat, spes, vigilantium hominum esse somnia.*' Furthermore should one translate the *elpis* of the Greeks by hope? A. Gauthier tends to present the risks of such a translation: 'This notion is strictly *undetermined* because *elpis* refers indiscriminately to good or bad, with or without foundation: it is the idea that one has, rightly or wrongly, of what will happen, good or bad. So one finds with the Greeks two series of phrases on *elpis*, some favourable (the unhappy man is saved by *elpis*), some unfavourable (nothing worse than the *elpis* which loses the happy man through pride).'
    This ambivalence can be found in our own analysis.
    On hope in Aristotle, cf. A. Gautier, *Magnanimité*, pp. 33–55 and 194–6, Vrin, Paris, 1951, and *Aristote, l'Ethique à Nicomaque*, Louvain, 1959 (2nd edn 1970).
9 R. Caillois and G. E. von Grunebaum, *Le Rêve et les sociétés humaines*, pp. 22–44, N.R.F., Paris, 1967. (*Dream and Human Societies*, University of California Press.)
10 Our emphasis.
11 F. Dumont, *La Vigile du Québec*, pp. 180–1, Montreal, 1971. (*Vigil of Quebec*, University of Toronto Press, 1975.)
12 R. Bastide, 'Sociologie du rêve' in *Le Rêve et les sociétés humaines*, op. cit., pp. 177–8, and 'Sociologie du rêve' in *Universitas*, 6–7, pp. 109–22, May-December 1970. Cf. also *Le Rêve, la transe et la folie*, op. cit.
13 'Dreaming, a creative process' in *American Journal of Psychoanalysis*, 24, 1, 1964.
14 O. L. Burridge, *Mambu, a Melanesian Millennium*, London, 1960.
15 In the discourse and discussion of February 1906 published in *Sociologie et philosophie*, p. 45. (E. Durkheim, *Sociology and Philosophy*, trs. D. F. Pocock, Free Press, New York, 1974.) For a more extended commentary, cf. Henri Desroche, 'Retour à Durkheim. D'un texte peu à quelques thèses méconnues', in *Archives de Sociologie des Religions*, 79–88, *(A.S.R.)* 27, 1969, and 'Pour une sociologie des idéations collectives' in *Social Compass*, XIX, 1972, 2, pp. 199–212.

16 This text, 'Le Sentiment religieux à l'heure actuelle', dates from winter 1913–14. It has been re-published twice, once in *A.S.R.* 27, 1969, once in E. Durkheim, *La Science sociale et l'action*, pp. 305–13, P.U.F., Paris, 1970 (our emphasis).

17 Particularly in the final pages of *Formes* and in the first work *Le Socialisme* (recently re-published: P.U.F., 1971).

18 Another gloss: 'which is above all warmth, life, enthusiasm, exaltation of mental activity, transport of the individual above himself'. Ibid., p. 607.

19 In M. Mauss, 'Sociologie et anthropologie', pp. 306–8, P.U.F., Paris, 1950.

20 J. Lacroix, *L'Echec*, ch. 1, P.U.F., Paris, 1964, 3rd ed., 1969, 'Psychologie de l'échec', pp. 3–51.

21 Cit. in N. Wachtel, *La vision des vaincus*, pp. 45–6, Gallimard, Paris, 1971. (*The Vision of the Vanquished: The Spanish Exploration of Peru through Indian Eyes*, trs. Ben and Siân Reynolds, Harvester Press, Brighton, 1976.)

22 Ibid., pp. 257, 272.

23 This theme is approached elsewhere: cf. Henri Desroche, *Les Dieux Rêvés. Théismes et Athéismes en Utopie*, Desclée, Paris, 1972.

24 Cf. ch. 2.

25 R. Bastide, op. cit. *supra*.

26 A. Gramsci, *Oeuvres choisies*, p. 102, Éditions Sociales, Paris, 1959. (*Selections from Political Writings 1910–20*, ed. Q. Hoare, trs. J. Mathews, Lawrence & Wishart, London, 1977.) A welcome commentary on the sociology of Gramsci in E. Salamini, *La Sociologie de la connaissance dans l'oeuvre de Gramsci* (multigraphed thesis, Paris, 1972) (our emphasis).

27 The quotation chosen by Jean Lacroix for his book is significant:
   I was referring to all those who live with an obsession with success, who feign success which is transformed into failure at each moment, because each moment brings them closer to death, which is a failure with no remedy. Happy is he who feels a failure! The feeling of our own failure is the beginning of our only possible success . . . where is the success of the satisfied? They are the great failures and their obsession with success comes from there.
   (J. Sales, op. cit., p. 5).

28 *Formes*, pp. 604, 597.

29 Cf. F. Engels, *La Guerre des paysans.* (*Peasant War in Germany*, Lawrence & Wishart, London, 1969.)

30 E. Bloch, *Thomas Münzer, théologien de la Révolution.*

31 Mega, 1, 2, 443, French version of this text in Henri Desroche, *Marxisme et religions*, pp. 88–9, P.U.F., Paris.

32 His invective to the victorious nobles: 'The peasants have been conquered, that only proves that the peasants do not yet deserve to be free' (p. 279). His warning to the peasants: 'I see with pain and despair that you are not worthy of being free . . . I see, alas, that it

was madness to entrust the defense of freedom to men who do not have inner freedom' (p. 276). And his final statement to his executioners: 'Do not believe that all this will last. One day, unless you are enlightened by the Gospel, I shall be avenged. I wanted too much; but patience, a man like me does not die' (p. 282). Attributed by A. Weill, *Histoire de la grande guerre des paysans* (2nd ed.), Paris, 1860. These pages, which were first published in *La Phalange*, were borrowed from Zimmerman's work, which also served as a source to Engels.

33 E. Durkheim, *Sociologie et philosophie*, pp. 134–5, P.U.F., Paris, 1953.

34 H. Cox, La *Fête des fous*, Seuil, Paris, 1971. (*Feast of Fools: A Theological Essay on Festivity and Fantasy*, Harper & Row, New York, 1972.)

35 The slogan was not Marx's monopoly. It was used implicitly or explicitly by d'Holbach (1761), Goethe (1828), H. Heine (1840), R. Bauer (1841–2), Feuerbach (1838 and 1841), M. Hess (1843). Cf. H. Gollwitzer, *Athéisme marxiste et Foi chrétienne*, p. 25, Castermann, Paris, 1965. (*The Christian Faith and the Marxist criticism of Religion*, trs. D. Cairns, St Andrews Press, Edinburgh, 1970.)

36 D. Mothé, *Le métier de militant*, Paris, 1971. Unpublished diploma thesis to be published by Seuil.

37 A post-factum remark: these three types of alterity, to which one is thus led, are not without analogies with the three passions dear to Fourier. Even if the analogy is fanciful, it is worth a brief mention. In fact, what Fourier calls *fluttering*, or 'alternating', in the absence of which man falls into tepidity and boredom, corresponds to *alternance*. Obviously the *cabbalist*, 'speculative enthusiasm', 'passion for intrigue', 'far from the flat calm praised by ethics for its gentleness', corresponds to *altercation*. Less obviously, the *composite*, that 'enthusiasm that excludes reason' and that fulfills *together* the needs of the senses and the aspirations of the soul, corresponds to the *alternative*. Bread and roses. Without this composite, in other words if a society keeps its material or spiritual hunger, then that society 'becomes insipid to itself and will not go far without dying of its lovely death'. (L. Fourier, *Théorie de l'unité universelle* I, pp. 145, 434–6; III, pp. 406–10; IV, p. 399.)

38 J.-P. Sartre, *L'Être et le néant*, p. 717. (*Being and Nothingness*, trs. H. Barnes, Methuen, London, 1969.)

39 H. Bergson, *Évolution créatrice*, pp. 248, 250. Or again, p. 246: '*Life is an effort to climb up the slope that matter descends* . . . .' 'It is like an effort to lift up the weight that is falling. It is true that it only succeeds in delaying the fall. At least it can give us an idea of what it was like to lift the weight.' One could paraphrase this as follows: Hope is an *energy in which the imaginary climbs up a slope that reality descends*. It is like the effort of grace to lift up a weight. It is true that it only succeeds in checking it. At least it gives us an idea of what the snatching was like (just as one says of a weight lifter that he 'snatches' the weight). (*Creative Evolution*, trs. M. Arthur, Greenwood Press, Westport, Ct, 1976.)

## Chapter 2: A panorama of millenarian phenomena

1 Chaix-Ruy, J., *J.-B. Vico et l'illuminisme athée*, Del Duca, Paris, 1970.
2 Henri Desroche, *Les Dieux rêvés, Théismes et Athéismes en Utopie*, Desclée, Paris, 1972.
3 This investment of the millenarian phenomenon, which eventually is revolutionary, is particularly well emphasised by Jean Baechler, *Les phénomènes révolutionnaires*, P.U.F., Paris, 1970. (*Revolution*, trs. Joan Vickers, Blackwell, Oxford, 1976.)
4 Cf. Henri Desroche, Preface to *Dieux d'hommes. Dictionnaire*, Mouton, La Haye, Paris, 1969. One can find references in this dictionary which it would have been tedious to mention here. Universal references are provided, *infra*, cf. ch. 4.
5 One exception: '*Paradise*' (1736–43), a community founded by a Saxon immigrant, Christian Priber, who settled with the Cherokee Indians, learnt their language and, in order to protect them from the Whites, planned to organise them into a society with the name of 'Paradise'. His extra-confessional inspiration came from Plato and Thomas More. Accused of conspiring with the French, Priber was arrested by the English colonial powers and thrown in prison where he died.
6 I mention this 'Messiah of the Year XIII' to satisfy the curiosity of Ernst Bloch, who, with a mutual friend, wonders what these communising and messianising followers of the French Revolution could be. A work has been devoted to them, Claude Hau, *Le Messie de l'An XIII*, Denoël, Paris, 1955.
7 Already mentioned in ch. 1. One should note that the Church that came from this Kimbanguist prophecy is today only one of the 250 new churches found in a recent study in Zaire. Furthermore, on the series of messianisms in Angola, cf. the recent study of Maria Helena Gil, *Les Messianismes d'Angola*, 191 + xxviii pages, Diplôme E.P.H.E., Paris, 1972.
8 Cf. 'Les Christs Noirs', preface by R. Bastide to the work of Martial Sinda, *Le Messianisme congolais*, pp. 7–13, Payot, Paris, 1972.
9 The gaps concerning Asia (China, Japan, Indonesia . . .) are particularly unforgivable. Cf. the contributions of J. Chesneaux.
10 Bloch, E., *Thomas Münzer, théologien de la révolution*, Jullard, Paris, 1964 (our italics).
11 Cf. *infra*, ch. 5 – And earlier, in the same sense: Jean Bérard, 'L'Homme fait-il son histoire', *Revue historique*, October 1957.
12 Paul VI, in an apostolic letter to Cardinal Roy on the occasion of the eightieth anniversary of *Rerum Novarum*, 14 May 1971. Quotations in *Le Monde*, p. 14, 15 May 1971. French text in *La Croix* (our italics).
13 'It would be dangerous to ignore it. The call to utopia is often a useful pretext for those who want to flee from real duties and take refuge in an imaginary world. Living in a hypothetical future is an easy alibi for driving off immediate responsibilities' (ibid.).

## Chapter 3: Exile and the kingdom in eternal return

1 Métraux (A.), *Le Vaudou haïtien*, Gallimard, Paris, 1958. (*Voodoo in Haiti*, trs. H. Charteris, Deutsch, London, 1972.) 'Le mariage mystique dans le Vodou', *Cahiers du Sud*, October 1956. The chapter quoted here: 'La Possession', in *Haiti. La terre, les hommes et les dieux*, p. 84, La Baconnière, Neuchâtel, 1957 (our italics).

2 Analysed in Jacqueline Nicolas's study, *Les 'juments des dieux'*. Rites of possession and the feminine condition in Hausa. C.N.R.S.I.F.A.N., *Études nigériennes*, no. 21, 1969, also *Anthropos*, Paris, 1972.

3 Cf. M. de Certeau, *La Possession de Loudun*, Julliard, Paris, 1970.
A strange meeting associates in a great number of cases the possessed or the 'possessionists' (who are convinced of the reality of the possession) and the communities of 'spirituals'. On the French map of the mid-seventeenth century one often finds in the same places the cases of possession and the most pious groups: *during its years of madness, Loudun was also a school of spirituality.* At the centre of this demonological fair was, for three years, one of the greatest mystics of the seventeenth century who was both the Don Quixote and the Hölderlin of this 'extraordinary adventure'. The theatres of the devil are also mystical centres. More fundamentally, Alfred Jarry is right in saying about Loudun, that *possession by the Holy Spirit or by the devil are manifestly symmetrical. The two 'possessions' present an analogous structure.* Mystique and possession often form pockets in a society whose language is being dulled, which is losing its spiritual porousness and becoming impervious to the divine. *The relationship with a 'hereafter' wavers between the immediacy of a diabolical stranglehold and the immediacy of a divine illumination.* (pp. 12–13).

4 Psalm 73; 22.

5 Sic humana voluntas in medio posita est, ceu jumentum, si insederit Deus, vult et vadit, quo vult Deus, ut Psalmus dicit: Factus sum sicut jumentum et ego semper tecum. Si insederit Satan, vult et vadit, quo vult Satan, hec est in ejus arbitrio, ad utum sessorem currere aut eum quaerere, sed ipsi sessores certant ob ipsum obtinendum et possidendum (*De servo arbiyrio*).
One edition of this Lutheran treatise refers to the Hypomnesticon attributed to St Augustine and attributable to Pelagius (P.L. 43, 1611–64). One does indeed find the image of mounting (III, 20): 'Recte namque arbitror comparari liberum arbitrium *jumento* . . . .' It seems that St Augustine himself was familiar with this image.
F. Berrouard has pointed out several passages to me: 'domat Deus jumentum cui insidet . . . .' En. in Ps. 31, P.L. 36, 272 . . .
'Jumenta mansueta vult habere Dominus: esto jumentum Domini'. Ibid, 33, P.L. 66, 310. 'Si enim tu ad domanda jumenta tua profers virgam, profers flagellum, Deus non profert ad domanda jumenta sua, quod sumus nos, qui de jumentis suis faciet filios suos?' Sermo 55, 4.4, P.L. 38, 376. 'Sedeat supra nos Dominus, et quod vult nos docet. Jumentum ipsius sumus, ad Jerusalem imus . . . .' etc. *Sermo*

*Frangipane*, 4, 4, I, p. 211. G. Morin, *Miscel. Agost.*

6 Cf. *Father Divine*, in C. Braden, *These also Believe*, the MacMillan Company, New York, 1953.

7 Cf. the strategy of John of Leyden in Münster, or of Tanchelm in Antwerp, or of Father Enfantin in Saint-Simonism.

8 Cf. E. Sarkisyanz, *Russland und der Messianismus des Orients*, Tübingen, 1955. In an analogous way, G. Gurvitch said:

> Although I do not belong to any religion, I shall all the same allow myself to remark that the Russian theology of the immanence of the Holy Spirit in humanity, which implies a call to humanity to help God continue to create the world, seems to me to be much closer to collectivism and is perhaps one of the secrets of communism in Russia.

*Revue de l'Institut de Sociologie*, p. 30 (Brussels), no. 2–3, 1967.

9 V. Lanternari's thesis emphasised this with much documentation, *Movimenti religiosi di liberta e di salvazzo dei populi oppressi*, Milan, Feltrinelli, 1960.

10 Cf. Eliade (M.), 'Méphistophélès et l'Androgyne ou le mystère de la totalité' in *Méphistophélès et l'Androgyne*, p. 95, Gallimard, 1962. In particular his putting this theme in perspective in the continuity of the mystical theme in the 'coincidentia oppositorum'.

11 M. Éliade, op. cit., ch. 3, 'Renouvellement cosmique et eschatologie', p. 155.

12 Cf. the recent speculation of J.-C. Pichon, *Le Royaume et les prophètes*, in which he founds his chronosophy on the fact that an *astral* rhythm determines *historical* events or advents, Laffont, 1963.

13 Cf. the case of the message given by the millenarianising person that was Thomas Münzer – Cf. *supra* ch. 1.

14 Tuveson, *Millennium and Utopia*, Berkeley, Los Angeles, 1949.

15 Cf. *supra*, ch. 1.

16 On monasticism and utopia, cf. J. Séguy's contribution, 'Les Sociétés imaginées, Monachisme et Utopie', *Annales*, 26, 2, pp. 328 and 354, March–April 1971.

17 (Our italics). Cf. R. Bastide, 'Le messianisme raté' . . . *Archives de Sociologie des Religions*, 5, pp. 31–7. The following analysis could also be compared to the stimulating essay of J. Lacroix, *L'Echec*, P.U.F., Paris, in particular p. 46.

18 Among many Durkheimian texts we have already quoted one of the most topical, cf. *supra*, ch. 1. To the 'relapse' described in this text, there is eventually the opposition of the cycle of a new take-off like the one evoked by R. Bastide, following the ecclesification of 'Black Christs': 'At each juncture of history, there is a specific response. Today the Black Christs have been placed on the altars and have thus lost their dynamic powers as agitators of the people; but the ancient gods, whose voices one had wanted to stifle, start to speak again through the bodies of mediums in trance.' 'Christs Noirs', in Sinda, *Le Messianisme congolais et ses incidences politiques*, Payot, Paris, 1972.

19 L. Festinger, *When Prophecy fails, An account of a modern group that predicted the destruction of the world*, Minneapolis, 1956.
20 G. Duveau, *Sociologie de l'Utopie*, P.U.F., 1961.
21 Basco B., 'Lumières et Utopie. Problèmes de recherches', *Annales*, p. 555, 355, 26, 2, March–April.
22 The most important thing in this literature is to set the social imagination in motion, to keep one's distance. One should say that in these imaginary journeys, the pleasure of travelling is often more important than the countries one discovers (ibid.).

## Chapter 4: Revolutionary ideologies and religious messianisms

1 Cf. Henri Desroche, XIV, on Durkheim and the 'collective ideations' so dear to him. Cf. M. Rodinson on Marxism: 'Marxist sociology and Marxist ideology', *Diogène*, October–December 1968. The same definition of ideology in terms of action. Cf. *infra* for Durkheim. For Rodinson: 'The function of an ideology is to give directives of individual or collective action' (p. 79). Which is not, any more than it is in Durkheim, an end of non-receiving: *'Ideology can just as easily blind as light the way'* (p. 83).
2 In contrast with 'revolution' sublimated, definitions of the revolution by Simone Weil or Jeanne Deroin, cf. *supra* ch. 1. Cf. elsewhere, A. Decouflé, *Sociologie des Révolutions* and his analyses of the *Paris Commune*, as well as J. Baechler, *Les Phénomènes revolutionnaires*, P.U.F., Paris, 1970.
3 Cf. *supra*, ch. 2 and 3.
4 Durkheimians defined religion as the *administration* of the sacred. After examining Durkheim's texts, I prefer the *making viable* of the sacred, this *sacred path* either going or returning; going to the sacred but also returning from it, for if one goes too far, one does not return, one loses one's life and one's reason. The remarks of a psychologist, H. Diekens, are also relevant: 'Approche psychologique des rites religieux mystiques et de leur symbolisme', in *Eschatologie et Cosmologie*, Institut de Sociologie, U.L.B., Brussels; he distinguishes in all the states of trances 'rituals of induction' and 'rituals of return', rather like compression and decompression devices in diving.
5 René Dumont, *Développement et socialismes*, Seuil, Paris 1969. (*Socialism and Development*, trs. R. Cunningham, Deutsch, 1973.) Thus reproducing the postulate of an 'imperfect society' formulated at the same time, although in a different register, by Milovan Djilas, *La société imparfaite*, Calmann-Lévy, Paris, 1969.
6 Also relevant, there is among many recent positions, the analysis of ideologies and apparatuses made on both Christianity and communism by C. Wagon, 'Des biens célestes et de leur propriété' in *Églises en crise*, Cahiers d'étude du Centre Protestant de Recherches et de Rencontres du Nord, no 31, July–August 1969, pp. 7–42. Also more

spectacularly, Michel Garder's 'point of view', 'Une théocratie matérialiste' in *Le Monde*, 4 April 1970, p. 4.

7 Cf. Alfred Willemer, *L'image-action de la société ou la politique culturelle*, Seuil, Paris 1970, and his exploration of what he calls 'The imaginaction' in comparative themes such as student action in May 1968, Dadaism, surrealism, Free Jazz or the Living Theatre. (*The Action-Image of Society*, trs. A. M. Sheridan Smith, Tavistock Publications, London, 1970.) Concerning the events of May 1968 precisely as a conjunction of a millenarianism without religion and a revolution without ideology, cf. the suggestions of P. Vidal-Naquet, *Journal de la Commune étudiante* p. 50, Seuil, Paris, 1969. (*The French Student Uprising, November 1967–June 1968*, ed. A. Schnapp and V.-M. Pierre, trs. M. Jolas, Beacon Press, Boston, 1974.) 'These contradictions are perhaps summarised in another more basic one, which, it seems, is part of the "apocalyptic" and "millenarian" character of the revolutionary movement . . .' ibid., p. 66, note 169: 'There is much research to be done on this presence of millenarianism in the movement'.

8 Bakunin, *God and the State*, pp. 60–1.

9 Chapman, Walcker, *Le Rêve doré (les Conquistadores)*, Albin Michel, Paris, 1970.

10 J.-E. Monast, *On les croyait chrétiens, les Aymaras*, Cerf, Paris, 1969.

11 Cf. R. L. Moreau, 'Les Marabouts de Dori' in *Archives de Sociologie des Religions*, 17, pp. 113–14.

12 Cf. Henri Desroche, I.

13 There are some indications in W. D. Morris, *The Christian Origins of Social Revolt*, London, 1949.

14 Cf. *supra* ch. 2.

15 Cf. the list in *Socialismes et Sociologies Religieuses*, pp. 45–8.

16 Cf. G. L. Tuveson, *Redeemer Nation. The Idea of America's Millennial Role*, University of Chicago Press, Chicago, 1968.

17 E. Sarkisyanz, *Russland und der Messianismus des Orients, Sendungs – Bewusstein und politischer Chiliasmus des Ostens*, Mohr, Tübingen, 1955.

18 V. Lanternari, *Movimenti religiosi di liberta e di salvezza dei populi oppressi*, Feltrinelli, Milan, 1960. Complemented in *A.S.R.* 19, pp. 99–116; 24, pp. 105–20.

19 W. E. Muhlmann, *Chiliasmus und Nativismus*, D. Reiner, Berlin, 1961.

20 M. P. De Queiroz, *Réforme et Révolution dans les sociétés traditionelles. Histoire et ethnologie des mouvements messianiques*, Anthropos, Paris, 1968.

21 N. Cohn, *The pursuit of the Millennium*, Secker & Warburg, London, 1959.

22 D. B. Barrett, *Schism and renewal in Africa, an analysis of six thousand contemporary religious movements*, Oxford University Press, 1968. A bibliographical sketch in R. Kaufman, *Millénarisme et acculturation*, Brussels, 1964 (who elsewhere studies Kitavala more especially), and also a recent substantial thesis: J. Girard, *Dynamique de la religion et de l'église Deima*, three volumes (roneo), Paris, 1970.

23 The Congolese 'Joan of Arc' of the eighteenth century described in

G. Balandier, *La vie quotidienne au royaume du Congo*, Paris, 1965. Depicted on stage at the Festival of Avignon: 'Béatrice du Congo'.

24 Many of R. Bastide's contributions to this 'messialogy' are to be found in his work *Le prochain et le Lointain*, essays on the meetings of civilisations, 'L'orange mystique', p. 245 et seq. Ed. Cujas, Paris, 1970.

25 Sartono Kartodirjo, 'The peasants of Banten in 1888'.

26 Le Grip, 'Le mahdisme en Afrique Noire', *L'Afrique et l'Asie*, XVIII, 1952, 3–16.

27 E. Hobsbawm, *Primitive Rebels*.

28 A recent contribution from J. F. C. Harrison, *Robert Owen and the Owenites in Britain and America. The Quest for the New Moral World*, Routledge & Kegan Paul, London, 1969. In particular the chapter on 'Millenarianism. The Millennial Heritage. Disciples and Prophets'. Cf. also Henri Desroche, 'Messianismes et utopies': a note on the origins of western socialism in Henri Desroche, III, p. 117. I have since prepared a deeper analysis of the central case of E. Cabet and his Icarian communism as 'true Christianity'. It will be published shortly under the title *Odyssée d'une Utopie*: written and practised Icaries in the 'Christian communism' of E. Cabet.

29 M. Rodinson, op. cit. p. 20.

30 The one that, in contrast and related to the '*sollicitatio ad turpia*' which is well-known in canonical law, I have called the '*sollicitatio ad sublimia*'.

31 I am using the Durkheimian categories of 'volume' and 'density'.

32 *Being and Nothingness*.

33 Cf. 'La caractérisation de cepalier', in Rodinson, op. cit. p. 91.

34 *Sociologie et philosophie*, pp. 134-5, P.U.F., Paris 1963.

35 Cf. C. Wittke, *The Utopian Communist. A biography of W. Weitling, nineteenth century reformer*, ch. VII, pp. 105, 1950. Also Henri Desroche, 'Marx-Engels, La circulaire contre Kriege', pp. 313–33.

36 *Oeuvres*, III, p. 245.

37 *Oeuvres*, III, p. 544.

38 Ibid., p. 541.

39 E. Durkheim, *Le socialisme*, p. 350, Éd. M. Mauss, 1928 (our italics).

40 *Elementary Forms* (our emphasis). The same commentary is to be found elsewhere: 'action is always more or less urgent and cannot wait . . . . The theories that are therefore subordinated to the demands of practice are thus hastily and summarily constructed.' *Science sociale et l'action*, p. 112.

41 'The revolutionary movement . . . is restricted to the dimensions of a revolt, and once this upheaval has been realised, the prophets teach their followers . . . how they should work and play together in truth . . . so that the Scriptures can be fulfilled and that some visionaries should not have prophesied in vain.' Cf. *Circulaire contre Kriege*, op. cit.

42 A letter written 17 May 1846.

43 'According to M. Renan, Jesus said he was the Messiah. According to me, we made him be one.' Jesus, according to Proudhon, is a

messiah despite himself, an 'anti-messiah', 'anti-messianist' . . . 'an individuality to be rediscovered, reinstated, remade almost, so much has he been dissolved and pulverised by the very religion that he created'. *Écrits sur la Religion, passim.*

44 M. Rodinson, op. cit. on the laws of ideology:
   Maximum valuation . . . of the struggle and of the objective of the struggle . . . ; devaluation of all struggles other than the one one is engaged in . . . ; a tendency towards a Manichean vision of reality. *The positive agent of the struggle is idealised to the maximum . . . . The enemy is systematically vilified to the maximum* (pp. 84–7).

45 Cf. *supra.*

46 M. Djilas, *La société imparfaite*, Calmann-Lévy, Paris, 1969. (*The Unperfect Society: Beyond the New Class*, trs. Dorian Cook, Allen & Unwin, London, 1972.) Henri Desroche, 'La foi perdue et retrouvée', *Esprit*, pp. 553–8, March, 1970.

47 L. Althusser, *Pour Marx*, pp. 238, 239, Maspéro, Paris, 1966.

48 Pascal: 'Reasons for which one prefers the hunt to the catch . . . .'

## Chapter 5: Religious phenomena and collective imagination

1 G. Le Bras, *Études de sociologie religieuse*, II, p. 798. (*Studies in Religious Sociology* (2 volumes in 1), Arno Press, New York, 1975.)

2 *General introduction to the critique of political economy* (1857) . . . Furthermore:
   Our attraction to the art of the Greeks does not contradict the underdevelopment ('unentwickelt Gesellschaftstufe') of the society in which this art flourished. It is more likely the result of it; it is more likely indissolubly linked to the fact that the unrealised social conditions in which this art was born and in which it could only have been born, can never return.

3 Cf. G. Le Bras, 'Religion légale et religion vécue', pp. 15–20, *Archives de Sociologie des Religions*, 29, January–June 1970. Questions and answers pp. 18–19. The image of the believer: 'We can all create a certain *image* of God, we have not created God, but His image'. The image of the founder:
   There is the religion of the founders. In other words, one cannot say that a Moslem has created his God, but one can say that his God has been not created, but preached by a man that he knows and whose thought he believes he follows. There are therefore elements other than men in the creation of gods. There are the founders. . . .

4 Henri Desroche, 'Dernière instance et premier rôle', *A.S.R.*, 23, pp. 153–8, January–June 1967.

5 First short recapitulation in Henri Desroche, *Dieux d'hommes. Dictionnaire*. A collective larger edition is being prepared, as is a dictionary of written and practised utopias. Cf. elsewhere the documentation collected in *A.S.R.* and index *infra*, note 40.

6 E. Durkheim, 'Le sentiment religieux à l'heure actuelle', in *A.S.R.*,

27, 1969, 71–7, reproduced as 'L'Avenir de la religion' in *La Science sociale et l'Action*, pp. 305–13, P.U.F., Paris 1970:

> The man who lives religiously is not only a man who *represents* the world to himself in one way or another . . . . He is above all a man who feels a power within himself . . . which he does not feel within himself when he is not in a religious state. Religious life implies the existence of very special *forces* (op. cit., pp. 306–7).

7 In his replies to Marc Boegner, exhumed by E. Poulat, pp. 89–90, *A.S.R.*, 30, July–December 1970.

8 'Jugements de valeur et jugements de réalité', p. 134 (April 1911), reproduced in *Sociologie et Philosophie*. (*Sociology and Philosophy*, trs. D. F. Pocock, Free Press, New York, 1974.)

9 'Doubtless we ignore how movements can, in combining, give rise to a representation. But we do not know how a movement of transfer can when it is stopped, be changed into heat or vice versa.' p. 38, E. Durkheim, *Sociologie et Philosophie*.

10 Cf. H. Desroche, XIV, for a wider commentary.

11 Montreal Conference: Raymond Prince, *Trance and Possession States*, Montreal. R. M. Bucke, *Memorial Society*, 1966 (*A.S.R.* 26, no 148). Paris Conference: October 1968 with contributions from R. Bastide, 'Prolégomènes à l'étude des cultes de possession'. Erika Bourguignon, 'World distribution and patterns of possession states', etc. Cf. L. de Heusch, 'La folie des dieux et la raison des hommes' in *Pourquoi l'épouser?* p. 245, N.R.F., Paris 1971.

12 The bibliography would be never-ending. The main works are to be found in the catalogue drawn up by R. Bastide in the second part of his recent work, *Le Rêve, la Transe et la Folie*, pp. 55–105, Flammarion, Paris, 1972.

13 'The fact is that among these good things, the greatest are the ones that come from a delirium ($\delta\iota\grave{\alpha}\ \mu\alpha\nu\acute{\iota}\alpha\varsigma$), which without doubt brings us a divine gift', *Phaedra*, 244a . . . . 'We must demonstrate that on the contrary the gods wanted their supreme happiness when they made them the gift of a similar delirium. Doubtless this demonstration will not convince those with strong minds, but it will convince the wise', 254b-c.

14 And the circumspect analysis in *Elementary Forms* pp. 226–7:

> It will be objected . . . that . . . in this hypothesis, religion remains *the product of a certain delirium*. Indeed what other name can one give to the state in which men find themselves when, because of a collective effervescence, they believe themselves to be transported into a world which is completely different from the one that they have under their eyes? It is true that religious life cannot achieve a certain degree of intensity without implying a psychological exaltation which is not unconnected *to delirium* . . . . But if, for this reason, one can say that religion goes with *a certain delirium*, one must add that *this delirium*, if it has the causes that we have attributed to it, *is well-founded*. The images that it is made of are not pure illusions . . . they correspond to something in reality.

Doubtless it is in the nature of moral forces that they express the fact of not being able to affect the human mind with some energy without putting it outside of itself, without plunging it into a state that one can describe as *ecstatic*, as long as the word is understood in its etymological sense . . . but it does not in any way follow that they are imaginary (our emphasis).

15 Cf. the quotation from Durkheim, *supra*, note 14, on 'images' implying 'moral forces', that may be 'ecstatic', but are not for all that 'imaginary'. For a more recent case study cf. G. Althabe. *Oppression et libération dans l'imaginaire*, p. 359, Maspéro, Paris, 1969, and its review in R. Bastide, op. cit. One should also refer to the works of G. Bachelard (*Poétique de l'Espace, Le droit de rêver*, etc.) (*Poetics of Space*, trs. M. Jolas, Beacon Press, Boston, 1969.), P. M. Schuhl (*Imaginer et réaliser, l'Imagination et le Merveilleux*), J. Duvignaud (*Spectacle et Société . . . La fonction de l'imaginaire dans les sociétés*), and perhaps especially André Breton, *Les Vases communicants*. Also worth mentioning is the recent work of R. Christinger, *Le voyage dans l'Imaginaire*, Mont Blanc, Geneva, 1971. And the research done for the review *Circe*. Among psychiatric works, one is comparatively useful, on the pathology of the imagination, H. Faure, *Hallucinations et Réalité perceptive*, P.U.F., Paris, 1969. To be added to this short list: the American works mentioned by H. Cox, in particular: Bundy, Caligor and May, Hart, Kelsey, Kollman, Leonard. Cf. Bibliography.

16 Maurice Halbwachs, *La mémoire collective*, P.U.F., second edition, Paris, 1968. *La topographie légendaire des Évangiles en Terre Sainte. Étude de mémoire collective*, P.U.F., Paris 1941. New edition, 1972, preface by F. Dumont, *Les cadres sociaux de la mémoire*, P.U.F., Paris 1925.

17 There is no universal memory. All collective memory is supported by a group limited in time and in space. One cannot gather together in one frame alone the totality of past events, unless one detaches them from the memory of the groups that remembered them, unless one cuts the bonds which tie them to the psychological life of the social milieus in which they are produced, and unless one retains only the chronological and spatial diagram (*Mémoire Collective*, p. 75).

18 'The historian is himself historical, in other words he historialises himself in illuminating "history" with the light of his plans and those of his society. Thus one must say that the meaning of the social past is continually being adjourned.' *L'Être et le néant*, p. 582. (*Being and Nothingness*, trs. H. Barnes, Methuen, London, 1969.)

19 Cf. E. C. Tuveson, *Millenium and Utopia*, Berkeley, Los Angeles, 1949.

20 A theme that was over-abundantly developed by the great Polish messianists of the nineteenth century: Towianski, Mickiewicz, Wronski.

21 Title of the work by N. Berdiaev, *L'Idée russe*, Mame, Paris, 1969. Berdiaev's work on Russia is, as has already been indicated, the counterpart of Tuveson's work on America. Cf. *supra* ch. 2.

22 J. Séguy, *Introduction à la sociologie historique*, P.U.F., Paris. Cf. J.

Séguy, '*Sociologie de la connaissance et sociologie des religions*', pp. 91–107, *A.S.R.* 30, July–December 1970:
> The sciences themselves appear to be socially conditioned. We feel that the sociology of knowledge has not yet delved deeply enough into this problem. There is only proof in a logical framework, not a social one. *If the non-theological sciences of the religions relativise their object, doubtless one should also relativise the relativisers.*

(op. cit. p. 106). There is also the important contribution from Adam Schaff, *Histoire et Verité, essai sur l'objectivité de la connaissance historique*, Anthropos, Paris, 1971.

23 M. Halbwachs, *Topographie légendaire*, op. cit.
24 R. Hertz, 'Sainte Besse. Etudes d'un culte alpestre', in *Mélanges de Sociologie religieuse et Folklore*, pp. 131–91, Paris, 1928, recently re-published.
25 P. Delooz, *Sociologie et canonisation*, pp. 7–8, Liège, 1969. Cf. the discussion on this important research in *A.S.R.*, pp. 109–15, 30, 1970.
26 The case of Simon Kimbangu, who was messianised by Kimbanguists or Kimbangologists, and who was a reluctant messiah. Cf. our Kimbanguist file in *A.S.R.* 31.
27 J. Guiart, *Un siècle et demi de contacts culturels à Tanna*, New Hebrides, Musée de l'Homme, Paris, 1956.
28 R. Bastide, *Les Amériques Noires*, in particular chapter V, Payot, Paris, 1967. *Religions en conserves et religions vécues*, pp. 95–155. (*African Civilisations in the New World*, trs. P. Green, Hurst, London, 1971.)
29 All these remarks tend to justify our principle of cleavage . . . . What we had already foreseen – the break between the economic infrastructures, which are explained by adaptation to the surrounding environment, and the superstructures, which are explained by African traditions – is even more pronounced here. The black American lives in two worlds which each have their own rules; he adapts himself to the surrounding environment, yet he also keeps up, in another area, the religions of his fathers (ibid., p. 132).
Cf. also R. Bastide, *Les Religions africaines du Brésil*, P.U.F., Paris 1960: 'The first movement that was seen to occur is not one of the action of the economic on the religious, but *on the contrary, one of the secretion of infrastructures from superstructures*', p. 543.
30 *Morphologie sociale*, Colin, Paris, 1938.
31 K. Marx, *The 18th Brumaire of Louis Bonaparte*, 1st edition, 1852.
32 Ibid., pp. 7–8.
33 P. Ansart, 'Marx et la théorie de l'imaginaire social', *Cahier International Sociologique*, XIV, 1968, p. 99.
34 Ibid., p. 114.
35 Cf. our preface to Saint-Simon, Henri Desroche, V.
36 E. Tuveson, *Millennium and Utopia*, op. cit.
37 The notion of History as a process moving from the bottom to the top in a series of majestic phases culminating inevitably in some great transformation which should settle the dilemmas of society, is the concept destined to dominate modern thought. I believe that

these preliminaries can be found in the apocalyptic phenomena of
the eighteenth century (ibid., p. 75).

38  On the second point, cf. J. Baechler, *Les Phénomènes révolutionnaires*,
P.U.F., Paris, 1970 (*Revolution*, trs. Joan Vickers, Blackwell, Oxford,
1976).

39  Cf. W. D. Wallis, *Messiahs, Christian and Pagan*, Boston, 1918. *Messiahs,
their role in Civilization*, Washington, 1943. Cf. the remarks by
P. Demiéville, cit. *supra*, ch. 1.

40  An inventory on this subject, if not an inquiry, has been drawn up
over the last fifteen years, in the *Archives de Sociologie des Religions
(A.S.R.)*. It is far from complete, but here is an idea of its scope.

    *A.S.R.* inaugurated this inventory in no. 4, 1957 (July–December).
Over the years, fifty articles representing some 600 pages, have been
published on this theme of messianisms millenarianisms found in the
most diverse cultural areas or religious contexts: Fiji (J. Guiart, 4,
3–30); South Africa (J. Eberhardt, 4, 31–6); North America in the
seventeenth–eighteenth centuries (H. Desroche, 4, 57–92); in
Bahaism (P. Berger, 4, 93–107); in South America (A. Métraux, 4,
108–12 and R. Bastide, 5, 31–7); among the Pawnees (M. Wax, 4,
113–22); in contemporary Japan (H. van Straelen, 4, 123–32); in the
Chinese sects (G. Dunstheimer, 4, 133–42 and J. Chesneaux, 16,
122–4); in Donatism (J. Hadot, M. Meslin, 4, 143–8); in the Book of
Revelations (S. Giet, 4, 149–57); in Brasil (M. I. Pereira de Queiroz,
5, 3–30 and 11–120, 16, 109–21); in Melanesia (J. Guiart and P.
Worsley, 5, 38–46); in Russia (P. Kovalesvsky, 5, 47–70 and 108–10);
in Italy (Lazzaretists) (J. Séguy, 5, 71–87); in the Congo (G.
Balandier, 5, 91–5); in Europe in the nineteenth century (F. Isambert,
5, 96–8); in the origins of Western socialism (H. Desroche, 8, 31–46),
at the Chicago conference, April 1960 (J. Guiart, 9, 105–10); in the
Mourides in Senegal (V. Monteil, 14, 77–102); in the 'Selette' in the
nineteenth century (E. Appolis, 14, 103–22); in the Middle Ages (A.
Werner, 16, 73–6); in a meeting at Bouake in 1963 (H. Desroche,
16, 105–8); in black mahdism (R. L. Moreau, 17, 113–34); in
Ruanda (L. de Heusch, 18, 133–46); in Basutoland in the nineteenth
century (C. H. Perrot, 18, 147–52); in the Mariavite Church (E.
Appolis, 19, 51–68); in a contemporary Senegalese visionary (V.
Monteil, 19, 69–98); in Black Africa (V. Lanternari, 19, 99–116 and
21, 101–10); in Saint-Simon (J. Dautry, 20, 7–30 and H. Desroche
26, 27–54); in Ernst Bloch (P. Furter, 21, 3–22); in the Jehovah's
Witnesses (J. Séguy, 21, 89–100); in the Shabbatai Zevi movement
(W. P. Zenner, 21, 111–18); in Judeo-Christianity (J. Hadot, 24,
35–48); in the Black Muslims (V. Lanternari, 24, 105–120); in the
dissident churches of sub-Saharan Africa (D. R. Barrett, 25, 111–40);
in science fiction (C. Renard-Cheinisse, 25, 141–52); in Paraguay
(M. Haubert, 27, 119–30); in Kimbanguism (H. Desroche and P.
Raymaekers, 31).

    Other works include Sylvia Thrupp, *Millennial Dreams in Action*,
Mouton, The Hague, 1962. V. Lanternari, *Movimenti religiosi*, Milan,

Feltrinelli, 1960. Also Guariglia, Mühlmann, M. I. P. de Queiroz, etc. Cf. *supra* and bibliography.

41 Cf. H. Desroche, IX.

42 Cf. M. Leenhardt, *Do Kamo. La personne et le mythe dans le monde mélanésien*, Gallimard, Paris, 1947. *Mythe et rationalité, modes complémentaires de connaissance*, pp. 252–5.

43 Could one wish for a more uncompromising and 'utopian' utopia than *Voyage en Icarie* written by Cabet during his exile in London? And yet this adventure found its audience. And what an audience! Without granting the 500,000 'communists' with whom Engels thought he could endow it in 1844, the archives enable one to estimate at least 200,000 members of the Icarian organisation, which was the first prefiguration of a French communist *party*. H. Desroche, XV.

44 A. E. Morgan, *Nowhere was somewhere. How history makes utopias and how utopias make history*, Chapel Hill, 1946.

45 H. Desroche, XI.

46 R. Fakkar, *Sociologie, socialisme et internationalisme pré-marxistes*, Delachaux and Nestlé, Neuchâtel, 1968. Cf. bibliography, pp. 305–12, on the diffusion of Saint-Simonism in and beyond Europe.

47 J. F. C. Harrison, *Robert Owen and the Owenites in Britain and America*, H. Desroche, VII, 'Owénisme et Utopies Françaises' (30 July–December 1971) in *A.I.S.C.*

48 Wittke, *The Utopian communist. Biography of W. Weitling, nineteenth century reformer*, Baton Rouge, Louisiana, 1950.

49 Cf. N. Eurich, *Science in Utopia*, 1967.

50 Cf. O. Lutaud's thesis, presently being completed.

51 Cf. *Beschreibung*, 1844. Edited with commentary in H. Desroche, IV, pp. 87–115.

52 Cf. E. Morin, *Journal de Californie*, Seuil, Paris, 1970.

53 For this see the *Dictionnaire des Utopies*, currently in preparation.

54 One can concur with E. Cobham Brewer, author of *A Dictionary of Miracles* (1966), who says: 'Dreams are realities for as long as the mental conditions which produce them last.'

55 According to the neologism suggested by A. Willener, *L'Image Action de la société ou la politique culturelle*.

56 In the extension of a *sociology of expectation* sketched by M. Mauss in his communication (10 January 1924) to the Société de Psychologie. Cf. *supra*, ch. 1.

57 E. Morin, *La rumeur d'Orléans*, Seuil, Paris, 1969. (*Rumour in Orleans*, trs. P. Green, Blond, London, 1971.)

58 W. Chapman, *The Golden Dream*, 1967.

59 *Le Centenaire du Capital* (11–20 July 1967), Lahaye, Paris. 'Freud at first thought that all the hysterical girls had *really* undergone scenes of paternal seduction, in other words that they had all been seduced by their fathers. But when he found in a series of fantastic stories, seduction scenes that became more and more unbelievable, he began to think (I believe this was a turning point in Freudian thought),

that the seduction did not really exist, had not occurred; but that does not stop it from being *represented* as such.' Catherine Backès, p. 182. 'Let us distinguish between reality and the effectiveness of reality. It is all the more determinative in that *it does not exist*', p. 183.

60 Ibid., p. 187.

61 E. Steiner, *Treblinka*, Fayard, Paris, 1966. In *Les religions africaines au Brésil*, R. Bastide drew up an empirical inventory of another series of types of behaviour, *including* millenarian behaviour. Cf. ch. III, *La protestation de l'esclave et la religion*, p. 107 et seq.

62 Maimonides's principle stipulates that 'no soul should devote itself to idolatry' . . . 'Well, it's not his soul you're being asked for, it's his body.'

63 Ibid., p. 234.

64 Ibid., p. 99.

65 The conditions made hanging very difficult . . . . Later on, when the beginnings of social relations were established between the prisoners, the technique was improved. A friend was chosen to pull away the box . . . . The man stood on the box . . . passed his belt round his neck and tied it to a beam. When everything was ready, he said 'Go ahead.' His friend pulled the box away, and *recited the Kaddish* (p. 129).

66 This would indeed pre-suppose a sociology that was in some way 'idealistic'. Why not? Durkheim does not hesitate to use the term: 'There is therefore an area in nature, where the formula of *idealism* is applicable almost to the letter: it is the social kingdom. Here more than anywhere, the idea makes the reality.' *Elementary Forms*, p. 228. Curiously enough, Adler, cit. *supra*, ch. 4, says the same of socialism: 'As a movement, socialism is a current made of actions, positions and value judgments. *Idealism can and should prevail*', op. cit.

67 Cf. Harvey Cox, *The Feast of Fools: A Theological Essay on Festivity and Fantasy*, Harper & Row, New York, 1972. Cf. R. Bastide, *Les sciences de la folie*, Mouton, 1972, on this experience as a 'compensation ritual'.

68 In the sense, for example, that the narration of the trances incurred by the Cevennes prophets is called *The sacred theatre of the Cevennes*. This implication is also studied by M. Leiris, *La possession et ses aspects théâtraux chez les Éthiopiens de Gondar*, Plon, Paris, 1958 in particular, chap. V. *Théâtre joué et théâtre vécu dans le culte des Zar*, p. 96: Experienced by the actor . . . this special kind of theatre, which can never admit its theatrical nature, is also experienced by the spectator. Any moment he too may well be possessed . . . . In short it is a matter of privileged moments *in which the collective life itself takes the form of theatre*.

69 A. Artaud, *Le Théâtre et son double*, p. 45, Gallimard, Paris, 1964. (*Theatre and its Double*, trs. V. Corti, Calder, London, 1970.) Ibid., pp. 106, 126.
To do that, to link the theatre to the possibilities of expression by forms and by everything that is movement, noise, colour, plastic,

etc., is to return it to its primitive destination, to re-site it in its religious and metaphysical aspect, to reconcile it with the universe . . . A theatre . . . which at first presents itself as an exceptional force of diversion. A theatre which produces trances . . . and which addresses itself to the organism with precise methods, and with the same methods as the healing music of certain peoples which we admire on record, but which we are incapable of engendering ourselves . . . .'

In this perspective, an interesting comparative commentary on the *crisis* of possession in the cults, and the *hold* of possession in the theatre, is made by Louis-Jean Antonio, *La crise de possession et la possession dramatique*, Éditions Léméac, Ottawa, 1970.

70 It is indeed the image of a miracle, the miracle of the rope, which best illustrates this constitutive dialectic. Cf. M. Éliade, 'The miracle of the rope' in *Méphistophélès et l'Androgyne*, p. 200, Gallimard, Paris, 1962. This image should elucidate a sociology of 'collective ideations' which Durkheim said regretfully was 'still to be created'. Cf. *supra*, Introduction.

## Conclusion: The sociology of hope and the hopes of sociology

.1 Author of *Theologie der Hoffnung*, Kaiser Verlag, Munich, 1964.

2 Cf. *Figures et Idoles de l'Espérance*, Cahiers de Villemétrie, 88, 89, 90, 1971–2, p. 79.

3 Comte is quoted and discussed in P. Arbousse-Bastide, 'Auguste Comte et la Sociologie des Religions', *Archives de Sociologie des Religions*,. pp. 3–58, 22, July–December 1966.

4 E. Durkheim, in *La Science sociale et l'action*, P.U.F., Paris, 1970.

5 *Elementary Forms*, pp. 427–8.

6 Text of Marx's, presented and discussed by M. Rubel, 'Socrate et le Christ', *La Nef*, p. 57, June 1948.

7 H. Lefèbvre, *La Somme et le reste*, p. 83.

8 A. Gramsci. On the 'determinism' attributed to Marxist materialism: When one does not have the initiative in the struggle, and the struggle itself ends up being identified with a whole series of defeats, mechanical determinism becomes a *formidable force of moral resistance* . . . . I am momentarily beaten, but in the long run the force of things works for me, etc. . . . Real will disguises itself as an act of faith in a certain historical rationality, as an empirical and primitive form of impassioned finalism, *which appears as a substitute* of predestination, of providence, etc., of confessional religions . . . a popular version of the cry 'It is God's wish . . . .'
(*Selections from Political Writings 1910–20*, ed. Q. Hoare, trs. J. Mathews, Lawrence & Wishart, London, 1977.)

9 M. Adler, who speaks against any attempt to camouflage Marxism as a millenarianism: 'Marxism as such is not a millenarianism'.
However if one distinguishes Marxism as a *theory* and as a *movement*, Adler admits as far as the movement is concerned:

If one wishes to say that the followers of Marxist socialism are often attached to their cause with *a kind of religious enthusiasm*, and that they are calling with their vows for the realisation of the socialist ideal . . . with the same fervour with which the first Christians awaited the Kingdom of heaven, and of all those who hungered for salvation and dreamed of their messianic era, one is merely expressing a truth which characterises the psychology of all the great revolutions.

Quoted in Y. Bourdet, *Le Communisme. Réalité et Utopie*, Cahiers, I.S.E.A., 1971.

10 The editorial of the 'Gazette de Cologne' no 179 in the *Gazette Rhénane*, July 1842, in *Marx, Engels, Sur la religion*, pp. 33–5, Éditions Sociales, Paris, 1960.

11 M. Weber, 'Politics as a Vocation', in H. H. Gerth and C. W. Mills (eds), *From Max Weber*, Routledge & Kegan Paul, 1948.

12 J. Séguy, 'Max Weber et la sociologie historique des religions', *A.S.R.*, 33, 1972.

13 Extracts reproduced in *Le Monde*, 1 June 1972.

14 R. Bastide, *Le Rêve, la Transe et la Folie*, pp. 61, 92–3.

15 Ibid., p. 91.

16 M. Weber, 'Politics as a vocation', op. cit., p. 127.

# Bibliography

ALTHUSSER, L., *Pour Marx*, Maspero, Paris, 1966.
ANSART, P., 'Marx et la théorie de l'Imaginaire social', *Cahiers Internationaux de Sociologie*, XLV, p. 99 et ss, 1968.
ARBOUSSE-BASTIDE, P., 'Auguste Comte et la sociologie religieuse', *A.S.R.*, 22, juillet–décembre 1966.
ARTAUD, A., *Le théâtre et son double*, Gallimard, Paris, 1964. (*Theatre and its Double*, trs. V. Corti, Calder, London, 1970.)
BACHELARD, Gaston, *Le droit de rêver*, P.U.F., Paris, 1970.
BAECHLER, J., *Les phénomènes révolutionnaires*, P.U.F., Paris, 1970. (*Revolution*, trs. Joan Vickers, Blackwell, Oxford, 1976.)
BALANDIER, Georges, *La vie quotidienne au royaume de Congo*, Hachette, Paris, 1965.
BAROJA, J.-C., *Les sorcières et leur Monde*, Gallimard, Paris, 1972.
BARRETT, D., *Schism and Renewal in Africa, An Analysis of six thousand contemporary religious movements*. Oxford University Press, 1968.
BASCO, B., 'Lumières et utopie. Problèmes de recherche', *Annales*, p. 555 et ss., 26, 2, mars–avril 1971.
BASTIDE, R., *Les religions africaines du Brésil*, P.U.F., Paris, 1960. *Les Amériques Noires*, Payot, Paris, 1967. *Le prochain et le lointain*, Cujas, Paris, 1970. *Le Rêve, la Transe et la Folie*, Flammarion, Paris, 1972.
BERDIAEV., N., *L'Idée russe*, Mame, Paris, 1969.
BLOCH, E., *Das Prinzip Hoffnung*, Suhrkamp-Verlag, Frankfurt-am-Main, 1959.
BLOCH, E., *Thomas Münzer Théologien de la Révolution*, Julliard, Paris, 1964.
BRADEN, Ch. S., *These also Believe*, The MacMillan Company, New York, 1953.
BRETON, A., *Les Vases Communicants*, Gallimard, 19 (coll. Idées), Paris, 1955.
BUNDY, M., *The Theory of Imagination in Classical and Medieval Thought*, University of Illinois Press, Urbana, 1927.
BURRIDGE, K., *New Haven. New Earth. A Study of Millenarian Activities*, Basil Blackwell, Oxford, 1969.
*Cahiers de Marxologie*, 'Le Communisme. Réalité et Utopie', IV, II, novembre 1970.
CAILLOIS, R. et GRUNEBAUM, G. E. von, *Le Rêve et les Sociétés humaines*, N.R.F., Paris, 1967. (*Dream and Human Societies*, University of California Press.)

# Bibliography

CALIGOR, L., MAY, R., *Dreams and Symbols Man's unconscious language*, Books, New York, 1968.

*Centenaire du Capital (Le)*, Décade de Cerisy la Salle, Mouton, The Hague, Paris, 11–20 juillet 1967.

CERTEAU, M. de, *La possession de Loudun*, Julliard, Paris, 1970.

CHAIX-RUY, J., *J.-B. Vico et l'illuminisme athée*, Del Duca, Paris, 1970.

CHAPMAN, W., *Le rêve doré. Les conquistadores*, Albin Michel, Paris, 1970.

CHESNEAUX, J., *Les sociétés secrètes en Chine*, Julliard (coll. Archives), Paris, 1965.

CHRISTINGER, R., *Le Voyage dans l'Imaginaire*, éd. Mont-Blanc, Genève, 1971.

COHN, N., *The Pursuit of the Millennium*, Secker & Warburg, London, Londres, 1957.

COX, H., *The Feast of Fools: A Theological Essay on Festivity and Fantasy*, Harper & Row, New York, 1972.

DELOOZ, P., *Sociologie et Canonisation*, Liège, 1969.

DESROCHE, Henri, I, *Les Shakers américains. D'un néochristianisme à un pré-socialisme*, Minuit, Paris, 1955.

H.D., II, *Marxisme et religions*, P.U.F., Paris, 1962.

H.D., III, *Socialismes et sociologie religieuse*, Cujas, Paris, 1965. *(S.S.R.)*

H.D., IV, *Sociologies religieuses*, P.U.F., Paris, 1968. *(S.R.)*

H.D., V, *Saint-Simon. Le Nouveau Christianisme et les écrits sur la religion*, Seuil, Paris, 1969. *(S.S.N.C.)* (Préface: 'Genèse et structure du christianisme saint-simonien', in *A.S.R.* 26, p. 27–54, 1968.)

H.D., VI, *Dieux d'Hommes. Dictionnaire des messianismes et millénarismes de l'ère chrétienne*, La Haye, Paris, Mouton, 1969 (Préface: 'Dieux d'Hommes. Contribution à une sociologie de l'Attente.'). *(D.H. Dict.)*

H.D., VII, *Owénisme et utopies françaises*, *A.I.S.C.D.*, 30 juillet–décembre (no spécial), 1971.

H.D., VIII, 'Dissidences religieuses et socialismes utopiques'. *Année Sociologique*, P.U.F., Paris, 3e série, 1952, p. 393–429, 1955.

H.D., IX, 'Fouriérisme écrit et fouriérisme pratiqué', *in* E. POULAT, *Les cahiers manuscrits de Fourier*, p. 5–36, Éd. de Minuit, Paris, 1957.

H.D., X, 'Fouriérisme ambigu. Socialisme ou religion?' *Revue Internationale de Philosophie*, 60, 1962.

H.D., XI, 'Écriture et tradition de l'utopisme pratiqué', p. 3–18, *A.I.S.C.D.*, 19 janvier–juin 1966.

H.D., XII, 'Voyages en Utopie', *Esprit*, numéro spécial 'Prospective et Utopie', p. 222–45, février 1966.

H.D., XIII, 'Dernière instance et premier rôle', *A.S.R.*, p. 153–8, 23 janvier–juin 1967.

H.D., XIV, 'Thèses durkheimiennes sur la religion comme idéation collective', *A.S.R.*, 27, p. 79–88, 1969.

H.D., XV, 'Genèses de l'Icarie écrite', préface à Et. Cabet, *Oeuvres, Voyage en Icarie*, 1970, p. IX–LX, Éditions Anthropos, Paris.

H.D., XVI, *Les Dieux rêvés. Théismes et Athéismes en Utopie*, Desclée, Paris, 1972.

H.D., XVII, *L'Homme et ses religions. Sciences humaines et Expériences religieuses*, Cerf, Paris, 1972.

DJILAS, M., *La Société imparfaite*, Calmann-Lévy, Paris, 1969. (*The Unperfect Society: Beyond the New Class*, trs. Dorian Cook, Allen & Unwin, London, 1972.)

DUMAS, A., *Dietrich Bonhöffer, une théologie de la Réalité*, Labor et Fides, Genève, 1968.

DUMONT, R., *Développement et socialismes*, Seuil, Paris, 1969. (*Socialism and Development*, trs. R. Cunningham, Deutsch, 1973.)

DURKHEIM, E., *Le socialisme*. Éd. par Marcel Mauss, Alcan, Paris, 1928.

DURKHEIM, E., *Les formes élémentaires de la vie religieuse*, Alcan, Paris, 1912. (*Formes.*)

DURKHEIM, E., *Sociologie et philosophie*, P.U.F., Paris, 1953. (*S. Ph.*) (*Sociology and Philosophy*, trs. D. F. Pocock, Free Press, New York 1974.)

DURKHEIM, E., *La science sociale et l'action*, P.U.F., Paris, 1970 (*S.S.A.*).

DUVEAU, G., *Sociologie de l'utopie*, P.U.F., Paris, 1961.

DUVIGNAUD, J., *Spectacle et société*, Du Théâtre grec au happening. La fonction de l'imaginaire dans les sociétés, Gonthier-Denoël, Paris, 1970.

ELIADE, M., *Mythes, rêves et mystères*, Gallimard, Paris, 1957.

ELIADE, M., *Méphistophélès et l'Androgyne*, Gallimard, Paris, 1962.

ENTRALGO, P. L., 'La Espera y la Esperanza', *Revista de Occidente*, Madrid, 1958.

EURICH, Nell, *Science in Utopia. A Mighty Design*, Harvard University Press, 1967.

FAKKAR, Rouchdi, *Sociologie, socialisme, internationalisme prémarxistes*, Delachaux et Nestlé, Neuchâtel, 1968.

FAURE, Henri, *Hallucinations et réalité perceptive*, Bibliogr. psych., p. 251–67, P.U.F., Paris, 1969.

FESTINGER, L., *When prophecy fails*, An account of a modern group that predicted the destruction of the World, Minneapolis, 1956.

FOURIER, Ch., *Oeuvres*, Réédition anastaltique, 11 volumes, Éditions Anthropos, Paris, 1966.

FUCHS, J., *Rebellious prophets*, A Study of Messianic Movements in Indian religions, Asia Publishing House, London, 1965.

GOLLWITZER, H., *Athéisme marxiste et Foi Chrétienne*, Castermann, Paris, 1965. (*The Christian Faith and the Marxist criticism of Religion*, trs. D. Cairns, St Andrews Press, Edinburgh, 1970.)

GOUHIER, Henri, *La jeunesse d'Auguste Comte et la formation du positivisme*, t. II *Saint-Simon jusqu'à la Restauration*, Vrin, Paris, 1936.

GRAMSCI, *Oeuvres choisies*, Éditions Sociales, Paris, 1959. (*Selections from Political Writings 1910–20*, ed. Q. Hoare, trs. J. Mathews, Lawrence & Wishart, London, 1977.)

GUARIGLIA, G., *Prophetismus und Heilserwertungsbewegungen als völkerkundliches und religionsgeschichtliches Problem*, F. Berger, Horn-Vienne, 1959.

GUIART, J., *Un siècle et demi de contacts culturels à Tanna (Nouvelles-Hébrides)*, Musée de l'Homme, Paris, 1956.

GUIART, J. et WORSLEY, P., 'La répartition des mouvements millénaristes en Mélanésie', *A.S.R.*, 6, p. 38–46.

HALBWACHS, M., *La Mémoire Collective*, P.U.F., 2e éd., Paris, 1968. *Les cadres sociaux de la mémoire*, P.U.F., Paris, 1925. *Morphologie sociale*, Colin, Paris, 1938. *La topographie légendaire des Évangiles en Terre Sainte*, Étude de mémoire collective, P.U.F., Paris, 1941.

HARRISON, J. F. C., *Robert Owen and the Owenites in Britain and America. The Quest for the New Moral World*, Routledge & Kegan Paul, London, 1969.

HART, R. L., *Unfinished Man and the Imagination*, Herder and Herder, New York, 1968.

HAU, Claude, *Le Messie de l'an XIII*, Denoël, Paris, 1955.

HEDGEPETH, W., STOCK, D., *The Alternative. Communal Life in New America*, MacMillan Company, New York, 1970.

HERTZ, R., 'Saint-Besse. Étude d'un culte alpestre' in *Mélanges de sociologie religieuse et folklore*, Paris, 1928.

HOBSBAWM, E. J., *Primitive Rebels*. Trad. fr. *Les primitifs de la révolte dans l'Europe moderne*, Fayard, Paris, 1963.

HUIZINGA, J., *Homo ludens: Essai sur la fonction sociale du jeu*, Gallimard, Paris, 1951.

ISAMBERT, F., *Buchez ou l'âge théologique de la sociologie*, Cujas, Paris, 1967.

KELSEY, M. T., *Dreams, the dark Speech of the Spirit: a christian Interpretation*, Doubleday, New York, 1968.

KOLLMAN, C., *Studies in the modern theory of Imagination with especial reference to its development from the Renaissance to Kant* (thèse non publiée), Harvard University, 1950.

LACROIX, Jean, *L'échec*, P.U.F., Paris, 1964.

LANTERNARI, V., *Movimenti religiosi di liberta e di salvazzo dei populi oppressi*, Milan, Feltrinelli, 1960. Trad. fr. *Les mouvements religieux des peuples opprimés*, Maspero, Paris, 1962.

LE BRAS, G., *Études de sociologie religieuse*, t. I, 1955, t. II, 1956, P.U.F., Paris. (*Studies in Religious Sociology*, Arno Press, New York, 1975.)

LE BRAS, G. 'Religion légale et religion vécue', *A.S.R.*, 29, p. 15–20, janvier–juin 1970.

LEENHARDT, M., *Do Kamo*. La personne et le mythe dans le monde mélanésien, Gallimard, Paris, 1947.

LE GRIP, 'Le Mahdisme en Afrique Noire', *L'Afrique et l'Asie*, XVIII, 1952, 3–16.

LEIRIS, M., *La possession et ses aspects théâtraux chez les Éthiopiens de Gondar*, Plon, Paris, 1958.

LEONARD, G., *Education and Ecstasy*, Delacorte Press, New York, 1968.

LÉON-PORTILLA, M., *Vision de los Vencidos*, Mexico, 1961, trad. fr. *Le Crépuscule des Aztèques, Récits indigènes de la Conquête*, Castermann, Paris, 1965.

LOISY, A., *L'Évangile et l'Église*, Nourry, Paris, 1929, 5e éd.

MANNHEIM, K., *Ideology and Utopia*, Kegan Paul, London, 1936 (1960).

MANNONI, O., *Clefs pour l'Imaginaire*, Seuil, Paris, 1969.

MANUEL, F. E., *The New World of Henri de Saint-Simon*, Harvard University Press, Cambridge Mass., 1956.

MARCUSE, H., *La Fin de l'Utopie*, Seuil, Paris, 1968.

MARX, K., *Le 18 Brumaire de Napoléon Bonaparte* (1re édition 1852), Éditions Sociales, Paris, 1945.

MAUSS, Marcel, *Oeuvres* (3 tomes), Minuit, Paris, 1970.

MERTON, E. K., *Éléments de théorie et de méthode sociologiques*, Plon, Paris, 1957.

MÉTRAUX, A., *Haïti. La terre, les hommes et les dieux*, La Baconnière, Neuchâtel, 1957.

MÉTRAUX, A., *Le Vaudou haïtien*, Gallimard, Paris, 1958. (*Voodoo in Haiti*, trs. H. Charteris, Deutsch, London, 1972.)

MOLTMANN, J., *Theologie der Hoffnung* (8e éd. 1969), Kaiser Verlag, Munich, 1964, trad. fr., *Théologie de l'Espérance*, Cerf, Paris, 1970.

MONAST, J. E., *On les croyait chétiens. Les Aymaras*, Cerf, Paris, 1969.

MORE, Thomas, *L'Utopie*, Dent, 1951.

MOREAU, R. L., 'Les marabouts de Dori', *A.S.R.*, 17, p. 113–34.

MORGAN, A. E., *Nowhere was Somewhere. How History makes Utopias and how utopias make History*, Chapel Hill, The University of North Carolina Press, 1946.

MORIN, Edgar, *La rumeur d'Orléans*, Seuil, Paris, 1969. (*Rumour in Orleans*, trs. P. Green, Blond, London, 1971.) *Journal de Californie*, Seuil, Paris, 1970.

MORRIS, W. D., *The Christian Origins of Social Revolt*, Allen & Unwin, London, 1940.

MÜHLMANN, W. E., *Chiliasmus und Nativismus*, Dietrich Reimer, Berlin, 1961. Trad. fr. (abridged) *Messianismes révolutionnaires du Tiers-Monde*, Gallimard, Paris, 1968.

NICOLAS, Jacqueline, *Les 'juments des dieux'. Rites de possession et condition féminine en pays Hausa. C.N.R.S.-I.F.A.N. Études nigériennes*, no 21, s.d. (ronéo). *Anthropos*, Paris, 1972.

PRINCE, R. ed., *Trance and Possession States*, R. M. Bucke Memorial Society, Montreal, 1966.

QUEIROZ, M. I. P. de, *La guerre sainte du 'Contestado'*, Universidad de Sao Paulo, 1957.
*Réforme et révolution dans les sociétés traditionnelles*, Histoire et ethnologie des mouvements messianiques, Anthropos, Paris, 1968.

SARTRE, J.-P., *L'Imagination*, P.U.F., Paris, 1950. *L'Imaginaire* (coll. Idées), Gallimard, Paris, 1970.

SARTRE, J.-P., *L'être et le néant*, Gallimard, NRF, Paris, 1943. (*Being and Nothingness*, trs. H. Barnes, Methuen, London, 1969.)

SCHLOSSER, K., *Propheten in Africa*, A. Limbech, Brunchwich, 1949.

SCHUHL, P. M., *Imaginer et réaliser*, P.U.F., Paris, 1963. *L'imagination et le merveilleux. La pensée et l'action*, Paris, 1969. (*Poetics of Space*, trs. M. Jolas, Beacon Press, Boston, 1969.)

SÉGUY, J., *Utopie coopérative et oecuménisme. Pieter Cornelisz Plockhoy Von Zürik-Zee, 1620–1700*, Mouton, Paris, La Haye, 1968.

SÉGUY, J., 'Les sociétés imaginées. Monachisme et utopie', *Annales*, 26, 2, mars–avril 1971, p. 328–54.

SILVER, A. H., *A History of Messianic Speculation in Israel*, New York, 1927.

SINDA, M., *Le Messianisme congolais et ses incidences politiques*, Payot, Paris, 1972 (préface de R. BASTIDE: 'Les Christ Noirs').

SOURIAU, E., *L'ombre de Dieu*, P.U.F., Paris, 1955.

STEINER, E., *Treblinka*, Fayard, Paris, 1968.

THRUPP, Sylvia L., *Millennial Dreams in Action*, Mouton, La Haye, 1962.

TOURAINE, A., *Le mouvement de mai ou le communisme utopique*, Seuil, Paris, 1968.

TUVESON, E. L., *Millennium and Utopia, A Study in the Background of the Idea of Progress*, Berkeley, Los Angeles, 1949.

TUVESON, E. L., *Redeemer Nation. The Idea of America's Millennial Role*, University of Chicago Press, Chicago, 1968.

VIDAL-NAQUET, P., *Journal de la Commune Étudiante*, Seuil, Paris, 1969. (*The French Student Uprising, November 1967–June 1968*, ed. A. Schnapp and V.-M. Pierre, trs. M. Jolas.)

WACHTEL, N., *La Vision des Vaincus. Les Indiens du Pérou devant la Conquête Espagnole*, Gallimard, Paris, 1971. (*The Vision of the Vanquished: The Spanish Exploration of Peru through Indian eyes*, trs. Ben and Siân Reynolds. Harvester Press, Brighton, 1976.)

WALLIS, W. D., *Messiahs. Christian and Pagan*, Boston, 1918. *Messiahs. Their Role in Civilization*, Washington, 1943.

WILLEMER, A., *L'image-action de la société ou la politique culturelle*, Seuil, Paris, 1970. (*The Action-Image of Society*, trs. A. M. Sheridan Smith, Tavistock Publications, London, 1970.)

WITTKE, C., *The Utopian Communist. A Biography of W. Weitling, nineteenth Century Reformer*, Baton Rouge, L. 1950.

WORSLEY, P., *The Trumpet shall sound. A Study of Cargo Cults in Melanesia*, MacGibbon and Kee, London, 1957.

# Index